ROMAN LAW

An Historical Introduction

ROMAN LAW

An Historical Introduction

BY

HANS JULIUS WOLFF

UNIVERSITY OF OKLAHOMA PRESS
NORMAN AND LONDON

ERNESTO LEVY

SEPTUAGENARIO

D.   D.   D.

ISBN: 0–8061–1296–4

PREFACE

THIS BOOK does not deal with the institutions of Roman law. It is rather an attempt to describe the political, intellectual, and—if the expression be permitted—mechanical forces which were responsible for the growth of Roman law and for its lasting impact on our civilization. With this, the author hopes to have filled a gap that still exists in English and American literature.

The book was not written for specialists, but for practical lawyers and others interested in historical problems as they are related to law. The author also hopes that his book will prove useful as an introductory text in courses in jurisprudence and on Roman law, and as supplementary reading in courses on ancient and medieval history.

The author is obliged to Professors John P. Dawson of the University of Michigan and Wolfgang Kunkel of the University of Heidelberg for many valuable criticisms and suggestions. Professor James J. Hayes, head of the English Department at Oklahoma City University, was kind enough to read the manuscript and to suggest a number of stylistic improvements. To all these the author wishes to express his deep and sincere appreciation.

HANS JULIUS WOLFF

Kansas City, Missouri

v

CONTENTS

ABBREVIATIONS

BIDR: *Bullettino dell'Istituto di Diritto Romano*
Cod.Just.: Code of Justinian
Cod.Theod.: Theodosian Code
Dig.: Digest of Justinian
Gai.: *Institutes* of Gaius
RE: Pauly-Wissowa-Kroll, *Realenzyklopädie der Klassischen Altertumswissenschaft*
Z.Sav.St.:*Zeitschrift der Savigny Stiftung für Rechtsgeschichte, Romanistische Abteilung*

The Codes and the Digest are divided into "books," and the "books" into "titles." Each title contains a number of fragments which are often again subdivided into paragraphs. The first paragraph of a fragment is called the *principium* (*pr.*), so that the paragraph numbered "one" is really the second paragraph within the fragment. Citations from the Codes and the Digest are given here in the manner usual in modern Romanist literature, i.e., by giving the numbers of book, title, fragment, and paragraph in this succession. Only three numbers are used when the fragment cited is not subdivided into paragraphs.

The two numerals used in citations from Gaius indicate the "book" and the paragraph within the "book." There are no "titles" in Gaius.

ROMAN LAW

An Historical Introduction

CHAPTER I

THE PLACE OF ROMAN LAW IN WESTERN CIVILIZATION

ROMAN LAW occupies a unique place in the history of our civilization. Originally the law of a small and insignificant rural community, then that of a powerful city-state, it became in due course the law of an empire which embraced almost the whole of the known civilized world of its time. When political, economic, and military exhaustion and the invasions of Huns and Germanic tribes put an end to this greatest political organization the world has ever seen, its law remained in force both in its eastern half, where the Byzantine Empire as the direct continuation of the old Roman Empire survived till 1453, and in its western regions, where new kingdoms under Germanic rule came into existence. In fact, it was only then—in Constantinople, the new, eastern Rome—that Roman law was for the first time laid down in a final and comprehensive statement.

Later many of its conceptions and institutions lived on in the legal systems which evolved in the Orthodox church in the East and in the Catholic church in the West. In the late Middle Ages it was considered as the supreme law of the new empire in the West, which claimed to be the successor of the Roman Empire of old. It was studied in the universities of Europe; and through the medium of university-trained jurists in chancelleries and courts, it exerted a deep influence on the development of legal institutions and doctrine in all continental European countries inside and outside the Empire, from Spain to Poland. Only in England was this influence kept within narrow limits because of the early rise of a national legal profession and the early organization of a national common law.

The influence of Roman law, moreover, in original or adapted form, extended into modern times. The *Corpus Iuris Civilis,* as the codification made in Constantinople under the auspices of Emperor Justinian in the sixth century was called in more recent times, remained an immediate source of law in wide areas of Germany until 1900. Modified forms of Roman law are even now the law of the land in Scotland, in Ceylon, and in the Union of South Africa (where it is called the Roman Dutch law). Less direct but no less important was the impact of Roman doctrines on the great codifications of private law which have come into existence in Europe, America, and Asia since the eighteenth century.[1]

The achievement of the Romans in the field of law has thus become one of the foundations of Civil law, i.e., of one of the two main groups of legal systems governing the nations of Western civilization (the other being Anglo-American Common law). We are therefore entitled to call Roman law one of the strongest formative forces in the development of Western civilization. This alone justifies the study of Roman law. But there are more reasons which make such studies significant, for Americans no less than for Europeans.

One of these reasons is of a practical nature; it concerns primarily the American lawyer and follows directly from the historical facts just outlined. Roman law, forming an im-

[1] The most important and original of these are the French code—*Code Napoleon* or *Code Civil*—of 1804, the Austrian code of 1811, the German code of 1896, and the Swiss codes of 1889 and 1907. From the French code were derived, among others, Italian, Spanish, Portuguese, Dutch, Belgian, Romanian, and Egyptian codes; the codes of Louisiana and Quebec; and most of the Latin-American codes. German law exerted a strong influence on Hungarian, Brazilian, Japanese, and Greek laws; Swiss law was recently adopted in Turkey. For a complete list, see E. Rabel, "Private Laws of Western Civilization," *Louisiana Law Review,* Vol. X (1949), 1.

portant part of the intellectual background of so many modern legal systems, supplies a basis for comparative studies and a common ground for discussing questions of co-ordination or unification in international economic and political intercourse. This importance reaches beyond the bounds of private law, the field in which the juristic art of the Romans celebrated its greatest triumphs and where the lasting influence of their achievements is most immediately felt. General jurisprudence derived from sources of Roman law played its part in shaping the Natural law of the seventeenth and eighteenth centuries and thereby had its impact on International law. We may thus say that the very fact that Anglo-American law was far less subject to Roman influences than was Civil law, and that, consequently, Romanist concepts and doctrines are not immediately familiar to the common lawyer, makes a foundation in Roman law all the more imperative for him if he wishes to find a common basis of discussion with the European or South American lawyer—whether this discussion aims to establish new legal principles in private or public international relations, or deals with problems of practice involving foreign law.

The other reason is of a more theoretical character, but perhaps of even greater importance. It touches on the interests of the historian, political scientist, and sociologist, as well as of the lawyer. Roman law is not only the best-known, the most highly developed, and the most influential of all the legal systems of the past; apart from English law, it is also the only one whose entire and unbroken history can be traced from early and primitive beginnings to a stage of elaborate perfection in the hands of skilled specialists. If studied in the light of the modern historical-comparative method, it is particularly suited to give insight into the interrelations of law and other social forces and into the psychological and intellectual processes that contribute to the growth and progress of law.

Thus legal history leads, in the last analysis, into the realm of philosophy. Its ultimate goal has been aptly described by a recent writer as a new kind of natural law:[2] not in the sense of the eighteenth-century school of Natural law, which strove to work out a system of positive principles based on pure reason and therefore supposed to be eternally valid, but in the more relative sense of discovering typical notions and techniques by which the law may react to given conditions. If due allowance is made for the multiplicity of possible reactions and for variety in detail, the fact that such reactions conform to types can be accepted as a result of research already done. The importance of this aspect of legal history in general—and of the history of Roman law in particular—to anyone who wishes to understand the social and legal phenomena of his own time and country need not be demonstrated.[3]

[2] P. Koschaker, *Europa und das römische Recht*, 345 f.

[3] To mention just one example, the earliest methods of substituting judicial litigation for the free use of force are strikingly parallel to those employed in most recent efforts to establish machinery for the peaceful solution of international controversies or of labor disputes. Concerning international controversies, see H. J. Wolff, "The Origin of Judicial Litigation among the Greeks," in *Traditio*, Vol. IV (1946), 86.

CHAPTER II

THE HISTORICAL AND CONSTITUTIONAL BACKGROUND OF ROMAN LAW

I. A BRIEF SURVEY OF ROMAN HISTORY

ARCHAEOLOGICAL DISCOVERIES have established that there existed in the centuries after 1000 B.C. several settlements on hills adjoining the Tiber River in Central Italy, thirteen miles inland from the mouth of the river. The population of these settlements was partly of Latin and partly of Sabine stock—two different branches of the Italic group of peoples. This group, whose language indicates their membership in the ethnic class known as Indo-European, had migrated into Italy during the second millennium B.C. and superimposed themselves on a pre-Indo-European population. At one time, probably in the seventh or sixth century B.C., the Tiber region fell under the domination of the Etruscans, a powerful and highly-civilized nation of non-Indo-European origin which lived in numerous cities situated to the north in the area between the valley of the Po and the Tiber River. When the Etruscan domination of the Tiber region ended around 500 B.C., there had arisen on the Tiber hills a city-state, the city of Rome.

According to legend, this city had been founded in 753 B.C. by Romulus, its first king. But this story deserves no more credit than the romantic details with which it is embroidered.

The beginnings of the city of Rome in fact are unknown. It is not impossible that the first organization of the various settlements into a state centered in a fortified city was an achievement of the Etruscans. However this may be, the name of the new community, Roma, is of Etruscan origin.

In its early days, Rome was ruled over by kings. The names of seven kings are reported, but their personalities, perhaps with the exception of the last three, are legendary. These last three kings, Tarquinius Priscus (the Old), Servius Tullius, and Tarquinius Superbus (the Arrogant)—or perhaps only the two Tarquinii—formed the Etruscan dynasty, which as such is certainly historical. In 510 or 509 B.C., the Etruscan dynasty was overthrown, and the Republic of historical times was established.

The revolution that expelled the last king was not a popular uprising but a revolt of the aristocracy. It may also have been a national reaction of the Latin-Sabine element against the Etruscan domination. Whether or not this was so depends on the question, unanswerable for us, as to who were the aristocrats staging the revolt. At any rate, what followed was a state controlled by the aristocracy. Only the aristocracy could hold offices in the state or participate in its religious cults; and at the very beginning it was probable also that only the aristocracy, voting in the assembly of the *curiae* (see below, page 39), could elect officials and exercise legislative powers. Aristocracy and commoners were strictly separated. In the early days they even lacked the *conubium;* in other words, between a noble person and a commoner no valid marriage, giving a son born of the union the status of a member of his father's family, was permitted.

The aristocracy were called the patricians, the commoners were called the plebeians. Who they were—and the cause of their inferior status—are as yet unsolved riddles. Many hypotheses have been proposed by scholars of the highest rank, ranging all the way from one which considers the patricians

8

as the old Etruscan aristocracy continuing its rule over the Latin peasants, to the opposite which holds that the patricians were the Latin peasants and the plebeians Etruscan craftsmen and businessmen who had lost their former privileged status in the national revolution of the Latins. There are theories defining the plebeians as originally aliens who had settled in Rome and on Roman soil, and others which seek the explanation in social differences, considering the plebeians simply as the smaller peasants and the little townspeople who were "clients" of the patrician clans and gave services and other contributions in return for protection.

It is not possible here to choose between these various theories. Perhaps all of them contain some grain of truth. It is not likely, however, that either class should simply be identified with one or another of the national elements of the people. In fact, it seems that the patricians were mostly of Italic stock but that some of the patrician clans were of Etruscan origin, although perhaps already Latinized when the Republic began. It is certain that the patricians were a landowning class, and it can be assumed that those few craftsmen and businessmen who existed in those early days were plebeians. But there were landholders among the plebeians, too. The general assumption is that originally only the patricians were organized in *gentes* (see below, page 23). But at a somewhat later time, at least, there were also plebeian *gentes*. Possibly those are right who think that the richer ones among the plebeian peasants succeeded in forming *gentes*. However, the *gens* at that time had already lost whatever original importance it may have had. Therefore a better explanation may be that there were a few old *gentes* which for some reason had not joined in the self-governing political community after the expulsion of the last king.[1]

At any rate, even at the earliest stage recognizable to us, we find that the plebeians were not aliens but part of the Ro-

[1] The point needs investigation.

9

man people. They held membership in the military-political organization of the citizenry in the *centuriae* and in the *tribus*, local subdivisions of the state (see below, pages 40, 41). The *tribus* in fact formed the basis for a separate organization of the plebs, under its own officers (the tribunes of the plebs), which made the plebs almost a state within the state. According to Roman tradition, this occurred in 494 B.C.

The plebeians very soon began to strive for equality with the patricians. Gradually they achieved, besides the *conubium*, a power of veto for their tribunes over decisions by officials and Senate, and admission to offices. A momentous victory came when the Licinian-Sextian law of 367 B.C. stated that at least one of the two consuls, the highest officials in the state, should be a plebeian. The Hortensian law of 287 B.C., at the latest, even provided that *plebis scita*—i.e., resolutions passed by the plebs in its special assembly under the presidency of its tribunes—should be binding on the whole citizenry, thus elevating plebiscites to the rank of full-fledged laws.

Some privileges of the patricians remained, however, chiefly with regard to priestly offices and religious functions. But these were almost all of a purely formal nature, at least after 300 B.C. Thus the struggle between patricians and plebeians, which filled the first century and one-half of the Republic, ended with the almost complete equality of the two classes. This resulted in the formation of a new aristocracy of mixed patrician and plebeian origin, the *optimates* or senatorial class. This class consisted of a number of families possessing almost a monopoly of the high offices in the state and of membership in the Senate.

During this time Rome was a small but not entirely insignificant state. It was already the dominating power in the lower Tiber Valley; as a matter of fact, as early as the establishment of the Republic it held the leading position in a league of Latin cities. In the following century it slowly pushed forward against the declining Etruscans and others. About 390

B.C., Rome was brought to the verge of catastrophe by an invasion of Gauls who burned the city but could not take the Capitol. However, after the repulse of the Gauls, Rome resumed the offensive. In a series of almost incessant wars against Etruscans, Sabines, and other Italic peoples, and finally (281–275 B.C.) against King Pyrrhus of Epirus, a Greek invader of Italy, Rome made herself the mistress of the whole Italian peninsula south of the Apennine Mountains.

A new era began in 264 B.C. Rome was now one of the great powers. For the first time it ventured out of Italy proper, intervening in internal troubles in Messana (Messina), a Sicilian town just opposite the mainland. This brought it into conflict with the Phoenician city of Carthage, the dominating commercial and maritime power of the western Mediterranean. In two immense wars (264–241 and 218–201 B.C.), Rome undermined the strength of Carthage (after a third war, 149–146 B.C., Carthage was completely destroyed) and emerged as the dominating power of the ancient world. During the third century, it had already extended its dominion over areas outside of Italy proper (Sicily, Sardinia, the present northern Italy, parts of southern France and Spain); and during the half-century following the second Carthaginian War, it reached out into the eastern Mediterranean, making war on the Hellenistic kingdoms of Macedonia and Syria and on the states of Greece.

At the same time, further progress was made in the West. By 146 B.C., Rome was the only surviving great power in the whole area of the Mediterranean, ruling over wide regions that were either directly subject as provinces or attached to Rome as satellite states, and intervening constantly in the foreign affairs of the remaining independent states. The century following that year saw the extension of Rome's direct rule over most of the lands of western North Africa and of Asia Minor, over the remainder of Spain, and over Gaul to the Rhine River. After the incorporation of Egypt in 30 B.C., nearly every country bordering on the Mediterranean Sea was dominated by Rome.

Still later followed the conquests of England, of parts of Germany, of the Balkan peninsula up to the Danube River and beyond, of Mauretania (Morocco), and of more lands in Asia as far as Mesopotamia and Armenia. The Roman Empire reached its greatest extension under Emperor Trajan (A.D. 98–117).

The building of such an empire could not occur without tremendous domestic changes and convulsions. As early as the fourth and third centuries B.C., the expansion of Roman power had changed Rome's original character of a closely knit community based on an economy of small-scale agriculture. After the second Carthaginian War, Rome became one of the leading economic centers of the ancient world and somewhat later one of the leading centers of culture. The wealth of the world and many foreigners, both free and slave, poured into Rome. Most important among the foreign elements were numerous Greeks who brought with them the refinements of Greek culture and Greek interest in art, literature, and science. The Roman upper class—save for a small, conservative minority —was eager to take full advantage of all these imports.

But the changes were not all beneficial. The new wealth was absorbed by the landed governing aristocracy and by a new and quickly rising business class, the so-called equestrians (*equites*). The masses saw little of it. On the contrary, heavy military burdens created an ever increasing indebtedness of the peasant class, which resulted more and more in the loss of their land to creditors. The small-farm economy of old Italy changed during the second century B.C. into one of huge *latifundia* owned by the aristocracy, worked by large gangs of slaves, and producing oil and wine instead of grains. Ever larger masses of the former free rural population moved into the city where they formed, together with great numbers of freedmen of foreign origin, a proletariat maintained by grains imported from the provinces, chiefly Africa; part of these grains were distributed free by the state.

In 133 B.C., under the leadership of Tiberius Sempronius Gracchus, a revolutionary movement directed at sweeping social reforms broke loose, centering in a redistribution of the land in Italy. It failed, was resumed in 123 B.C. by Tiberius's brother, Gaius, and failed again. However, this unsuccessful attempt at social reform brought to a head all the tensions produced by a century of growing social and economic dislocation. The Roman people were divided into three hostile camps, the landowning senatorial aristocracy, the rich business class of the equestrians, and the proletariat.

The old political order, which had rested on the willing acceptance by the masses of the political leadership of the aristocracy, broke down, and a century of revolution followed which saw bloody civil wars and the rise to dictatorial power of ambitious leaders—Gaius Marius, Lucius Cornelius Sulla, Gnaeus Pompeius, and Gaius Iulius Caesar—with unsuccessful efforts by others to reach the same goal. (It is remarkable —and significant for Rome's position in the world—that nevertheless its foreign expansion and the development of its culture continued unchecked.) Domestic peace returned after 31 B.C., when Caesar's nephew and heir, Gaius Octavius, defeated the last serious seeker of power, Marcus Antonius. In 27 B.C., Octavius, who, as Caesar's adopted son, called himself Gaius Iulius Caesar Octavianus, was given the title *Augustus* (the Majestic) and subsequently was granted sweeping powers which made him a virtual monarch.

This was the beginning of Rome's imperial period. Theoretically, it was a re-establishment of the republican constitution, the emperor (from *imperator*—the commander—the military title held by Augustus) being only one of the chief officials of the state and the commander in chief of the army. But, as a political fact, the new state was a monarchy in the beginning and became more so as time went on. The extraordinary civil and military powers of Augustus[2] and his over-whelming personal prestige (*auctoritas*) made him a real ruler. He was designated *princeps senatus,* leader of the Senate, with the right to speak first on any question under debate (there-fore this form of state is commonly called the Principate). As *Divi filius,* i.e., as the son of the deified Caesar (*Divus Iulius*), he was able to drape his rule with a religious cloak. The hold-ers of high offices, in name republican, were hand-picked by the emperor. The popular assembly, which in the last decades of the Republic had degenerated into a tumultuous gathering of the rabble of the capital, lost its importance. Under Au-gustus's successor, Tiberius, its right to elect officials was trans-ferred to the Senate; soon its legislative activity also ceased. The Senate retained for a time its functions as a governing body. In spite of the fact that many of its members were the emperor's henchmen, it was able for some time to uphold the conservative ideal of Rome as a Republic led by its aristoc-racy.

But the old senatorial nobility was gradually dying out, partly as a result of bloody persecutions staged by emperors of the first century A.D. in retaliation for real or alleged con-spiracies against their rule. Moreover, from the time of Clau-dius (A.D. 41–54), the membership of the Senate included in-creasing numbers of provincial notables who owed their digni-ty to imperial grace. In the second century A.D., the Senate be-came an assembly of mere yes-men.

Even more than in Rome itself, the emperor was truly an absolute ruler in the provinces. Several of these remained nominally dependent on the Senate, but their governors were chosen by the emperor. Others which required military garri-sons were kept by Augustus under his direct administration. Egypt was from the beginning placed under a special regime

---

2 The word became part of his name: Imperator Caesar Augustus. These three words remained as the imperial title, to which later emperors added their individual names.

which excluded any senatorial influence upon its administration and gave the emperor, in the eyes of the natives, the position of a successor to their former kings.

Both for Rome and the Empire the ascendance of Augustus was a blessing. Not only did it bring an end to the civil wars, but to the provinces it also brought honest and just administration, a thing unknown to them under the rule of the corrupt nobility of the period of the dying Republic. During the Principate there were wars at the frontiers of the Empire, which included most of the civilized world. But inside the Empire a rarely interrupted peace reigned for more than two hundred years. As a result, comparative prosperity was enjoyed by a relatively large proportion of the population. The Principate was also a period of high, though slowly declining, culture and of widespread education.

The social complexion of the Empire was different from that of the times preceding it. The political importance of the senatorial class faded away. Instead a new class of imperial officials, taken from the equestrian class—i.e., the upper middle class—gained in importance and prestige, especially from the reigns of Hadrian and Antoninus Pius on. The fact that many of the highest equestrian officials obtained senatorial rank contributed to the transformation of the senatorial class.[3] Peace and prosperity and an active world trade made the Principate a time of the middle class and of an urban civilization.

This and the prevailing authoritarian form of government changed the relative importance of capital and provinces; the provinces moved steadily toward a position of equality with the capital. It was at first chiefly Roman citizens, living in the provinces in considerable numbers since republican times, who profited from the new conditions; some of the most

[3] Equestrians received senatorial rank by imperial grant. In addition, senators were in the imperial period required to show a fortune of at least 1,000,000 sesterces ($50,000). The minimum census for equestrians was 400,000 sesterces ($20,000). Any freeborn citizen eighteen years old and possessing property valued in this amount was eligible to the equestrian class.

prominent men of the first two centuries A.D., among them several emperors, were natives of Spain, for example. But Roman citizenship itself was extended. Individual grants of citizenship had of course always occurred. The imperial period witnessed a large-scale spread of citizenship among provincials who retained their foreign residence and nationality. The beginnings of this development lay actually in the republican period when, as a consequence of a bloody rebellion of Rome's Italian allies (the Marsic or Social War, 90–88 B.C.), the citizens of the Italian cities received the status of Roman citizens.

Under the Principate, citizenship was often given to outstanding men in provincial cities. More important, it was regularly given to honorably discharged veterans of the army which then consisted largely of non-citizens. The effect of this policy was a change in the character of Roman citizenship. In theory, it was still conceived as that of the city of Rome, thereby retaining some of its old splendor; in actual fact, it became an Empire citizenship. The last step was taken by Emperor Caracalla, who in A.D. 212 bestowed citizenship on the bulk of the free inhabitants of the Empire. The whole evolution resulted in making an empty dignity of Roman citizenship— once the proud privilege of participating in the government of the city that ruled the world—and in making the citizen a mere subject. But it also produced a feeling of unity and a sort of Empire-patriotism throughout the Empire.

The period of the Principate lasted about three hundred years. For almost two generations the emperors came from Augustus's own family (the Julian-Claudian dynasty, A.D. 14–68, ending with the death of Nero).[4] Then, after a brief troubled interlude in which three emperors were proclaimed within the space of little more than one year, came the Flavian

---

[4]The emperors of this dynasty were Tiberius (A.D. 14–37), Gaius, better known by his nickname Caligula (A.D. 37–41), Claudius (A.D. 41–54), and Nero (A.D. 54–68).

dynasty of Vespasian (A.D. 69–79) and his two sons, Titus (A.D. 79–81) and Domitian (A.D. 81–96), the latter a bloody tyrant; Domitian was murdered, as was the insane Caligula before him. After the brief rule of the aged Nerva (A.D. 96–98), honest and well-meaning but ineffective, Rome saw a succession of four excellent emperors: Trajan of Spain (A.D. 98–117), the first provincial on the throne, Hadrian (A.D. 117–138), Antoninus Pius (A.D. 138–161), and Marcus Aurelius (A.D. 161–180).

This long period of good government became possible by the fact that neither Nerva nor any of his first three successors had a son, so that they were able to select worthy successors through the formal step of adopting them. However, during the reign of Marcus Aurelius there occurred a turn for the worse. Difficult wars against the Parthians (Persians) and the Marcomanni, a group of Germanic tribes, and a terrible plague did much to interrupt the long enjoyed prosperity. Heavy taxes, necessary for the maintenance of the army, had been slowly draining the wealth of the middle class and had become a very heavy burden on the rural population. Now the economic situation began to decline sharply. This was coupled with the mistake of Marcus Aurelius in choosing his son, Commodus (A.D. 180–192), as his successor; Commodus turned out one of the worst emperors Rome ever had.

The death of Commodus, who was murdered, plunged the empire into confusion and civil war. Septimius Severus (A.D. 193–211), after years of fighting, succeeded in establishing his authority. He represented a new type of emperor. A Roman citizen of equestrian rank, he had had a distinguished career in the administration and in the army and had been raised to senatorial status by Marcus Aurelius. His ruthless but good rule was founded on the army, now exclusively composed of provincials (Septimius Severus himself was a native of Africa, of Phoenician stock), which received many special favors. His reforms wiped out the last vestiges of senatorial

17

participation in the government and marked the decisive step toward imperial absolutism, although the outward forms of republican institutions which characterized the Principate were preserved.

Septimius Severus founded a new dynasty which lasted till A.D. 235.[5] After this date the Empire suffered a complete collapse. Fifty years followed which were an almost constant period of civil and foreign war, interrupted only at times by capable emperors who for brief periods brought internal peace by ruling with an iron hand. Deterioration of the coinage, begun as early as under Septimius Severus, and ever increasing taxes with their consequences of inflation and decline in economic activity, were among the causes of the catastrophe.

But the ultimate cause of all evils was the dominant position of the soldiery, a soldiery that included no longer any Roman elements and had long lost its sense of patriotism and duty. A practice which had made itself felt occasionally in earlier times, especially after the death of Nero and after the death of Commodus, became the order of the day. The army, or sometimes individual armies stationed in different parts of the Empire, became accustomed to raising popular generals to emperorship. The unavoidable effects were anarchy and an ever deepening economic depression; for the emperors of this period, the so-called soldier-emperors, were forced to make concession after concession to the soldiers, with all the devastating consequences such a situation could not fail to have for the finances of the Empire.

This terrible period came to an end when a general-emperor, Diocletian (A.D. 284–304), succeeded in establishing his rule firmly and in reorganizing the Empire which, surprising-

---

[5] Septimius Severus was succeeded by his sons, Marcus Aurelius Antoninus, better known as Caracalla (A.D. 211–217), who had been his father's coemperor since A.D. 194, and Publius Septimius Geta (murdered in A.D. 212 at Caracalla's instigation); and, after a brief interruption, by his nephews, Marcus Aurelius Antoninus, better known as Elagabalus (A.D. 218–222), and Marcus Aurelius Severus Alexander (A.D. 222–235).

ly enough, had survived the storm with its main structure intact. With his rule, the final period of Roman history began. It is called the Dominate because the emperor now in law as well as in fact was absolute, the master (*dominus*) of his subjects. Under the new order as established by Diocletian, all governmental functions were concentrated in the hands of the emperor, who was recognized as a god;[6] the last vestiges of authority of the Senate were gone. However, in view of the political situation during the last century of the Principate, this was a change in form rather than in fact.

Actually, Diocletian's reorganization of the Empire was more a consolidation than it was a new departure. He even tried to return to old Roman concepts by adapting these to the conditions of the times. But the ancient world emerged from the period of anarchy entirely changed. Rome had lost its pre-eminent status and had become just one city among others. Diocletian had, in fact, scattered the central offices of the government over four provincial cities (Milan, Trier, Sirmium, and Nicomedia), each having equal rank with the others, and each being the capital city of one of the two emperors (*Augusti*) and two subemperors (*Caesares*). His successor, Constantine, made Byzantium (named Constantinople after him) the New Rome.

Declining productivity and heavy taxes had brought loss of incentive and deterioration of civic responsibility. The intolerable taxes had in fact induced the upper classes in the cities to seek escape by every means possible; later emperors actually had to make membership in the *curiae* (the bodies in

6 The emperors had from Augustus been worshipped as gods in the provinces. In the East they posed as successors of the divine Hellenistic kings. In Rome itself the living *princeps* was not a god, but the Senate had power to proclaim a dead emperor as *divus*, i.e., as elevated to the gods. This was done for Caesar, Augustus, and for most of the succeeding emperors. Diocletian's demand of divine honors from all his subjects was not in the Roman tradition, although Caesar and some emperors—Caligula, Domitianus, Commodus—had tried to raise similar demands. It was part of Diocletian's redefinition of Roman emperorship in terms of divine and absolute Hellenistic kingship.

which the local nobility was organized) compulsory for families of the required standing.

Even more disastrous, however, was the plight of the rural population. The "colonate," a type of semiservitude, formerly known only in some provinces, was spreading over the Empire, because many peasants saw no other way of escaping the exactions of creditors and rapacious officials than by turning their land over to some large landholder who could protect them, and receiving it back as tenants under conditions which severely curtailed their personal freedom.

Culture, too, had suffered. Education had deteriorated. Instead of the highly intellectual spirit of the stoic philosophy which had permeated the upper and middle classes during the first centuries of the imperial period, more emotional movements, expressing themselves in new religions, had made steady progress since the beginning of the Principate. But one of these religions attained world-historic importance. At the time of the accession of Diocletian, the most successful of them, Christianity, was on the verge of triumph. It underwent a last great persecution under Diocletian, but his successor, Constantine, through the famous Edict of Tolerance issued at Milan in 313, gave it equality with the other religions of the Empire. He took an active interest in the Nicene Council of 325 and eventually became a convert himself. Theodosius I, by the end of the fourth century, made Christianity the official religion of the state.

On the whole, the reforms of Diocletian and Constantine brought improvement. The fourth century compares favorably with both its predecessor and successor. Internal peace was better secured. Economic conditions improved. A tremendous inflation, comparable to that in Europe after the first World War, was arrested. Education and culture reached a higher level. But all these improvements were paid for with a general loss of individual freedom and with a rising spirit of religious and political intolerance.

New dangers arose soon in the form of invasions by Huns and Germanic tribes. The Migration of Nations reached the borders of the Empire. This was a shock that the Empire, weakened as it was, could not stand. Diocletian had found that the Empire had become too unwieldy to be governed by his new bureaucracy from one central point and had divided it into two halves, one comprising Italy and the lands to the west, the other the eastern countries. In 286 he made another general, Maximianus, his co-Augustus and entrusted him with the government of the western half of the Empire, reserving for himself the eastern half and the final decision in matters concerning the whole Empire. During the remainder of the fourth century, the Empire was sometimes divided and sometimes united. But the division became permanent when in 395 Theodosius I divided the Empire between his two sons, Arcadius and Honorius.

The Western Empire, left with its own insufficient resources and torn by intrigue and strife at the top, could not stand the impact of the invasions. Germanic kingdoms were established in Africa by the Vandals, in Spain and southwestern France by the Visigoths, and in southeastern France by the Burgundians. Italy itself several times was the victim of invasion. In 476, the last West Roman emperor, Romulus Augustulus, was deposed by Odoacer, the leader of a mixed group of barbarians which took Rome. Odoacer who made himself king of Italy recognized, it is true, the nominal overlordship of the emperor in Constantinople, as other Germanic leaders had done before him and as Theodoric, the leader of the Ostrogoths, did when he conquered Italy from Odoacer in 488–493. Nevertheless, the accession to power of Odoacer marked the end of the Roman Empire in the West.

The Eastern Empire, richer, more civilized, and better organized, succeeded in fighting off the invaders. Justinian (527–565) even succeeded in re-conquering Africa, Italy, and parts of Spain, and thus in partly restoring, for a brief spell, the old Empire. However, most of the gains were surrendered by his immediate successors, and from then on East and West remained separated. The Roman Empire of the East, which we call the Byzantine Empire, carried on for almost another millennium, constantly fighting against Persians, Arabs, and Turks. In the thirteenth century, as a result of one of the crusades, it was for some time attached to the new western, medieval Empire. It reached its end in 1453 when the Turks conquered Constantinople.

II. THE ROMAN STATE

1. PRIMITIVE ROME

The Romans credited Servius Tullius, the sixth of the seven Roman kings, with the establishment of important institutions of their government. But the truth of this tradition is doubtful. Most of the institutions attributed to him certainly originated at a later date and were ascribed to the regal period to make them appear more venerable. The role of Servius Tullius in the history of the Roman state, if he ever lived at all, cannot be ascertained.

Later Roman historians described the early city as the "Rome of the four regions." This comprised the *Septimontium* (i.e., the "Seven Hills"), Mounts Viminalis and Quirinalis, and the low ground in between (the *Subura*). It is hard to say what the four regions represented. It may be that they were originally separate villages, but it is also possible that from the beginning they were mere parts of the town. The latter possibility would gain in probability if the theory is correct which holds that in the Etruscan period Rome was a thriving center of trade and commerce.[7] It is certain that the territory of the Roman state was not confined to the city itself and that

7 See F. Bozza, *La possessio dell'ager publicus*, in *Fondazione Guglielmo Castelli*, XVIII, 141 f.

the early Romans—and particularly their nobility which in
the earlier republican era alone formed the political community—were a peasant people.

The population had presumably from pre-Roman times
been organized in *gentes*. The word *gens* may be translated as
"clan." A *gens* was a group of families which in the beginning
had probably lived together in one or several villages—or at
any rate as neighbors occupying a coherent territory—believed themselves to be the descendants of a common ancestor,
and performed certain religious cults in common. They had a
common name, the *nomen gentile*, while as a rule each of the
families belonging to the *gens* had its own name, the *cognomen*
or surname, and each individual member of a family a given
name in addition.[8] This is all that can be said about the *gens*
with a reasonable amount of probability, although it is not
unlikely that at a very early time, before any state had come
into existence, the *gens* was an independent political unit. As
a matter of fact, it seems that some residue of this original
condition persisted as late as the time of the earliest Republic;
for we are told that in 479–477 B.C. the *gens Fabia*, with the
permission of the Roman Senate, waged war against the Etruscan city of Veii.[9]

But it is impossible to answer the question of the internal
organization of the *gens* at that time. It is especially difficult
to accept the theory that the *gens* was at one time a closely knit
group ruled over by a chief, the *pater gentis* (father of the
clan), which only after the consolidation of the state split up
into individual families. A recent suggestion that the *gens* was
a loose association of families which chose a common leader

---

[8] For instance: Publius Cornelius Scipio; Publius is the given name *(praenomen)*, Cornelius the *nomen gentile*, and Scipio the *cognomen*. To be sure,
in the earlier period it was mainly patricians who had all three names. Most
Romans had only a *praenomen* and *nomen gentile*, and it was not until the
imperial period that *cognomina* became common.

[9] Livy, *Ab Urbe Condita Libri* 2.48.8–50.11. See also H. Siber, "Die ältesten
römischen Volksversammlungen," in *Z. Sav. St.*, Vol. LVII (1937), 256.

only when confronted with an emergency seems to be nearer the truth.[10] Whatever its original nature may have been, in historical times the *gens* had no longer any legal importance except for the right of the members of a clan to seize the estate of a fellow-member who had died without leaving any will or natural heir, and to claim the guardianship over a minor or insane fellow-member without relatives.

Servius Tullius is said to have organized the whole Roman people into thirty *curiae*—ten in each of the original tribes of the Ramnes, Tities, and Luceres—with each *curia* consisting of ten *gentes*. In this tradition the only certain element is the existence of the *curiae*, which were associations performing religious functions and acting as the voting units in the oldest form of Roman legislative assemblies. Little is known about the three tribes just mentioned except that they had nothing to do with the later local "tribes."

Nor is any definite statement possible about the character of the office of the king (*rex*) except that it existed. This fact is proved by the existence in the Republic of a *rex sacrificulus* or "offering-making king," then a minor religious official, and by the institution of the *interregnum*—the word may in this instance be translated by "stopgap kingship"—which served to bridge a vacancy in the highest office of the state (the Senate designated as *interrex* for five days one of its members, who designated a successor for five days, and so on, until new consuls were elected). Perhaps the king was elected for life by the assembly of the *curiae* or by the Senate, but it is also possible that he designated his own successor. He may have been regularly taken from one particular family. His functions were those of chief priest, general, and protector of domestic peace.

10 This is the theory of P. Frezza, "La costituzione cittadina di Roma ed il problema degli ordinamenti giuridici preesistenti," in *Scritti in Onore di Contardo Ferrini Pubblicati in Occasione della Sua Beatificazione*, I, 275–98.

2. THE ROMAN REPUBLIC

While all statements concerning the regal period are necessarily uncertain, the constitutional history of the Republic is, as a whole, well known. Its institutions and underlying concepts, which in modified form survived in the imperial period, are the foundation on which the historical legal system of Rome rested.

The Roman "constitution" was never expressed in a document which, like the American Constitution, set forth with the authority of the highest law of the land the forms, functions, powers, and mutual relations of the organs of government. The Roman "constitution" was, like the English, a complex of ancient principles and developing practices, supported by some specific enactments, which in their totality defined the powers and functions of government. Before we enter upon a description of its main institutions, however, a few observations about its character and spirit may be in place.

Rome was never a democracy in the sense of either Greek or modern democracy. The transition from monarchy to republic probably meant no more than the passing of the powers of a lifelong king to annually elected officials. This gave the patrician *gentes* security against such attempts at tyrannical government as had been made by Tarquinius Superbus, but left the whole fabric of the state unchanged. The effect of the plebeian movement was similar. It gained for the plebeians as a class full participation in the direction of the state and produced some institutions devised to check oppression by patrician officials, but it did not change the aristocratic character of Roman government. Though in theory offices now were open to every citizen, they remained in fact in the hands of a number of families, of both patrician and plebeian stock, who, being the bigger landowners, were able to devote their time, without salary, to public affairs and were held so high in social esteem that they could practically monopolize the business of government. Only rarely did a *homo novus,* a "new man" from the outside, succeed in attaining the highest office; Gaius Marius and Marcus Tullius Cicero, the famous orator and statesman, are outstanding examples.

Nor were the popular assemblies which elected the officials and passed laws truly democratic; for they were organized in such a way as to give effective control to the rich, and particularly to those whose wealth consisted in land. Furthermore, the power of the popular assemblies was strictly limited (see below, page 38). Political power was thus concentrated in the hands of the landed upper class which filled the offices and thereby the seats in the Senate; it is for this reason called the senatorial class. Only during the revolutionary first century B.C. did the masses have greater influence, but even then they were really only a tool in the hands of the demagogues (usually aristocrats) who led them; and the period ended in the establishment of a new form of state which deprived the masses of the last shred of power and increasingly reduced the aristocracy to impotence in favor of a bureaucracy serving the emperor.

Nevertheless, the Roman Republic achieved a stability seldom paralleled in history and maintained the strength to weather mortal dangers and ultimately to make herself the mistress of an enormous Empire. One contributing factor was the character of the Roman aristocracy in the period down to the third Carthaginian War. Although producing very few great men, it maintained until then, in addition to a dignified reserve *(gravitas),* an unusually high level of ethical standards and statesmanlike wisdom, a tenacity in adversity, and a spirit of disinterested patriotism which both justified and secured its claim to leadership. The other factor was the machinery of government which, although certainly not consciously planned in this way, resulted in an ingenious system of checks and balances. It was this characteristic of the Roman constitution which elicited the ardent admiration of the great Greek historian, Polybius, who was a close friend of Publius Cornelius Scipio Aemilianus, the conqueror of Carthage and most highly esteemed Roman statesman of the later second century B.C.

This system of checks and balances was not the result, as in the American Constitution, of a division of power between the legislative, executive, and judiciary branches of the government. On the one hand, it consisted in a combination of practically unlimited powers of the highest officials with powers of veto by officials of equal or higher rank. On the other, it lay in the political control of the officials by the Senate, the tribunes of the plebs, and the people. For the people could reject a bill brought by an official, and the official depended on their votes when later running for another office.

Three elements must be considered in discussing the Roman constitution: the officials, the people, and the Senate.

A. THE OFFICIALS. The magistracy was the most important and most characteristic element in the Roman constitution. The word denotes the governing office; it comes from the Latin *magistratus*, meaning both the official and his office. In the Roman terminology the word "magistrate" includes all political officials, from the consuls down.

In the magistracy the strong Roman sense for authority found expression. In the Roman conception, differing from the modern, the powers of the magistrate were not clearly limited by law. It is true that magistrates below the highest rank were charged only with certain functions. But within the confines of these functions, their authority, called *potestas*, was unlimited; they could issue and enforce by fines—up to a legally fixed limit—any order which in their discretion was fit to achieve their purpose, and they could be stopped only by the veto of a colleague, a higher official, or a tribune of the plebs.

The three highest officials—dictator, consul, and praetor —were not even restricted in their functions. In so far as special duties were assigned to them, such as the administration of justice to the praetor, this followed from the necessity of dividing governmental work among several officials rather than from the nature of their office (the praetor was, of course, restricted by the superior authority of the consul who would prevent him from meddling in matters not his concern). The authority of the magistrates was so great that they might even disregard the law, except when it specifically ordered or forbade them to act. We shall have opportunity to observe the decisive influence this particular aspect of the magistrate's *potestas* had on the evolution of the Roman legal system.

In addition to the general *potestas* of every magistrate, the three highest officials—dictator, consul, and praetor—possessed a further power described as *imperium*. This power originated and was properly at home in the military sphere where it meant the absolute power of the commander in chief to issue and enforce orders, a power which existed with respect to the soldiers under his command as well as to the population in the area of military operations. It involved the authority to take any measure of coercion the commander saw fit to take, including corporal and even capital punishment. In the Roman conception of the state, the command of the army was the primary function of the highest magistrates, and from this function, in which the magistrate's power found its fullest expression, the Romans derived the nature of his office and authority in general. The concept of *imperium* was the pivot of all Roman constitutional thinking. It is possible but not certain that it was brought to them by the Etruscans.

As an awe-inspiring sign of their power, magistrates vested with *imperium* appeared in public accompanied by their lictors, who carried the *fasces*—i.e., a bundle of rods surrounding an ax (like the sign on the American dime).

In principle, the *imperium* was effective inside no less than outside the city of Rome. Inside the city, however, it was somewhat limited by the fact that even the magistrate, with all his power, was under the authority of the *populus Romanus,* the Roman people conceived as a political community. Accordingly, the magistrate's power to impose fines was from very early times restricted by law; and against an order by which he was to suffer corporal or capital punishment—except when issued by a dictator—a citizen had a right to appeal to the popular assembly, the *comitia centuriata,* which had the final decision. This appeal was called *provocatio ad populum.* As a symbol of this limitation of the *imperium,* the lictors concealed the ax when they displayed the *fasces* inside the city limits (*pomerium*).[11]

The Romans considered the *provocatio* as the palladium of the liberty of the citizen and cherished the belief that its introduction coincided with the establishment of the Republic. This, however, is very doubtful. It is almost certain that the institution was an innovation of the earlier republican period, although the circumstances and time of its introduction are matters of conjecture.

These were for a long time, however, the only legal restraints on the *imperium.* The magistrate was free to take any other measure of coercion, and the restrictions named benefited only Roman citizens (and, till the second century B.C., among citizens only those within the city). Outside the city lay the sphere of military law, and there the *imperium* remained absolute until a late date. It was not before the early second century B.C. that a *lex Porcia* allowed the *provocatio* against coercive steps taken by magistrates outside the city— at first only in the interest of civilians. Later in the same century, the principle was liberalized to the extent that even soldiers were permitted to have disciplinary actions referred to the popular assembly.

[11] The *pomerium* had originally been the true line of defense for the city. In republican times, however, it was not extended when the city grew, and it came to be situated within the actual city. It became an imaginary line, playing its part in some old religious and legal traditions, but no longer of any military importance.

This conception of the magistrate's power was, of course, fraught with danger, although in the earlier period this danger was usually mitigated by the high sense of duty which was then characteristic of Roman officials. But the constitution itself provided for an effective safeguard in the right of veto mentioned before, or—to express it in the Roman manner— in the right of the tribunes of the plebs and of magistrates of equal or higher rank to intercede against any act of a magistrate.

In connection with the right of "intercession," another very characteristic principle of the Roman constitution should be mentioned, namely that of "colleagueship." This means that offices were given to several men simultaneously who held equal *potestas* and, where this was in question, *imperium*. This arrangement permitted not only a division of the burdens of their office between the incumbents for the sake of greater efficiency; for example, in time of war each of the consuls could go to a different theater of military operations. More interesting from the standpoint of constitutional law was the effect of providing a safeguard against misuse of the *imperium* by either of the two colleagues. For it was a principle of Roman law that whenever a power or right was shared by several persons, each partner was entitled separately and independently to exercise to their full extent the powers involved in the right. This included the power to prevent anybody else, even the other partner, from encroaching upon the right.

The effect was that partners who disagreed could completely check one another; *partes concursu fiunt,* "the clash makes the parts," was the Roman way of describing the situation. It was this principle—applicable to public office as well as to private rights—which furnished the legal basis for the mutual right of veto among colleagues.

Normally offices involving *potestas* were elective and annual. As is usual when the highest positions are filled with politicians serving only short terms of office, the Roman magistrates needed the aid of a skilled technical staff. This aid came from the *apparitores,* professional salaried government workers who were appointed by the magistrates. The *apparitores* were, of course, responsible for much of the daily routine and for the clerical work, but they had no *potestas* and no political importance. They came from the lower social classes.

The early history of the republican magistracy is a matter of much controversy among modern students of Roman law. It is possible, but not very likely, that the highest office was dual from the beginning. Some scholars believe that originally there was only one chief magistrate, perhaps assisted by a junior colleague, with each having the *imperium.* The probable title of the highest official, whose position differed from that of the king merely by the fact that the office was now rotating annually among the patricians, was *praetor*—a word which in its original meaning indicates a military command. The office may have been doubled when increasing numbers of citizens permitted an enlargement of the army through the organization of a second legion.[12] This theory has in its favor the analogy of other Latin cities which were governed by a single *dictator,* as well as the later institution of dictatorship in Rome itself.

But we also hear of the existence in old times of a *praetor maximus,* and this has called forth the theory that the chief office was tripartite and only in the fourth century B.C.—when the praetorship of the later type (see below, page 33) was established—only then divided into the double-headed chief office of the *consules*[13] and the smaller magistracy of a single praetor. The expression *praetor maximus* may, as was recently sug-

12 This was recently suggested by P. de Francisci, "Dal regnum alla 'res publica,'" in *Studia et Documenta Historiae et Iuris,* Vol. X (1944), 150 ff.

13 The title was perhaps derived from the fact that they consulted the Senate.

gested,[14] simply refer to the oldest man among the three chiefs; this hypothesis seems preferable to the other that the *praetor maximus* was of higher rank than his colleagues, because in the latter case it would be difficult to imagine the transition from the earlier arrangement to that of historical times.

It is perhaps possible to combine the two main theories, in that the reorganization of the army may have brought about the doubling of the chief office, with the assistant of the original single chief remaining as a third colleague.

All this, however, is highly conjectural. It is certain only that in the early days the leadership of the state was an important issue in the struggle between patricians and plebeians and that its form underwent changes. For a time, in the fifth and fourth centuries B.C., the government was often in the hands of varying numbers of military tribunes with consular power. These tribunes, many of them plebeians, were the commanders of the cohorts into which the army was divided; after the organization of the two legions, each of them was composed of three cohorts of one thousand men each.

At the time of the fully developed republican constitution—i.e., from about the middle of the fourth century B.C.— the government consisted mainly of the following magistracies:

(a) *The Consul.* The two consuls were probably the heirs of the whole political position and power of the king. They had the highest *imperium,* except when there was a dictator. Such limitations as followed from the principle of colleagueship and from the restriction of the term of office to the brief space of one year were quantitative rather than qualitative; and further offices were created to relieve the consuls of administrative detail but not to confine their authority. Only the priestly functions of the king seem from the beginning to have been separated from their office. The task of the consuls

14 G. Wesenberg, "Praetor Maximus," in *Z. Sav. St.,* Vol. LXV (1947), 319–26.

was political leadership—in particular, the conduct of foreign affairs and the command of the army. The year was named after them, since the Romans had no era by which to number their years.

(b) *The Praetor*. A specialized magistracy with the title of praetor was established in 367 B.C. to relieve the consuls of the administration of justice. It remained at first reserved for the patricians, but thirty years later the plebeians gained access to it. In the beginning there was only one praetor, but by 242 B.C. a second one was added. Henceforth the first praetor was charged only with the administration of justice among Roman citizens, while the second one took care of the affairs between citizens and aliens and among aliens. Accordingly, the first praetor was called *praetor urbanus* (city praetor), the second *praetor peregrinus* (alien praetor).

When Rome acquired her first provinces, four more praetors were added to be sent there as governors. A law of the dictator Sulla, promulgated in 81 B.C., raised the total number to eight; at that time, however, the six additional praetors were also kept in the capital to preside over criminal courts, while the provinces were taken care of by promagistrates (see below, page 45).

Strictly speaking, the praetorship was not an office sharply distinguished from the consulship. The praetor was rather conceived as a kind of junior colleague of the consuls. He was vested with the same *imperium*, although the *imperium* of the consul was considered as *maius* (greater); that is to say, the consul could intervene against the praetor, but not vice versa. Accordingly, the praetor had only six lictors as compared to the consul's twelve.

By virtue of its connection with the administration of justice, the praetorship, as represented by the *praetores urbanus* and *peregrinus*, was of all the Roman magistracies the most important from the standpoint of legal history.

(c) *The Aedilis.* Also in 367 B.C., a new annual office without *imperium* was created for the purpose of keeping the state archives, of performing what we may call police functions (namely, the supervision of streets, buildings, bridges, and aqueducts), and of maintaining order in the public market place. Four functionaries, called the aediles, were charged with these duties. Two of them, the plebeian aediles, had long been in existence as officials of the plebs under the tribunes of the plebs. Now two more, at first patricians, were added as magistrates of the whole people. They were the "curule" aediles— so called, because, like consuls and praetors, they were entitled to the *sella curulis* (wheeled chair), one of the signs of the dignity of the patrician magistrate. In their capacity as market officers the aediles were responsible for important features of the Roman law of sales.

(d) *The Quaestor.*[15] This annual magistracy was established about the middle of the fifth century B.C., perhaps in imitation of an office which existed in South Italian Greek cities. The quaestors served as assistants of the consuls in financial and other administrative matters. Originally two, their number was gradually increased to as many as twenty. The quaestorship was the lowest of the magistracies. After a regular career had become customary, it was the first office usually sought by young men who wanted to devote their lives to politics.

The sources also mention *quaestores paricidii* (investigators of murder). These should be kept distinct from the financial quaestors. The *quaestores paricidii,* who seem to have made their first appearance in very early times, were not magistrates but special appointees of the chief magistrate. Their function was probably to ascertain whether a killing

---

15 The author follows K. Latte, "The Origin of the Roman Quaestorship," in *Transactions of the American Philological Association*, Vol. LXVII (1936), 24–33.

that had occurred in the community was intentional or unintentional; for under a very ancient rule, which possibly antedated the XII Tables, the accidental killer was not liable to the death penalty but only required to do religious atonement.

(e) *The Censor.* For military purposes, a census of the Roman citizens was regularly taken every five years. In 443 B.C., a new magistracy, the censorship, was established for this purpose, and henceforth two censors were elected every five years. The censors lacked the *imperium,* but their office was in some respects considered the highest dignity a Roman citizen could obtain; consequently, only *consulares*—i.e., men who had already served as consuls—were ordinarily chosen for the office, and censors enjoyed special honors not even given to the consuls. The reason for this was the fact that the officials who took the census had the power to decide the "class" and *tribus* to which each individual citizen was to belong. In view of the great differences between the classes and tribes, this implied the power to determine the political and social status of every citizen, a power which was the greater as there was no appeal from the decision of the censors. Furthermore—and this was even more important—the censors made up the list of the senators, with the power of excluding from the Senate a man held unworthy of this dignity.

Thus the censors became the watchmen over the moral behavior, in both public and private life, of the citizens; in fact, elaborating upon the activities mentioned, they developed a general jurisdiction in matters of morals, and the *nota censoria,* although in itself no more than an official censure, became their dreaded weapon. Possessing unlimited discretionary power, they were able to render decisions which could practically destroy a man politically and socially.

For centuries the censors, usually men of the highest character themselves, were responsible for the remarkably high moral standards of the Roman people and, especially, of their upper classes. Toward the end of the Republic, censorian control broke down, and the office finally disappeared. Augustus, however, assumed its powers and used them in his effort to restore the old standards which had been seriously impaired by the luxurious life and the unscrupulous political methods to which the Roman upper class had become accustomed during the last century of the Republic.

The activities of the censors lasted usually only about eighteen months out of every five years, being concluded by a public sacrifice called the *lustrum*.[16]

(f) *The Dictator*. In times of emergency the principle of colleagueship, the tribunician right of intercession, and the right of citizens to appeal to the people by way of *provocatio* might seriously hamper strong government. For such occasions the Romans had an extraordinary magistrate with *imperium,* the dictator, who was freed of these limitations. The dictator was not elected but named by one of the consuls. His authority was greater than that of the consuls. He had twenty-four lictors. However, he was supposed to resign as soon as the emergency was over; and in any event his office ended not later than the term of office of the consul who had named him or after six months had elapsed. The dictator in his turn named a deputy, the *magister equitum* (literally, leader of the cavalry), who also possessed the *imperium* and was subordinate only to the dictator himself.

In the old times, with their incessant wars near the city, the Romans made rather frequent use of this expedient. Gradually, however, the importance of the office declined. The consuls in actual fact named dictators only when so directed by the Senate; tribunician veto and *provocatio* became available against dictators; finally dictators were occasionally

---

[16] As this occurred every five years, it became customary to call a period of five years a *lustrum*. In this meaning the expression found its way into the modern languages.

elected; and after the second Carthaginian War the practice of turning the government over to a dictator was discontinued. An office of the same name appeared again, however, in the revolutionary troubles of the first century B.C., when Sulla and later Caesar were given the title and powers of dictator. But now its character was changed. Dictatorship was no longer the old emergency magistracy but an expression of the absolute political power these men had obtained.

(g) *The Tribunes of the Plebs.* Although not magistrates in the strict sense, the tribunes of the plebs should be mentioned here. This office was, probably in the early fifth century B.C., forced upon the patricians by the plebeians who needed an organ to protect them against the arbitrary use of the *imperium* by patrician magistrates. The tribunes—their original number was five, but soon raised to ten—were annually elected by the plebs. They had no *imperium* or *potestas* but an absolute power to veto any act of a magistrate; this power belonged, like every official power under the Roman constitution, to each tribune individually. To secure the exercise of their power the tribunes were recognized as "sacrosanct," that is to say, they were inviolable and not subject to the coercion of holders of the *imperium*. They were entitled to attend the meetings of the Senate, to submit bills to the *concilia plebis,* and to prosecute criminals before the *comitia centuriata;* this right was a potent weapon against patrician magistrates who overstepped their bounds in their dealings with plebeians.

Throughout the republican period, the tribunate never quite lost its importance as an office specially devised to guard the interest of the masses; as late as 133–123 B.C., it served the brothers Tiberius and Gaius Gracchi as the instrument by which they hoped to achieve their goal of social reform. Nevertheless, the democratic character of the office all but vanished in the later Republic. The requirement of plebeian descent of its holders became a mere formality. The tribunate degenerated into a political office sought by young members of the senatorial class; it took its place in the regular *cursus honorum* (political career) after the quaestorship, and more often than not incumbents were willing tools of the senatorial aristocracy in the pursuit of their most reactionary policies.

B. THE PEOPLE. The people exercised their power in assemblies (*comitia*)—held compulsorily on specified days and also whenever the governing officer saw fit to call them—in which every adult male citizen had a right to participate. The idea of delegating the power of voting on laws and political questions to parliaments of elected representatives was never conceived by any ancient people. This was a manageable system in the narrow confines of the old city-state. When Rome became a world power, however, this antiquated, but never changed, constitutional principle resulted in letting the people of the capital, who as a rule were alone able to attend the *comitia,* have the exclusive vote on all matters; in other words, a minority—and not of the best elements, at that—ruled at a time when thousands of Roman citizens lived all over Italy and many others were scattered throughout the Empire. This condition was not the least important among those responsible for the degeneration and eventual disappearance of the *comitia.* Furthermore, the assemblies were permitted to vote only on proposals made by the presiding officers, without the benefit of debate or the possibility of amendment (although informal, nonvoting assemblies—*contiones*—might precede the *comitia*). Voting was not by the individual citizens but by the units which constituted the *comitia.* Therefore all the ordinary citizen could do was to try to get his own unit to vote his way.

There were three kinds of assembly, with different functions, and differently constituted:

(a) The *Comitia Curiata*. This was the assembly of the afore-mentioned *curiae*. Originally only patricians belonged to the *curiae*, but the plebeians won access at an early time. The *comitia curiata* probably functioned as early as the regal period, although we are unable to determine the amount of their influence at that time. Under the Republic they lost their political importance to the assemblies described below.

They functioned chiefly in authorizing—or perhaps only in witnessing—acts of private citizens; citizens had to declare wills and *arrogationes*, i.e., adoptions into their families of fellow-citizens not subject to paternal power, before the *comitia curiata*. Besides, the *comitia curiata* retained into the early imperial period the right to bestow on newly elected officials their *imperium* (*lex de imperio*), although this function had degenerated to a mere formality and may never have been more than an act of homage and allegiance to the new military commander.

The *comitia curiata* were probably at no time a truly legislative body, but rather the Roman people organized for the purposes of election and acceptance of pronouncements made by kings or (later) elected officials and by private citizens—though it is conceivable and even likely that occasionally they deprived such pronouncements of their effect by refusing their co-operation. At any rate, they represented a form of popular participation in the government, which was not in line with the political conditions and conceptions of the fully developed Republic. The extent to which the *comitia curiata* fell into insignificance can be seen in the fact that even in the later republican period only thirty lictors acted as proxies for the thirty *curiae*.

(b) The *Comitia Centuriata*. The organization of the people in "centuries" ("hundreds") is one of the institutions attributed to Servius Tullius, but it probably had its origin under the Republic. The *comitia centuriata* gave expression to the idea that the *populus Romanus* and its army were one and the same thing. Their establishment possibly involved the recognition of the plebeians as members of the political community; for military service was compulsory for every able-bodied citizen, and there was no difference between patricians and plebeians as far as their military status and duty were concerned.

The military conception underlying the *comitia centuriata* was reflected in their ceremonial and arrangement (*centuria* was also the word for a company of soldiers). They were convened on the *Campus Martius,* a training and parade ground outside the *pomerium;* during the meeting the red war flag flew over the Capitol, and the approaches to the *Campus Martius* were patrolled by sentries. Their arrangement roughly followed the military organization, although they were not a true image of the army. The arrangement was based upon a division of the citizens into classes, according to their wealth and with preponderance awarded to the wealthier classes. The connection with the military organization lay in the fact that each citizen had to report for duty in a certain type of equipment, to be provided by himself, which was specified for each class in accordance with its means.

There were five classes, the first and wealthiest forming 80 centuries; the second, third, and fourth, 20 each; and the fifth, 30. In addition, there were 18 centuries of equestrians—i.e., men serving on horseback—above the first class, 4 centuries of artisans and musicians, and one for all those who were not able to meet the requirements even for the lowest class: a total of 193.

This tabulation will make it clear that the centuries in the various classes were of very different numerical strength, the wealthiest being the smallest but, in view of the voting system, the most powerful. The equestrians and the first class, with their combined 98 centuries, were a majority. Further discrimination came from the fact that the centuries of each class were divided equally into those of *seniores* and *iuniores,* i.e., men over and men under forty-five years of age; this of course gave the older men the greatest influence.

The influence of wealth was somewhat diminished when, between 241 and 218 B.C., a new distribution was made by which each of the 35 "tribes" was given one century of *seniores* and one of *iuniores* of each class for a total of 350, each of the five classes having an equal number of centuries. But the rich were still privileged by the retention of the 18 centuries of equestrians. Moreover, landed wealth was put at a distinct advantage; for the new arrangement gave only 40 centuries to the city, and only 8 of these 40 to the first class, thus discriminating against the rich businessmen in favor of the land-owning aristocracy.

The *comitia centuriata,* which could be called only by the consuls, elected the highest officials—consuls, praetors, and censors—and voted on bills proposed by the consuls. They were the most important among the various assemblies under the republican constitution.

(c) The *Comitia Tributa* and *Concilia Plebis.* Also from the time of Servius Tullius, the Roman territory was ostensibly divided into local districts, called *tribus.* Originally there were only four of them, and it is not clear whether they included only the town, or the surrounding countryside as well. They were, however, certainly restricted to the city when, a few years after the establishment of the Republic, about seventeen new tribes were added which covered the rural districts. Gradually more rural tribes were added, until their number reached, in 241 B.C., thirty-one rural and four urban tribes. There were no later additions.

Membership in the tribes originally depended on the possession of real property in a particular tribe, but a citizen could belong only to one tribe even if he owned land in several of them. Later the purely territorial principle was abandoned and membership in a particular *tribus* became hereditary. In 312 B.C., the tribes were opened also for admission of landless

41

citizens, but these were confined to the four urban tribes, as were also all freedmen and newly admitted citizens. This shows the political principle behind this organization: to give preponderance to the landowners.

The assembly of the tribes elected officials of lower rank. The legislative functions of the *comitia tributa* and *comitia centuriata* overlapped. The *comitia tributa* gave officials below the rank of consul an opportunity to bring bills before the people. All told, however, the importance of the *comitia tributa* was not great.

More important was the "tribal" organization in another direction. As mentioned before, it also provided the basis for the assemblies of the plebs, the *concilia plebis*, which under the Republic were very active in legislation, especially in matters pertaining to private law.

C. THE SENATE. The last of the three pillars on which the republican constitution rested was the Senate. The word *senatus* is derived from *senex* or "old man." Accordingly, the Senate presumably was originally a group of older men. It may have originated as an advisory council of the king, who would have picked the members of his council from the older and experienced men of the patrician *gentes,* the *patres.* At a very early date—possibly still in the regal period, and almost certainly before the plebeians had achieved full equality for eligibility to the magistracy—some plebeians were called in; they were called the *conscripti,* hence the formula *patres conscripti* by which the full Senate was addressed.

In early republican times senators were chosen by the consuls, but after the establishment of the censor's office, this right passed to the censors. The censors enjoyed great discretionary powers, although their hands were to some extent tied by a *lex Ovinia,* a statute enacted in the fourth century B.C., which directed them to prefer, so far as were available, men who had served as magistrates down to the rank of aedile; later even former quaestors were admitted. Admission to the Senate was for life, save for the power of the censors to expunge an unworthy man. The number of senators through most of the republican period was three hundred, but Sulla in 81 B.C. raised the number to six hundred; under Caesar there were as many as nine hundred members, but Augustus restored the normal complement of six hundred.

Under old constitutional law, legislative acts passed by the *comitia* had to be approved by the patrician senators (*auctoritas patrum*). This privilege, which, incidentally, was never extended to the whole Senate, soon became a mere formality. Thus—speaking in strictly legal terms—the Senate had only advisory functions. Magistrates were free to accept or reject its advice; and in the former case their decision was subject to possible intercession by a colleague or tribune. A resolution by the Senate was called a *senatus consultum* (Senate's counsel).

If not from the beginning of the Republic, however, constitutional practice soon produced a political situation which was very different from this legal theory. The Senate represented the accumulated experience and wisdom of the ruling class, and such things ranked very high with the Romans, who were a conservative people with an extraordinary respect for authority. Thus the Senate emerged as the truly governing body of Rome. Intercession, it is true, retained its full importance. In fact, it gave minority factions in the Senate itself a means to frustrate resolutions passed by the majority—if they were able to enlist the aid of some tribune of the plebs. But the magistrates themselves seldom dared to take steps involving questions of general policy without consulting the Senate, or to disregard its advice.

The fact that the consuls did not quite degenerate into mere executive organs, carrying out orders given by the Senate —as they did later in their relationship to the emperor—was due to the circumstances that in the Senate, as in the *comitia,*

43

the initiative had to come from the magistrates and that only issues brought by them before the Senate could be voted upon. The happy mixture of individual leadership and collective determination of policies, both tempered by the right of the people to reject proposals brought before them by the government, was one of the most important factors contributing to the stability of the Roman Republic from the fourth century B.C. to the middle of the second century B.C.

During that period, the Senate was in supreme control of all political and administrative matters, including those pertaining to the religious life of the state and people. To name only a few examples: the Senate legislated—for such was, for all practical purposes, the effect of its votes—on the admission of new religious cults or on the prohibition of alien cults;[17] on the expulsion of undesirable aliens;[18] on claims of subject or allied cities and on arbitration between such cities;[19] and on protection of sacred places or public establishments.[20] The Senate also directed the handling of public finances and, most important of all, was in complete control of foreign affairs; envoys of foreign states were received by it. The declaration of a state of emergency was a privilege of the Senate[21] and not the least of the Senate's powers was that of assigning to magistrates their specific competences in domestic administration, their military commands, and their provinces. This included the authority to vest magistrates who had served their terms

[17] The oldest *senatus consultum* known in its original text, the *sc. de Bacchanalibus* of 186 B.C., provided severe penalties for followers of an objectionable foreign cult.

[18] The *sc. de philosophis et rhetoribus* of 161 B.C. charged the praetor with the task of expelling from the city Greek philosophers and rhetors whose teachings displeased the conservatives in the Senate.

[19] For instance, the *sc. de Thisbaeis* of 170 B.C. granted certain requests made by the city of Thisbae in Boeotia.

[20] An example is the *sc. de aquaeductibus* of 11 B.C., which regulated the right of way for public aqueducts.

[21] It was done by the so-called *senatus consultum ultimum:* "*Videant consules ne quid detrimenti capiat res publica*" ("The consuls shall see to it that the state suffers no harm"). It extended the full *imperium* of the consuls into the city and suspended the machinery of *provocatio*.

of office with a prolonged *imperium* for specific purposes, such as the governorship of a province; such magistrates were known as promagistrates: proconsul or propraetor.

3. THE IMPERIAL GOVERNMENT

A. *The Principate.* From what was said in the first section of this chapter, it will be understood that the coming of the Principate involved not so much a change in constitutional theory as a radical concentration of political power. This, Augustus achieved through a clever use of the possibilities inherent in the constitution. He resigned, in 23 B.C., the consulship which he had held continuously since 27 B.C. But he retained a proconsular *imperium* which a law of 27 BC. had given him for ten years; repeated prolongations made this *imperium* an actual life office, and not long before his death Augustus had it conferred on his heir apparent (through adoption), Tiberius. The proconsular *imperium* involved the command of the army and, thereby, personal control of the imperial provinces; since it was declared to be an *imperium maius* it also gave the *princeps* authority over the promagistrates in the nominally senatorial provinces.

In Rome itself, Augustus secured his permanent supremacy more indirectly but no less effectively. When he resigned the consulship, he received for life the *tribunicia potestas,* i.e., the rights and powers of a tribune of the plebs—in other words, the rights of inviolability, of veto, of summoning the Senate, and of bringing bills before the assembly of the plebs. This power, too, was bestowed on Tiberius and became a regular attribute of the emperors.

Such was the constitutional position of the *princeps.* Its political effect was the transformation of the Roman state and Empire into a monarchy. The *comitia* were not abolished, but soon ceased to function. Popular legislation was replaced by senatorial legislation which Sulla had already made legally binding on the magistrates. But the Senate's influence was doomed, too, and even in the city itself supreme control was gradually passing to the emperor. In the second century A.D., approval by the Senate of bills submitted by the emperor became a matter of course—so much so that it became customary in the later Principate to refer to *senatus consulta* proposed by the emperor simply as speeches of that emperor. Consuls and praetors, although theoretically their office and *imperium* remained the same as before, sank to the level of mere executive officials charged with specific duties in connection with the administration and judiciary.

Alongside the old magistracies, there rose, from the time of Hadrian, to ever greater importance the new imperial officialdom—mostly men of equestrian rank—which was responsible only to the emperor himself and which administered the Empire along bureaucratic lines. This officialdom more and more overshadowed the traditional offices. A new financial administration sprang up in the form of an imperial treasury (*fiscus Caesaris*). Theoretically conceived as the private fortune of the emperor who therefore did not have to account for its management to the Senate, the *fiscus* became the real treasury of the Empire, while the old republican state treasury (*aerarium*), though continuing to function, became of secondary importance.

B. *The Dominate.* Naturally it was only the new imperial institutions which by conception and design fitted into the reorganization of the Empire by Diocletian and Constantine. Under the Dominate, to be sure, there were still consuls, praetors, quaestors, and senates in both old and new Rome (Constantinople). But the consulship was now only an honorary title, though of very high rank and often assumed by the emperors themselves. The year was still named after the consuls, one of whom was named by the emperor for the Western Empire and one for the Eastern Empire. Praetors and quaestors were officials charged with specific tasks in administration and judiciary under the emperor. The senates were aristocratic assemblies which at times were able to secure privileges for their class but as a whole had very little influence on matters of high policy. The government was exclusively in the hands of the emperors and their bureaucracy.

The government in each half of the Empire centered in the emperor, whose status as a divine ruler—or, in Christian times, as a ruler by divine grace—was emphasized by a strict court ceremonial, borrowed from earlier oriental monarchies, which symbolized the complete subjection of the people to him. He wore special garments and a diadem and those who approached him had to prostrate themselves. As regards the direction of the state, the emperor was aided by a state council (*consistorium*) composed of high military, civil, and ecclesiastical dignitaries.

Most important among these were the *praepositus sacri cubiculi,* the "chief of the imperial household," and the heads of four central agencies. These latter were the *magister officiorum,* or "master of the offices," who directed the administrative apparatus of the Empire; two finance officials, the *comes sacrarum largitionum,* or "count of imperial liberalities," who managed the finances of the Empire (deriving his title from the fact that one of his chief functions was the supervision of the frequent payments of bonuses to soldiers and officials), and the *comes rerum privatarum,* or "count of the private patrimony," who administered the imperial domain; and the *quaestor sacri palatii,* or "quaestor of the imperial palace," whose chief concern was legislation.

Local government was controlled by *praefecti praetorio.* Under the Principate the *praefectus praetorio* had been the commander of the *praetoriani,* the imperial guard stationed at Rome. Always a power in politics, this military officer had under Septimius Severus become the head of the civil administration and judiciary of the city of Rome. Diocletian bestowed the title of *praefectus praetorio* on the chiefs of the four main administrative districts into which he divided the Empire. They were the two eastern prefectures of the Orient (comprising Egypt, the Asiatic provinces, and Thrace) and of Illyricum (comprising Macedonia—which included Greece—and the Danube lands) and the two western prefectures of Italy (comprising Italy and Africa) and of Gaul (comprising Britain, Gaul, and Spain). The prefectures were subdivided into dioceses governed by "vicars," and these into provinces governed by "presidents" (*praesides*); for the sake of efficiency, the old provinces were divided into a large number of smaller units. Within this framework, a numerous hierarchy discharged the functions of administration and taxation, and of the judiciary.

In spite of the tight controls which theoretically existed, the system was rife with inefficiency and corruption. The latter, in particular, was in part provoked by increasingly oppressive regimentation which was necessitated by the growing inability—especially in the fifth century—of the Empire to meet the financial demands the government was compelled to make on it. Trade and commerce were widely subjected to state monopolies; the population was forced into closed occupational groups, or organized in corporations, each charged with specified duties, in which membership was made hereditary; and the rural population was tied to the soil. The urban upper class, organized in *curiae* with compulsory and hereditary membership, was ruined by its collective liability for taxes which could no longer be collected.

The consequence of all this was a trend toward feudalization, in that great landowners who were able to protect the peasants against the rapaciousness of the tax collectors succeeded in establishing themselves as semi-independent landlords ruling over semienslaved *coloni*. The Western Empire, where this trend was especially strong, collapsed under the strain when the barbarian hordes flooded over its borders.

CHAPTER III

THE EVOLUTION OF THE LAW

I. PRELIMINARIES

THE EARLIEST STAGES of Roman law are not known, although comparative research and the analysis of institutions of historical Roman law have enabled scholars to arrive at some conjectures, more or less plausible, concerning the character and underlying conceptions of the prehistoric legal order. It is impossible to say what part foreign or pre-Italic influences may have played in the legal development of those days. Some theories of a past age, which considered Roman law as wholly derived from ideas developed millenniums earlier in Egypt or elsewhere in the East and miraculously transplanted to Italy, were purely fantastic.

More serious is the question of Etruscan influences; the more so, since some religious practices of the Romans were undoubtedly Etruscan imports, such as the inspection of the entrails of sacrificial victims (*haruspicina*). It is in fact quite possible that the Romans inherited certain features of their constitution, such as the *imperium*, from their Etruscan rulers. No certain evidence, however, has yet been adduced to support the hypothesis of an Etruscan origin of institutions of Roman private law. Caution in suggesting such influences is the more advisable as Etruscan law is as yet quite unknown to us. In all probability, the development of their legal doctrines and institutions was an original achievement of the Romans in the beginning and remained so to the end. Etruscan and, later, Greek and other alien influences pertained to detail only and were assimilated without affecting the spirit and structure of the system as a whole.

ROMAN LAW

From the earliest times the Romans kept sharply distinct
the spheres of the secular law (*ius*) and of the divine law (*fas*:
literally, that which is said). This does not mean that rules pertaining to *fas* were considered as any less stringent than those
pertaining to *ius*, or that the state was not interested in the
former. But the state did not either allow the enforcement of
the *fas* through private suits or react to its breach by way of
criminal prosecution. The enforcement of religious duties
was left to priestly officials, who discharged their task in their
own way by means of coercion devised and administered by
themselves.

The difference between *ius* and *fas* was one of relevance
rather than of quality. *Ius*, as opposed to *fas* (*fas est* means:
not hampered by taboos),[1] belonged to the human sphere. In
historical Latin the word *ius* expresses both "right" and "law."
But it is probable that it originally signified only the rightful
power of a human being to act with reference to other human
beings. In a somewhat more general manner of expression, *ius*
was also that which is due in human relations. In the beginning, the existence of a *ius* was ascertained by securing, through
ordeal,[2] the approval of the gods. But the gods, in giving their
verdict, merely protected the human order; an action taken
without their approval did not, as such, violate a god; nor was
it supposed to provoke any hostile reaction of the deity, although the human and divine orders, *ius* and *fas*, might occasionally coincide. After the establishment in prehistoric

1 K. Latte, "Religiöse Begriffe im frührömischen Recht," in *Z. Sav. St.*,
Vol. LXVII (1950), 56f.

2 There is no direct evidence of an ordeal procedure in early Rome. But
its existence is suggested, not only by the evidence of comparable legal systems, but also by the structure of the oldest known form of Roman judicial
litigation, the *legis actio sacramento*. In historical times the *sacramentum* was
a deposit of money to be made by either party; the deposit of the party who
could not prove his claim was forfeited to the state treasury (Gai., *Instit.* IV
13). The literal meaning of *sacramentum*, however, is "oath"; this indicates that
the *sacramentum* of the historical period was the degenerated remainder of a
pledge by which each party exposed himself to the revenge of the deity whose
testimony he had invoked in vain.

times of a rational administration of justice, *ius* was, therefore, that which was capable of enforcement with the approval of those responsible for the preservation of the legal principles governing the life of the community.[3]

When the legal thinking of the Romans had matured to the point where they became able to see the various protected powers[4]—as well as the specific rights on which these powers rested—as a system, the meaning of *ius* was extended to include the system as such; in other words, *ius* assumed the additional meaning of "law." *Fas* came to imply those precepts of a religious or moral character which were enforced through priestly coercion (for instance, the duty of an heir to perform the rites of ancestor worship) or through censorial reproof (for instance, the prohibition of senseless cruelty of the chief of a family toward persons subject to his legally unrestricted paternal power).

It is true that the two spheres of *ius* and *fas* overlapped. For example, persons found guilty of theft or of certain kinds of behavior involving a gross breach of faith were considered as "ignominious" and suffered serious curtailment of their legal capacities.[5] In the imperial period, when there was no longer any censorial control, some of the reproachable acts formerly left to censorial action were given legal consequences.[6] As early as the time of the middle Republic, participation in certain objectionable religious cults was subjected

3 It was by a mere extension of the meaning of *ius* that the place where a *ius* had to be claimed—i.e., the tribunal of the praetor—was also called *ius;* hence the expression "proceedings *in iure.*" The occurrence of the term *ius* in connection with criminal justice is explained by the fact that the *comitia*, in rendering a verdict against the culprit, established the power *(ius)* of the magistrate to execute the penalty.

4 These are conceived in primitive law as powers of immediate seizure by self-help, either of the thing claimed or of the person liable to revenge.

5 They were not allowed either to represent others or to be represented by others in lawsuits. For a comprehensive treatment of the subject, see L. Pommeray, *Études sur l'infamie en droit romain.*

6 For instance, Emperor Antonius Pius (A.D. 138–161) decreed that masters who treated their slaves with intolerable severity should be compelled to sell those slaves (Gai., *Instit.* I 53).

to criminal punishment *(senatus consultum de Bacchanalibus)*. All this, however, concerned merely the question of where to draw the line between *ius* and *fas;* it did not blur the distinction between the two. From the standpoint of the history of Roman law, this distinction, consciously made from very early times, was of great importance, since it enabled the Romans to delimit the scope and the contents of strictly legal rules. This attitude may occasionally have caused a certain cold aloofness from purely human problems, but it undoubtedly contributed to the clarity of the legal system. It was only in the period of decadence that this clarity was blurred (see below, page 131).

It need hardly be said that at the time of its full development the Roman legal system provided rules for the punishment of criminals and for the administration of public concerns, as it did for the prosecution of private rights. However, historical conditions caused the Roman legal evolution to take its start from private law and procedure and kept these fields always in the foreground of Roman legal interest.

The establishment of domestic peace is, next to common defense, the most important task facing a primitive community. It is achieved when those who govern the community have become powerful enough to force into orderly channels the inclination of its members to seek realization of their claims by private force. Law emerges as such control assumes precise forms and brings forth the establishment of clearly conceived principles determining the admissibility of a desired self-help action. The formal and substantial problems involved in litigation—in modern technical terms, the problems of civil procedure and of private law—were therefore the starting points of the legal evolution, in Rome as elsewhere. This was the basis on which the concept of *ius* grew.

In the beginning, as at its more advanced stages, Roman law developed primarily as private law conceived as a system of actions—that is to say, as a system of rights and claims of individuals, each protected by its own, specific procedural remedy. Private law and the procedural means by which it was realized were the almost exclusive objects of the constructive and analytical work of Roman praetors and jurists; and it was Roman private law that in medieval and modern times put its indelible stamp on the legal evolution of Europe.

Criminal law and procedure were slow in their development and never attained an importance comparable to that of private law and civil procedure. Official punishment of offenders, especially in the military field, doubtless occurred from earliest times in the forms of disciplinary coercion, inherent in the magistrate's *imperium*. This, however, was entirely within the discretion of the magistrate and was no more "criminal law" than was in the old days the forfeiture (*sacratio*) of those who violated the *fas,* to a deity, who was expected to inflict punishment. From times immemorial—allegedly by virtue of a *lex regia* ascribed to Numa Pompilius (see below page 54 f.)—death was the penalty for premeditated homicide; while the XII Tables provided capital punishment for some wrongs committed against individual citizens, such as arson or the nocturnal theft of crops or evil incantation (*malum carmen incantare*). But in these instances the prosecution was possibly left to the wronged party and followed the general pattern of litigation among individuals, although it is likely that the penalties were executed by officials.

In the case of murder, the analogy of other primitive systems suggests that it was originally the murdered man's kinsmen who sought and, at least in the beginning, carried into effect the punishment of the murderer. The earliest public offense was treason. During the earlier republican period, grave violations of public interests and murder—then likewise classified as a public offense—were punished by the *comitia centuriata,* acting either as a last resort in cases of *provocatio* or as a trial court with magistrates or tribunes of the plebs as prosecutors. It was only in the later republican period that special criminal courts for a gradually increasing number of legally defined crimes came into being. Exile—in the earlier period merely an opportunity, granted to the culprit at the discretion of the magistrate, to escape capital punishment—now joined the latter as a form of punishment provided by law. A graduated system of penalties for numerous crimes appeared in the imperial era and became very elaborate under the authoritarian monarchy of the later Principate and of the Dominate, when criminal justice was administered by imperial officials.

The imperial period also witnessed the development of what may be termed an administrative law, namely, of general rules, issued by the emperors and applied by their officials, for the internal government of the Empire. Their chief purpose was to secure the fiscal interests of the state.

Criminal law and administrative law remained in the main outside the scope of juristic interest. The problems involved in criminal justice were of a factual rather than juridical nature. Moreover, both criminal justice and general administration were in imperial times the almost exclusive concern of officials following the directives of the emperors. Thus the two fields were ill-suited for the kind of authoritative counseling (*respondere*) by the great lawyers of Rome, which was so important in the field of private law and was the motive power for the growth of Roman jurisprudence. Only toward the end of the classical period of Roman jurisprudence did some of the lawyers pay a moderate amount of attention to them.

II. THE TWELVE TABLES

In their early days the Romans, like every primitive people, lived by unwritten, customary laws. It is not known when legal rules were first laid down in written form. We hear of *leges regiae*, i.e., regal laws, which are supposed to have emanated from some of the early kings. Romulus himself is credited with several of these rules; and there are also quite a few

54

attributed to Numa Pompilius, the second king, and to others. At some unknown time, probably not before the end of the Republic, the *leges regiae* were, according to the Roman tradition, collected by one Sextus Papirius; this book was known as the *Ius Papirianum*.

The *Ius Papirianum*, if it ever existed, is lost to us, but a number of rules ostensibly issued by kings have been preserved in works of later Roman and Greek writers. Their origin is unknown, although some apparently go back into an early, possibly prerepublican, period. As a whole, however, the tradition concerning them is no more trustworthy than that which credits King Servius Tullius with the chief institutions of the republican constitution. In any event, from the standpoint of the history of Roman law, their importance is small because, as far as can be seen from what purports to be their remnants, most of them pertained to matters of *fas* rather than to matters of *ius*.

The first true Roman legislation of which we know—and very likely really the first ever undertaken by the Romans—occurred about the middle of the fifth century B.C. It grew out of the struggle between patricians and plebeians. Roman historians give us the following account of this legislation: In 451 B.C. ten patricians, the so-called *decemviri* (ten-men), were charged with writing down the laws of the Roman people. They were granted extraordinary powers; the whole machinery of government, including even the right of the tribunes to intercede against their decisions, was suspended while they were in office. Their appointment was the result of years of agitation by the plebeians who felt oppressed by biased patrician magistrates, and it was made only after long delays due to the dilatory tactics of the patricians.

The decemvirs issued a code of laws written on ten (probably wooden) tablets. As these laws were considered incomplete, a second group of decemvirs—this time including some plebeians—was elected, who wrote two more tablets of laws.

These, however, were said to be unfair, mainly because they confirmed the ban on the *conubium* between patricians and plebeians. Furthermore, in defiance of the terms of their appointment—and against the vote of the proplebeian clan of the Valerians—the second decemvirs refused to resign after their legislative work was completed and tried to rule Rome in a selfish and tyrannical way. One Appius Claudius was responsible for the greatest abuses.

Finally an extreme outrage committed by Appius[7] brought about a secession of the plebs, who threatened to sever their relations with Rome, and the breach could be mended only by deposing and prosecuting the decemvirs. Despite all this, the code made by the two commissions of decemvirs was recognized from the date of its promulgation as a basic statement of the law of Rome. It was known as the law of the Twelve Tables.

Modern critical research has shown that this obviously inconsistent account is not trustworthy, especially in so far as it concerns the second decemvirs. But the fact that legislation of this kind occurred at some time during the early Republic is accepted by a majority of scholars. Similar legislation also occurred in other ancient city-states, such as the Solonian codification of the laws of Athens in 594 B.C. It is even more convincing that the Romans of a later period not only were familiar with the contents of the XII Tables but held them in high respect. Cicero states that in his own childhood schoolboys learned the XII Tables by heart. In the first century A.D., the Roman jurist Labeo and in the second century the Roman jurist Gaius wrote commentaries on them. We are told that a copy of the XII Tables, engraved in bronze, could be seen during the imperial period in the market place of Carthage, then a colony of Roman citizens.

---

[7] Appius had unjustly permitted one of his clients to seize as a slave Verginia, the beautiful daughter of a highly respected plebeian, in order that he, Appius, might get hold of her. In despair, Verginia's father had killed her because he saw no other way of saving her from ignominy.

All this would hardly be conceivable, if, as one scholar[8] suggested, the XII Tables had been no more than a mere literary fiction produced less than a century before Cicero. Even a less radical view[9]—which holds that what was known as the XII Tables was a compilation, made around 300 B.C., of a number of laws gradually enacted during the earlier Republic —has little in its favor. All that we know of the code, including a number of more or less literal quotations, shows that it was not a mere collection of several distinct enactments made at different times. Moreover, the prohibition of marriage between patricians and plebeians had been abolished by a *lex Canuleia* of 445 B.C. In a compilation made around 300 B.C. for the purpose of showing the Roman people the laws by which they lived, the inclusion of a provision obviously obsolete at that time would be incomprehensible.

As a matter of fact, no other period of Roman history offered conditions more propitious for such a codification than the time in which later Roman tradition placed it. The cleavage between patricians and plebeians, then at its peak, was not only political but also social and economic, at least as regards the majority of the plebeians. Many plebeians were small and poor people, often heavily indebted to the patricians. The procedure for enforcement of obligations, as in all primitive law, was harsh. It might lead to slavery and death for the debtor and his family. The magistrates who supervised the enforcement were members of the same class as the creditors. It was therefore only natural that the plebeians were interested in a clear statement of the limits to which creditors might go, and to which magistrates might allow them to go, in enforcing their claims. This is exactly what was done by the XII Tables. Their law of enforcement was still pitiless. But they also contained, right in the first sentences, elaborate

8 Édouard Lambert.

9 Ettore Pais. The writings of Lambert and Pais and other literature concerning the XII Tables are listed by S. Riccobono, *Fontes Iuris Romani Anteiustiniani. Pars Prima: Leges*, 23 f.

provisions concerning the methods to be used in bringing a defendant to court, the periods of grace to be granted a debtor, and so on. These provisions were obviously devised to protect debtors against unfair treatment and excessive cruelty.

The XII Tables, it is true, also contained much which had nothing to do with the question of how to protect the poor and the weak. But this affords no argument against our statement. The XII Tables represent an effort to codify the total of the rights and duties of the Roman citizen. The need of such a codification arose from the tension between the classes; but once the task was undertaken, the provisions necessary to alleviate this tension were perhaps the first and most important, but not the only, concern of those who wrote these laws. Solon's codification of the laws of Athens offers a close parallel regarding both its occasion and its execution.

The original text of the XII Tables is lost. In fact, it is said that the original tablets perished in the great fire of Rome which was caused by the Gallic invasion of 390–389 B.C. Roman literature, however, gives us a good deal of information about their contents, including a number of direct quotations. This information, of course, should be read with a critical mind. Not all of what later writers tell us about the XII Tables is true, and even where our ancient authorities appear to be basically trustworthy, we still have to reckon with possible modernizations of the text; certainly the language, if nothing else, was modernized, because the Latin of what purports to be literal quotations is that of the later Republic, not that of the fifth century B.C. Ancient times did not know such a thing as a copyright, and ancient writers had no strict views about scrupulous accuracy of quotations and saw no harm in adapting the texts of their authorities to the needs of their own time.

Nevertheless, enough is known to enable us to form an approximate idea of the character of the XII Tables and of the stage of development reached by Roman law at their time. The attempt has even been made to ascertain the original arrangement and distribution among the various Tables of the rules known that were supposed to have been laid down by the decemvirs. The results of this effort are, with few exceptions, hypothetical and often controversial, but scholars have adopted them, for convenience, in referring to individual provisions.[10]

The provisions of the XII Tables have the form of terse commands and prohibitions, sometimes brief to the point of obscurity. They concern procedure in court actions and enforcement, the law of family, of wills, succession, property, contracts, and torts, as modern lawyers would classify them. Others deal with questions of sacral law, public law, and criminal law, to adopt again a modern mode of classification. Some regulate the behavior of citizens, such as several provisions prohibiting, in the typical manner of ancient city-states, the display of excessive luxury in funerals. The XII Tables reflect the life of a primitive agricultural society which believed in witchcraft (*malum carmen incantare;* see above, page 53) and had rigid and often harsh concepts of liability. Yet, while archaic in form and thought, the law of the XII Tables had advanced considerably beyond the most primitive stage. It shows some development in legal technique; uncontrolled self-help was repressed and replaced by orderly forms of procedure; private vengeance was in some cases limited by the principle of retaliation, and in other cases public punishment or private composition had taken its place. Some ability to make more subtle distinctions appears in the different treatment provided for wilful and accidental homicide.

It is likely that the law of the XII Tables, like that of other primitive legislation, was largely a statement of long-observed principles sanctioned by immemorial custom. But it is difficult to imagine that fixed periods of grace for defaulting

[10] The author of this attempt at reconstruction was R. Schoell, *Legis XII Tabularum reliquiae.*

debtors or a tariff of compositions for injuries should have come into existence in any other way than by positive legislative act. The same may be said of such a thing as the rule that a father cannot recover his paternal power after thrice having sold his son. Another example is the provision concerning the *trinoctium;* this enabled a woman who had joined her husband without becoming, through prescribed formalities, subject to the domestic power of the head of his family, permanently to avoid such subjection by leaving her husband's house for three successive nights out of every year.

The possibility that some of these or like rules had been enacted by the people even prior to the XII Tables cannot, of course, be excluded. But it is reasonably safe to assume that most provisions of this type represent innovations by the decemvirs, or at least final formulations of rules which had not yet been crystallized.

It is not impossible that the decemvirs consciously took over some Greek ideas. According to the Roman tradition itself, a short time before the decemvirs were appointed, envoys had been sent to Athens to study Solon's laws, and the decemvirs are said to have been assisted by one Hermodorus from Ephesus. Modern critics may be right in discrediting these accounts; but this does not rule out the copying of some provisions found in the laws of the then still important Greek cities of South Italy. Generally speaking, cultural influences on early Rome by some of these cities are without question; one of them, Cumae, had developed the alphabet which the Romans used for the Latin language. At least one feature of the Roman constitution, the quaestorship, may have been an import from that area; and it is perhaps significant that the establishment of the quaestorship and the enactment of the XII Tables were approximately simultaneous events.

As a matter of fact, as far as the vocabulary and perhaps even the style of the XII Tables are concerned, a few traits of Greek origin can hardly be denied. As regards the contents, some features were described as of Greek origin by Romans writing in later centuries, and modern scholars have added more. All this may be true, although the existence of analogous provisions in Greek codifications is by no means proof that the Romans copied them and did not invent them independently. What is really important, however, is the fact that all these influences were in any event confined to detail or to matters of legal technique. The truly and exclusively Roman character of the XII Tables—both in spirit and institutions— was not affected by them.

For a thousand years the XII Tables remained the only attempt ever made by the Romans at a comprehensive codification of their laws; for the praetorian Edict, even in its final and statutelike form (see below, page 81), was not a true codification of the law but only a statement of the forms and conditions of judicial remedies. And for a thousand years this first attempt, which ushered in the recorded history of Roman law, was considered by the Romans as the basis of their whole social order, regardless of the fact that most of its provisions lost their practical importance. It was not until the time of Justinian in the sixth century A.D. that another successful attempt at codification—this time of an entirely different character—was made; and this second codification wrote the finale to the history of Roman law, in so far as it was the law of the Roman state.

III. THE *IUS CIVILE*

The XII Tables did not contain all that was Roman law at their time. In the typical manner of primitive legislation, they laid down, case by case, modes of procedure, consequences of certain acts, and a number of specified duties of citizens, as well as sanctions for noncompliance. But they merely presupposed and did not define, as would a modern codification, the forms and meaning of those institutions and transactions which were the substance of the legal order and provided the background for the specific situations considered in the law. There is no definition of such things as family, paternal power, marriage, succession, wills, modes of acquiring property or of contracting an obligation. All these not only existed but had their very distinct character, making them differ considerably, both in form and substance, from corresponding institutions of other peoples. But they were simply part of the heritage of national customs and their observance did not need to be ensured by a written statement.

The total body of traditional law was what the Romans in later times called *ius civile* or civil law—i.e., the legal order of the Roman citizenry. In other words, *ius civile* was that set of rights of the individual citizen which the community was prepared to protect through its constitutionally established organs, because they resulted from legal institutions and principles rooted in the collective conscience of the Roman people and sanctioned by ancestral usage, common recognition, or legislative fiat of the political community.

The XII Tables had given the *ius civile* a firm basis for its further growth. This growth came from several sources; namely, constructive interpretation of existing rules, recognition of usage, and legislation. Before entering into a description of these media of progress, one fact must be observed which should be kept in mind for a correct approach to the phenomena of Roman legal history. It was not until a late stage, when Roman law had ceased to be the law of the people of the city of Rome and had become, in theory as well as in fact, a universal law set forth and administered by the emperor for the whole Empire, that the law was deliberately and openly altered by abrogating obsolete rules. Modernization and change —very radical change—did occur, of course. But even when such change did not merely result from the peculiar Roman methods of administering justice and was incorporated in the *ius civile,* it had, in the legal conscience of the Romans, the character of modification or elaboration, of restriction or extension of traditional principles rather than that of innovation.

The Romans, like the English, retained a remarkable spirit of traditionalism; the authority of their law was rooted in the *mores maiorum*, the ways of the forebears. Their legal rules and institutions were part of the very life of the nation. They might be added to and moulded into something new, they might be allowed to fall into disuse when obsolete, but they could not be simply and arbitrarily abolished and replaced by something else. This conservative attitude accounts for the rather narrow limits within which the *ius civile* remained throughout its history. In particular, this traditionalism—together, to be sure, with the fact that even in advanced conditions the abstract effect of formal acts was often a practical advantage—explains the tenacious preservation, even at a late stage of legal evolution, of some of the rigid formalism of the primitive legal order.

Interpretatio iuris (interpretation of the law), recognized as an official source of *ius civile*, reaches back into very early times and must have begun soon after the enactment of the XII Tables. It aimed at taking advantage of the law by carrying it to consequences not envisaged by the decemvirs and really alien to their intentions, but capable of being drawn from their words. This was achieved in various ways. Archaic formalism excluded any change in the letter of the law or of the forms of action provided by it. But the meaning of words occurring in legal formulas might be extended beyond their literal sense.

The Roman jurist Gaius (second century A.D.) reports the following case which is supposed to have occurred in the early days:[11] A man lost his suit because he had described the wrong committed by the defendant as what it was—i.e., as a cutting of his (the plaintiff's) vines—while the XII Tables envisaged only the cutting of trees as a cause of action. He

[11] *Instit.* 4.11.

might, however, have won his case if he had used the correct formula as provided by the law, since the word "tree" could be understood to include vines.

Analogy was another means of filling gaps found in the written law. We are, for instance, informed that, despite the fact that the XII Tables were silent on this point, the former master (*patronus*) and his sons were acknowledged as the legitimate guardians of a freedman not of age; for the law gave the *patronus* and his sons the estate of a freedman who died without leaving an heir of his body or a will, just as it gave, under analogous circumstances, the estate of a citizen to his nearest agnate; and the agnate was expressly designated by the law as the young citizen's guardian unless the ward's father had named a guardian in his will.[12]

A third—perhaps the most archaic, but also the most ingenious—method was that of directly using provisions of the law, understood in a very formalistic and literal sense, to produce effects alien to their original purpose. It was this method which enriched Roman law without the necessity of recourse to legislation. As an example may be mentioned the invention of a way to emancipate a son from paternal power, a possibility not provided for in the law. This was accomplished by a clever use of the provision in the XII Tables which automatically terminated a father's power over his son whom he had sold for the third time. The father would alienate the son three times as a mere formality and for a token price. Twice the acquirer would free the son who would thereby be restored to his former status of *filius familias* (son of the family). However, after the third alienation and manumission (i.e., freeing), the son would no longer fall back into his father's *patria potestas;* instead he would become a freedman of the "buyer" who would become his *patronus*. To avoid this undesirable result, the "buyer" would now sell the son back to his former *pater familias* who would himself perform the final

12 Gai., *Instit.* 1.165.

manumission and thus acquire the status of his former son's *patronus*.

Yet mere *interpretatio iuris* proved insufficient, as life grew more complex. It could utilize, or mitigate the effects of, formalism, but it could not abolish it. None of the actions provided by the XII Tables or subsequent statutes (*legis actiones*) were available to protect claims acquired through agreements concluded without observance of traditional forms, or made with or among foreigners to whom the *ius civile* did not apply. Such agreements rested on a purely moral sanction of *fides* (faith, trustworthiness). Breach of *fides* was presumably regarded as a violation of the *fas* and expected to expose the offender to divine punishment, but it did not give rise to a *ius*. From some indeterminable time, however, praetors, acting on the strength of their *imperium*, acknowledged breach of *fides* as an extralegal cause of action. This, it is true, places the recognition of the *fides* as an element capable of bringing forth enforceable rights among the phenomena discussed in the next section. Nevertheless, the principle involved was firmly rooted in the Roman conscience, and once given legal recognition, it formed part of the *ius civile*. Far from being applied indiscriminately, it remained always confined to a limited number of specific contingencies. But it enabled the Romans to provide certain types of informal transaction, which had become common usage, with the power of producing actionable obligations.

Legislation was a third way of supplementing *ius civile*. Strictly speaking, a statute had the form of a *lex;* but since the Hortensian act of 287 B.C., at the latest, *plebis scita* (see above, page 10) were accorded validity equal to that of *leges*. The *lex* was an act duly passed by the people gathered in valid *comitia*. Bills had to be submitted to the *comitia* by the presiding magistrate after having received the approval of the patrician senators (*auctoritas patrum*). According to the kind of *comitia* which had passed the act, there were *leges curiatae, centuriatae,* and *tributae*; but only the latter two categories, and especially the second, were of importance in republican times.

The procedure in making plebiscites was the same, except that they needed no senatorial approval and were of course submitted by the tribunes of the plebs as presiding officers of the assembly of the plebs. Enactments were known under the *nomen gentile* of the magistrate or tribune who had submitted the bill (for instance: *lex Aquilia, lex Falcidia, lex Cornelia*, or *lex Iulia*); if the bill had been submitted by more than one official, say two consuls, the act would bear both their names (for example: *lex Papia Poppaea*). After the plebiscites had been given equal rank with the *leges* proper, it became customary to refer to them, too, under the title of *lex*. Consequently, it is sometimes doubtful whether an act mentioned in the sources was a *lex* in the technical sense or a plebiscite, but the question is of subordinate importance. All acts concerning matters of private law were plebiscites.

We know of a large number—about eight hundred—of *leges* (in both senses), although their number is surprisingly small when we consider that they extend over a period of several centuries. Even allowing for statutes not referred to in our sources, it seems clear that the Romans made only sparing use of popular legislation. Some of the known statutes have survived, wholly or partially, in their original texts, a few of them in the original inscriptions in stone or bronze, which were set up in conspicuous places, and others in literary quotations. Others are known from descriptions given by ancient authors. Of quite a few no more than the name is preserved. As regards their contents, they cover a wide range, dealing with constitutional matters, private law, criminal law, procedure, distribution of land, and other subjects. Some concern questions of lasting importance, while others were made to deal with passing issues of the day.

As a whole, Roman legislation was employed only to cope with specific issues. The Romans never made a constitution intended to set up comprehensively, once and for all, the principles and organs of government. After the XII Tables, which were themselves only a collection of various rules concerning specific issues, they did not codify again the whole of their *ius civile*. Only for a brief spell during the revolutionary first century B.C. did the idea of a codification of their legal system enter the Roman mind. Pompeius and Caesar entertained plans of this sort. But Pompeius met with overwhelming opposition, and Caesar was assassinated before he had an opportunity to attempt the realization of his plans.[13] Augustus refrained from using his powers in this direction. Codification had to wait until a radically different theory of government had given rise to a changed concept of law.

The reluctance of the Romans to apply legislation was a consequence of their conservative attitude toward law. Even the people had no authority to enact anything incompatible with the ancient concepts of the *ius civile*. As early as the XII Tables, this idea was set forth in a general provision forbidding *privilegia*—i.e., special laws made in favor or disfavor of particular individuals. Much later Cicero stated emphatically that no law was admissible that would deprive citizens of their status as free men. As a safeguard against undue change, many statutes were equipped with a salvatory clause, such as *"Si quid ius non esset rogarier, eius hac lege nihilum rogatum"* ("If there is anything which there is no rightful power to propose, of that nothing shall be proposed in this bill").

Thus Roman legislation served the purpose of adapting the structure of state and law to changed conditions, but never that of radically altering it. Statutes were needed, for instance, to incorporate in the constitution the gains made by the plebeian movement, to create new magistracies, or to define the nature of, and the penalty for, such offenses as the people saw fit to classify as public crimes. As regards private law and civil

13 See W. Kunkel, "Das Wesen des ius respondendi," in Z. *Sav. St.*, Vol. LXVI (1948), 423-57.

procedure, they were a means to supplement or delimit forms and contents of *ius civile,* when mere *interpretatio iuris* was unable to produce the desired effect. For instance, legislation was employed to introduce new *legis actiones* and to modernize civil procedure.

Among acts pertaining to substantive law, the most famous was the *lex Aquilia,* a plebiscite of 286 B.C., which defined the claims a master might raise against one who had inflicted death or bodily harm on his slaves or animals. Many enactments sought to protect deserving private interests from harm caused by the unbridled exercise of rights. Statutes regulating the rate of interest on loans, limiting or defining the liability of several sureties of one debtor to a creditor, restricting excessive bequests detrimental to the heirs, and others conceived in a similar vein belong in this category.

The subordination of statutory law to established *ius civile* also expressed itself in the fact that most if not all of the prohibitory enactments mentioned were, to use later Roman terminology, "imperfect"—i.e., they forbade, but did not render void, the objectionable transaction—or "less than perfect"—i.e., they provided a penalty for disobedience, without depriving a transaction made in violation of the law of its legal effect. It was the praetor who, by virtue of his *imperium,* gave these laws practical effectiveness. For instance, a *lex Falcidia* of 40 B.C. laid down that the total of bequests left in a will should not exceed three quarters of the estate; however, the lex was "imperfect" so that a will made in violation of its principle remained valid. The praetor made the statute effective by not allowing beneficiaries to claim their bequests from the heirs, unless they pledged themselves for the refund of whatever proportion of the value received would prove in excess of what the law permitted them to receive.

Conflicts between statutes were solved on the principle, laid down in the XII Tables, that the newest one had preference over preceding ones.

Legislation by the people had its day under the Republic, although Augustus still carried out his reforms by the means discussed above and some *leges* were enacted even during the first century A.D. But the mode of making law by vote of the people of Rome was no longer appropriate at a time when the political center of gravity was shifting into the provinces and when the government was being transformed into the bureaucratic administration of a world empire. Legislative activities passed to the Senate, whose enactments were accorded the authority of *leges*, though theoretically they were still, as under the Republic, mere advices to the magistrates. Under the Principate, the legislative development of the *ius civile* took the form of *senatus consulta*. Important reforms—especially with reference to the law of succession and wills—came about by this means.

Since the Senate was more and more becoming a mere mouthpiece of the emperor, it was to an increasing degree the latter who, from the second century A.D., was the real legislator. Under the Dominate, legislative powers definitely passed to the emperor.

The late period, however, saw a changed concept of *ius civile*. Theorists, it is true, still defined it as that portion of Roman private law which had its origin in immemorial custom and popular legislation, as distinct from those rules which had been laid down in the praetorian Edict and in imperial decrees.[14] Their conception, however, reduced the idea of *ius civile* to a mere shadow, namely, a mere systematic category within the one imperial law that had emerged. From the standpoint of the legal order of the day, it had little value. For the practical lawyer, "civil law" was simply "private law," spring-

[14] Several statutes of the later period make this theoretical distinction: see *Cod. Iust.* 2.52.5.3 (Constantine, A.D. 312), *Cod. Iust.* 7.37.2 (Emperor Zeno, A.D. 474–491), and *Cod. Iust* 6.28.4.*pr.* (Justinian, A.D. 531). That the Perpetual Edict remained in force as an imperial law throughout the late period has recently been shown by P. de Francisci, "Per la storia dell'editto perpetuo nel periodo postclassico" in *Revue Internationale des Droits de l'Antiquité*, Vol. IV (1950), 319–60.

ing from whatever source; and its opposite was that part of the legal system which concerned the interests of the state as distinct from those of individuals, primarily criminal law. As early as the time of Septimius Severus—in other words, from the very beginning of the absolute monarchy—we find the term *civilis* contrasted with the term *criminalis*.[15]

The new terminology, which became very common in the fourth and fifth centuries and has remained so ever since, reflects the transformation which the general concept of law had undergone as a consequence of changed political conditions. The original concept of *ius civile* was essentially connected with the state of the citizens of Rome and could not survive its passing.

IV. THE *IUS HONORARIUM*

The *ius civile* was the law true and proper of the Roman people, and for several centuries all the law by which Roman citizens lived was *ius civile*. From about the middle Republic, however, a new set of legal principles began to form which was not considered as part of the *ius civile;* these supplemented and partially superseded the *ius civile*. There was in Rome a dual origin of legal rules, comparable to, though certainly not identical with, the dualism of English common law and equity. Unlike the *ius civile*, the rules in question did not enjoy the full authority of those rooted in immemorial customs of the citizens or developed from duly enacted statutes expressing the collective will of the citizenry. As a matter of fact, in the strict sense of the word, they were not law at all. They rested entirely upon the discretionary authority of those officials—chiefly the praetor and in a limited sphere the aedile—who controlled the administration of justice.

15 The earliest instance is a rescript issued by Severus and Caracalla in A.D. 194: *Cod. Iust.* 2.1.2. Other early instances are: *Cod. Iust.* 9.20.1 (Caracalla, A.D. 213), *Cod. Iust.* 6.34.1 (Severus Alexander, A.D. 229), and *Cod. Iust.* 3.8.3. (Emperors Valerianus and Gallienus, A.D. 262).

In discharging this task, the magistrates found themselves confronted with the necessity of adapting the static *ius civile* to situations arising from more advanced social and economic conditions not originally envisaged. The great powers vested in the magistrates by the Roman constitution enabled them to cope with such situations by devising new remedies of their own. Gradually a body of established principles grew out of this practice, which in their totality make the *ius praetorium* (praetorian law) or, more properly,[16] the *ius honorarium*. The latter expression is derived from the Latin word *honos,* which denotes honor and, in a more technical sense, the office of the magistrate conferred upon him by the Roman people. The *ius honorarium* is the total of the legal principles applied by magistrates beyond the limits of the *ius civile*.

The probable starting point for this development was the praetor's jurisdiction over aliens. Rome, like other ancient city-states, adhered to the "personality" principle. This meant that the laws of the community were not conceived as applying within a particular territory—this principle is known as that of the "territoriality" of the laws—but only to the citizens of the community. In the very primitive period the stranger was entirely unprotected unless he succeeded in securing personal protection by a member of the community. Without such a protector, he was exposed to any kind of attack or injury, unable to defend himself or prosecute a claim before the authorities of the city.

When Rome grew in importance and foreign trade developed, protection of aliens was taken over by the state. The praetor, who shielded citizens from unwarranted attack and aided them in their justified claims, did the same for aliens, both in their relations among themselves and with Roman citizens. We cannot determine when praetors first began to extend their protection to foreigners, but we know that in

---

16 Actually, the praetors were only the most important but not the only officials responsible for its development.

242 B.C. alien business had grown to such dimensions that a new office, especially charged with jurisdiction over aliens, was created; namely, that of the *praetor peregrinus* or alien praetor.

This change of attitude, however, did not mean that the ancient principle of the restricted applicability of the *ius civile* was abandoned. Aliens were protected, but this protection rested wholly on the *imperium* of the praetor, with the result that its extension and the legal principles governing it were left to his exclusive discretion. We know nothing of the methods employed by the praetor in the beginnings of his regular jurisdiction over aliens, but we may surmise—and some institutions of later law positively point in this direction—that he followed the *ius civile,* except with respect to matters which by their nature were incapable of application to foreigners. However, the unlimited power implied in the praetor's *imperium* enabled him also to take account of new needs created by the growing intensity and complexity of economic life but not regulated by the *ius civile.*

The progressive spirit which thus characterized the jurisdiction of the *praetor peregrinus* could not fail to react upon the jurisdiction of the *praetor urbanus,* his colleague responsible for the affairs of citizens. The *ius civile,* as we saw, was slow in its development. The *praetor urbanus,* on the other hand, was vested with the same *imperium* as the *praetor peregrinus.* He possessed the power to set aside rules of the *ius civile* when their strict application would lead to results considered unfair or unresponsive to more advanced social conditions. Like his colleague, he might also provide legal relief in situations not envisaged by the *ius civile.*

The surprising amount of discretion allowed to the magistrate is explained by the nature of his role within the organization of justice under the republican constitution. He was not a judge pronouncing final judgment, but an official who undertook a preliminary examination of the claims and defenses advanced on either side. The aim of this preliminary examination (proceedings *in iure*) was to determine whether such claims and defenses involved any right or interest worthy of protection and therefore warranting trial. The trial itself (*iudicium,* or proceedings *apud iudicem*) was held by a private citizen, the *iudex privatus* (private judge), who rendered final judgment under the authority and instructions of the magistrate.

This separation of functions reflected the origin of judicial litigation. Such litigation had become possible when the political community first succeeded in preserving domestic peace by controlling, through its governing organ, the steps of private force taken by individuals in prosecution of their claims. The official permitted these steps, in such forms as he deemed proper, after the claim had been established by special means devised for this purpose. Since this control was based on the magistrate's *imperium*, his decision was unassailable, at least when he refused to authorize the trial; for even the veto of a tribune of the plebs, which might prevent a magistrate from taking action, could not compel him to act affirmatively.

Thus the magistrate's authority over the prosecution of private claims could override even the *ius civile*. The latter laid down the conditions under which a claim might be justified. But no claim was of any use unless the magistrate permitted the claimant to bring it to trial. And, by the same token, any claim recognized in this manner by the official was good, for all practical purposes, regardless of whether or not the *ius civile* provided for it.

In performing their function, praetors worked out an elaborate system of procedural devices by which they achieved their objective of "aiding or supplementing or correcting the *ius civile*," to quote the definition of the *ius praetorium* given by the Roman jurist Papinianus.[17] Some of these—for instance, prohibitory or mandatory injunctions (*interdicta*)—

17 *Dig.* 1.1.7.1.

73

were mere commands by which persons were forbidden to change, or ordered to restore or bring about, a certain state of facts; important institutions of substantive law, primarily those principles governing the protection of mere possession, as distinct from title, were developed by this means. Other devices had their place in the proceedings *in iure*. Their purpose was to safeguard persons against an abusive prosecution of rights existing under *ius civile,* or to remove disadvantages to which a lawsuit, admissible in itself, might expose a party.

We have already observed one of the techniques employed by the praetor to accomplish these ends: The pledge, required of the beneficiary of a bequest, to refund values received in excess of the limits allowed by the *lex Falcidia* (see above, page 68), was one of many "praetorian stipulations" imposed on parties, before permitting trial,[18] to provide against unfair consequences of formally correct judgments or to ensure the effectiveness of judgments. To illustrate the latter type: proxies for parties to a lawsuit were compelled to promise the payment of a penalty if the party represented by them would refuse to ratify their intervention. Another method consisted in setting aside by special decree *(restitutio in integrum)* harmful consequences of formal transactions valid from the standpoint of strict *ius civile.* It was employed to prevent unscrupulous persons from taking advantage of the inexperience of minors and to relieve debtors of obligations incurred under duress.

But the central part of the praetor's control over the prosecution of private claims was his examination of every claim on its particular merits. Here was his opportunity to enrich the *ius civile* itself by giving judicial recognition to concepts —such as the *fides*—that lived in the conscience of the citizens

18 If the plaintiff refused to comply with the praetor's order, the praetor would "deny the action" *(denegare actionem).* If the defendant refused, the praetor would grant immediate execution through permitting the plaintiff to seize the defendant's property *(missio in bona),* this seizure leading to a bankruptcy procedure.

but had no place in the formalistic legal system of old. Here also was the opportunity to erect a new system of legal concepts of his own, which partly modified, partly supplemented, and partly even superseded that of the *ius civile*.

The praetorian development of the legal system began early. Thus the *interdicta* certainly reach back into the archaic period when they were probably first employed to protect citizens in the use of tracts of public land assigned to them. The introduction into the law of the principle of *fides* also seems to have been a comparatively early achievement. The great period of the *ius honorarium*, however, was the last century of the republican era, when radical changes in the economic and social structure of Rome rendered many old institutions obsolete. A momentous change in the methods of judicial litigation, which occurred about the middle of the second century B.C., enabled praetors to meet the challenge.

The most characteristic feature of the archaic procedure of the *legis actiones* was its extreme formalism. The plaintiff had to state his claim in a solemn recital, every word of which was directly prescribed by the *lex* on which the action was based. The slightest mistake would effect the loss of his case. Interpretation might stretch the meaning of the words (see above, page 62 f.), but the words themselves were immutable, and no claim which could not in one way or another be made to fit the words was possible. It may be correct indeed that at a more advanced stage the praetor did admit the recital of formulas more freely conceived and not provided for by any enactment.[19] Even so, however, the range of possible reform remained limited by the rigidity of the procedure. In particular, the oral procedure offered no opportunity for any modification of the issue on account of objections made by the defendant, who could only admit or deny the plaintiff's claim but could not enter any demurrer.

All gates, however, were thrown open to the praetor when

[19] M. Kaser, *Das altrömische Ius*, 293.

a *lex Aebutia*—between 149 and 125 B.C.—permitted parties to a lawsuit to dispense with the recital *in iure* of rigidly prescribed oral statements of claim and denial and to draw up instead a written instruction (*formula*; hence the term "formulary procedure") for the *iudex,* which set forth the factual and legal questions involved in the issue and the conditions under which the judge was to pronounce judgment for the plaintiff or for the defendant. This reform marked the adoption, for the purpose of litigation among citizens, of a method which had already been occasionally employed by the Roman Senate in arranging arbitration of controversies between Greek cities. With respect to private litigation, this method had perhaps been worked out to some extent in the tribunal of the *praetor peregrinus.* A *lex Iulia* of 17 B.C., sponsored by Augustus, made the formulary procedure compulsory for all but a few specifically reserved types of lawsuit.

The written *formula* was the result of a free discussion of their claims between the parties and the praetor. Although the parties had to declare their acceptance of the *formula* when they agreed to submit their case to a judge (this procedure was called *litis contestatio*—approximately, the establishment of the issue in the presence of witnesses), the contents of the *formula* were determined by the magistrate. For the trial depended on the discretion of the praetor who might or might not authorize it, and who therefore, by virtue of his *imperium,* had the power indirectly to compel the acceptance of a *formula* approved by himself.[20] Freed of all verbal formalism, the written *formula* was a highly adaptable instrument which enabled the praetor to take into consideration any claim or objection he deemed worthy of his protection.

Let us consider, by means of a few examples, the methods employed by praetors.[21]

---

[20] See above, note 18.

[21] The following examples are not given in the chronological order of their incorporation in the legal system.

From old times Roman law was familiar with a formal transaction consisting in a solemn question put by one party to the other of whether the latter would pay or do something, followed by a solemn affirmative answer of the other party. This exchange of question and answer, known as the *stipulatio,* brought about an actionable obligation of the answering party under *ius civile.* Now it might happen that special circumstances made it unfair for the creditor to enforce the transaction. But the *ius civile* did not provide for any remedy in this case. From the strict point of view of the law, there was a valid contract, and that was all that counted. Here the praetor helped, on his own authority, by directing the judge to give judgment for the plaintiff (creditor) only if there were nothing in the circumstances of the case that would render the claim unfair. This was done by way of inserting in the *formula,* after the part stating the plaintiff's claim (*intentio*), an additional clause (*exceptio*) enabling the defendant to show cause why judgment should not go for the plaintiff.

When this clause was drafted in general terms so as to include any dishonest behavior (*dolus malus*) on the part of the plaintiff, it was called *exceptio doli.* In the case described, the *formula* would read: "Titius shall be the judge. If it is evident that Numerius Negidius (defendant) ought to pay Aulus Agerius (plaintiff) 10,000 sesterces, provided that in this matter nothing has been done or is being done through dishonesty on the part of A.A., the judge shall declare liable (i.e., sentence to pay) N.N. to A.A. for 10,000 sesterces; if it is not evident, he shall absolve (N.N.)."

Under *ius civile,* transfer of title to privately owned property in Italy, slaves, and certain animals required special formalities; the transaction was called *mancipatio.* If the formalities were omitted or if the transferee were not a citizen and therefore could not acquire property by *mancipatio,* no title was acquired by the transferee. The transferee could not recover the property from a third person holding it, unless he

77

had been in possession long enough to have a title through mere lapse of time. Even this way of acquiring title, which was called *usucapio*, was unavailable to foreigners.

In the early days this state of affairs caused no inconvenience. But when commercial intercourse increased and many aliens were doing business in Rome, the strictness of the law proved detrimental to many legitimate interests. A way out was found by a praetor by the name of Publicius—of unknown date, but certainly of the second or first century B.C.—who invented a *formula* by which the transferee was treated as though he had acquired title by *usucapio* (*actio Publicana*). Such a *formula*—in which the *condemnatio*, i.e., the instructions concerning the contents of the sentence to be pronounced by the judge, rested on an imaginary condition—was called "fictitious"; its *intentio* would read as follows: "If A.A. had for a year been in possession of the slave whom he bought in good faith and who was transferred to him, and if then this slave, who is the object of the action, ought to be his (viz., A.A.'s) according to the law of the *Quirites*,[22] then . . . ." In this way a new type of property right, based on the authority of the praetor and supplementing the law of property under *ius civile*, was introduced into the Roman legal system.

A praetorian remedy which in its practical consequences amounted to a direct change of the *ius civile* is known from the law of succession. The order of intestate succession under *ius civile* was tied up with its family system. Only sons who had remained under their father's domestic power till his death could be his heirs. A son released from paternal power was excluded from his succession. When, under the social and economic conditions of the later Republic, the old family system lost some of its importance and many fathers emancipated their sons to permit them to start businesses of their own, the strict law of succession led to undesirable consequences. The praetors began to treat such sons as though they were legiti-

22 The *ius civile*; *Quirites* was a term denoting the Roman citizens.

mate heirs. They achieved this by granting them what was called "possession of the estate" (*bonorum possessio*) and giving them preference to those who were heirs under *ius civile*.

To ensure execution of the decree of *bonorum possessio*, the praetor would issue, on the request of a *bonorum possessor* not in actual possession of the estate, an *interdictum* commanding the holder of the estate to turn it over to the *bonorum possessor*. If sued by the heir under *ius civile*, the *bonorum possessor* would be allowed an *exceptio doli;* and in relation to third persons, all actions and defenses available to the true heir were made available to him by means of fictitious clauses inserted in the *formulae*. Using this device, the praetors developed a new order of succession which superseded that of the *ius civile*.

These instances may suffice to suggest the techniques which produced the *ius honorarium*. This can be compared to English equity. Unlike English common law and equity, however, Roman *ius civile* and *ius honorarium* did not evolve as two separate legal systems, administered in separate courts and applicable in different situations. They were two sides of one legal system. For praetorian remedies were never conceived, as were the prerogative measures from which equity developed, as a means of extraordinary and, originally at least, extrajudicial relief. From the beginning the Roman *praetor urbanus*, presiding over the whole system of judicial administration, combined the two bodies of legal doctrine under one and the same procedure. Consequently, Rome never saw the establishment of separate courts of law and equity. A separate set of courts, it is true, did arise in the Roman Empire in the forms of the *cognitio extraordinaria* (see below, page 85), and its procedure was somewhat analogous to that of English equity courts.[23] Apart from this, however, the analogy to English developments is remote at this point, and in any case the *cognitio*

[23] In particular, the judgment was for specific performance, while in formulary procedure the judge could only assess damages.

extraordinaria had nothing to do with the relations of the *ius civile* and the *ius honorarium*.

Thus the principles which in the course of time were to make up the *ius honorarium* grew out of the practices of the praetors and aediles (what was said about the praetors is, to a lesser degree, applicable also to the aediles in their capacity as supervisors of the market). There is little doubt that in the beginning the officials developed new remedies from case to case, as they saw fit. There was no binding force in these measures, except for the case itself in which they were taken. A theory of judicial precedent comparable to that of Anglo-American law was never formally recognized at Rome.[24] If a praetor were dissatisfied with the effects of his decision, he might refrain from using it again; and his successor was free to decide whether he would follow his predecessor's example. This followed from the *imperium* with which the officials were vested.

It should be understood, however, that this characterizes the situation only from a strictly legal point of view. Continuity in decision, providing some basis for prediction, is essential to society. In actual fact, therefore, a number of remedies came into existence, which, often with some new additions, were taken over by each succeeding praetor—or aedile—and grew into a set of firmly established principles. Soon the officials began to lay them down in written form.

[24] This does not mean that precedent went entirely unheeded in Rome. (Concerning decisions by praetors, see above in text.) Decisions rendered by *iudices* in analogous cases might also be produced *in iudicio* and were given due attention. Cicero even listed *res iudicata* among the sources of law. It is very unlikely, however, that they were accorded binding authority, although one case is known of a ruling given by a judge of extraordinary renown having been generally accepted *(Dig.* 24.3.66 *pr.),* and a settled course of decision would be considered as recognized by law. See P. Collinet, "Le rôle des juges dans la formation du droit romain classique," in *Recueil d'Études sur les Sources du Droit en l'Honneur de François Gény,* I, 22–31, and H. F. Jolowicz, "Case Law in Roman Egypt," in the 1937 volume of *The Journal of the Society of Public Teachers of Law,* 1–16. Collinet and Jolowicz do seem to overrate the formal importance of precedent in Roman law.

This was done through publication by each praetor and aedile, at the beginning of his term of office, of a program, called his edict, in which he set forth the principles he expected to employ in discharging his duty. He would list the types of rights and claims, both of *ius civile* and of *ius honorarium,* which he was willing to protect and would indicate the kind of remedy he intended to grant in each case.

As many of the principles proclaimed in this way were adopted by succeeding magistrates, a standard edict gradually developed which was, so to speak, transferred from praetor to praetor and from aedile to aedile. It was called the *edictum tralaticium* on account of its "translative" character. It still was not strictly binding, to be sure. A magistrate might deviate from his own edict, and his successor was free to choose what he did and what he did not want to take over. Only toward the end of the republican period, in 67 B.C., was a law passed which forbade magistrates to deviate from their own edicts. The change was caused by Cicero's prosecution of Verres, the corrupt praetor of the province of Sicily.[25] This prosecution opened the eyes of the Roman people to the arbitrariness of unscrupulous magistrates who did not feel morally bound by their own programs as proclaimed in their edicts.

The practice of issuing edicts continued in the imperial period. But during the reign of Emperor Hadrian (A.D. 117–138), the praetorian and aedilician edicts were, by order of the emperor, drawn up in final form by the jurist Julianus. The edicts were still issued year after year by each new magistrate. But this was now a mere matter of form, for magistrates were bound, by a *senatus consultum,* to publish the edicts in the form they had received from Julianus. For all practical purposes, the praetorian edict—together with the aedilician edict—had become established law; later Roman jurists called it the "Perpetual Edict" (*edictum perpetuum*).

[25] Edicts were also issued by governors of provinces and likewise developed into a standard edict, the *edictum provinciale.*

The *ius honorarium*, like the *ius civile*, had run its course. The creative function passed into the hands of the emperors. The distinction between *ius honorarium* and *ius civile* was maintained as long as the judicial system with which they were connected continued in use. Roman legal scholars in fact were still able to develop further the *ius honorarium* by creative interpretation of maxims and institutions laid down in the *edictum perpetuum*. None the less, the importance of the distinction between the two bodies of law was now one of form rather than substance. When new methods of administering justice, reflecting the political changes that had taken place, finally replaced the traditional republican forms of procedure, the distinction—though still remembered by theorists—lost all meaning, and the fusion of *ius civile* and *ius honorarium* was accomplished.

V. THE *IUS GENTIUM*

Looking at the law itself rather than at the sources of its authority, the Romans also contrasted the *ius civile* with what they called the *ius gentium* or "law of the nations." From this point of view, the term *ius civile* was used with reference to those institutions which were, or were believed to be, peculiar to the Romans and not shared by any other people. Family organization and principles of succession, solemn forms of transactions devised for the conveyance of property rights and for the creation of obligations, forms of judicial action, and other matters belong in this category. These institutions were distinguished from those which were considered as common to all peoples. The Roman jurist Gaius, who wrote in the second century A.D., gave expression to this doctrine in the following words:

Every people that is governed by statutes and customs observes partly its own peculiar law and partly the common law of all mankind. That law which a people establishes for itself is peculiar to it, and is called *ius civile* (civil law), while the law that natural reason establishes among all mankind is followed by all peoples alike, and is called *ius gentium* (law of nations, or law of the world) as being the law observed by all mankind. Thus the Roman people observes partly its own peculiar law and partly the common law of mankind.[26]

Greek philosophy—popularized in Rome chiefly by Cicero in the first century B.C.—believed in the existence of legal institutions and conceptions inherent in human nature and therefore reasonable and shared by all mankind. This belief had been to some extent adopted by Roman jurisprudence and is reflected in the passage quoted.[27] The theory was merely an attempt to drape a scientific cloak around the fact that a number of principles developed by the *praetor peregrinus* had proved useful also in the jurisdiction of the *praetor urbanus;* the recognition of the *fides* as a basis for actionable obligations is an example.

But the Roman belief that the principles in question were common to all mankind was a mistake. The majority of the doctrines considered by them as *ius gentium* were in fact typical accomplishments of Roman legal thinking and were not shared by other nations.[28] Nevertheless, the concept of the *ius gentium* as a natural law common to all nations had a

26 Gai, *Instit.* I 1.

27 Cicero, following Greek philosophy, believed in the existence of a law inherent in human nature and therefore of higher authority than all positive customs and statutes. The classical Roman jurists did not ignore the existence of a natural justice, but, being interested primarily in the practical application of law, gave preference to those principles which followed positively from established traditions, statutes, and edicts. The problem has been discussed in E. Levy's recent article, "Natural Law in Roman Thought," in *Studia et Documenta Historiae et Iuris,* Vol. XV (1949), 1–23.

28 For instance, the "natural" notion that mere informal agreements (consensual contracts) are capable of producing actionable obligations was actually a result of the refined legal thinking of the Romans. Greek philosophy (Aristotle) had already arrived at the same conclusion, but not the positive law of the Greeks; see the author's article, "Consensual Contracts in the Papyri?" in *Journal of Juristic Papyrology,* Vol. I (1946), 55–79.

stimulating effect on the evolution of Roman law. In particular, it helped the Romans to overcome the rigidity of the early formalism of their law.

VI. THE IMPERIAL LAW

Imperial influence on the formation and administration of law began with the establishment of the Principate by Augustus. It is true that Augustus declined the power, repeatedly offered him by the Romans, of personally enacting public laws (*leges*) for the Roman people. But the magistracies with *imperium* which Augustus and his successors frequently held under the outwardly republican forms of the state, their power of command over the imperial bureaucracy, and their political prestige (*auctoritas*) made it possible for them to direct legal developments in many ways.

Under the Principate the emperors, as heads of the administration, laid down legal rules by means of edicts and of *mandata* or regulations for their subordinate officials. From the constitutional point of view, this was, of course, the same as republican magistrates had always done. The superior position of the emperors, however—and in particular their life tenure—greatly increased the importance of such orders. This was the more so since it became customary to consider those edicts of an emperor which were not revoked or changed by his successor as tacitly adopted by the successor, and thus to extend their validity indefinitely.

These direct methods of legislation were used in the provinces rather than in Rome itself. In the capital the emperors preferred indirect methods. Augustus and his first successor, Tiberius (A.D. 14–37), still made use of the old forms of legislation by the people. Later emperors rather availed themselves of the powers of the Senate. We have already observed, however, that this method degenerated more and more into a mere form, so that, for all practical purposes, measures enacted in this way were imperial law. The Perpetual Edict and a number of *senatus consulta* represent this type of imperial legislation.

Still, legislation through the popular assemblies and the Senate reflected, in theory at least, only the emperors' political influence and was not an expression of imperial prerogative. A real prerogative, however, was the power which the emperors exercised in the administration of justice, and it was in this area that their influence on the development of the law was most immediately and most strongly felt.

Generally in the provinces and to a limited degree even in Rome itself, courts acted under the authority of the emperors and thus were agencies of the imperial government. This was the *cognitio extraordinaria*. This expression denotes a form of administration of justice outside of the normal *ordo iudiciorum*—i.e., the organization of justice based on the constitutional concepts of the republican epoch (see above page 72 f).[29] In addition to this, and even more important from the standpoint of the present discussion, there was much direct interference by the emperors with the ordinary administration of justice by the existing courts. Emperors assumed the power to dictate the outcome of any pending lawsuit or criminal prosecution—that is, to take the decision out of the hands of the court concerned or to instruct the court how to decide.

In Rome itself, there was an imperial tribunal presided over by the emperor who could draw to himself any pending matter of criminal or private justice, either because he considered it important or because the parties had requested him to do so. It was up to the emperor to decide how much use he

[29] The chief difference between the procedure of the *ordo iudiciorum* and the *cognitio extraordinaria* lay in the fact that, in the latter, judgment was given by an official, not by a private *iudex*. Therefore the bipartition of the lawsuit was no essential of the *cognitio extraordinaria*, although in the earlier stages of this form of procedure the official with whom the action was filed regularly referred the trial to a subordinate *(iudex pedaneus)* in much the same manner as, under the *ordo iudiciorum*, the praetor referred the trial to the *iudex privatus*. Under the Dominate, the whole suit was carried through before the same official judge.

wanted to make of this opportunity; some emperors, such as Claudius (A.D. 41–54), liked this kind of activity and engaged in it extensively. The decision of the emperor, called *decretum* (decree), overruled all others.

Of greater practical importance and deeper influence, however, was the habit of the emperors of informing officials and private parties, at their request, concerning points of law. This was done by way of rescript (*rescriptum,* i.e., written answer). Officials would inform the emperor about their doubts and ask for instruction, and private persons would submit to the emperor a certain situation and ask for a decision. In the latter case the emperor would make it clear that his decision was conditional upon the truthfulness of the facts presented by the inquirer; the ascertainment of the truth the emperor would leave to the local judge. Again the decision rendered by the emperor was binding on all concerned.

Officials would submit questions of law by letter (*epistula*), their regular way of communicating with their superiors. Private subjects were required to submit a petition (*libellus*) either in person or through a personal representative in Rome. Two offices in the central imperial chancellery—the office *ab epistulis,* which handled the communications with subordinate agencies, and the office *a libellis*, which took care of petitions submitted by subjects—would write the rescript below the question. The document was returned to the inquirer after the emperor had affixed his signature.

In cases of exceptional importance or difficulty, the emperor would make the decision himself after deliberation with his council, and the bureau concerned would act only as a clerk. In routine cases the bureau must have prepared the decision as well, as the number of inquiries was much too large to be handled by the emperor personally. A record was of course kept in the imperial archive—as well as in some provincial repositories—and interested persons could obtain copies of such decisions.

The primary intention of the emperors in issuing rescripts was to dispense justice in individual cases. The expression "imperial legislation," sometimes used to describe this practice,[30] obscures its true character within the constitutional framework. But the cumulative effect of the judicial activities of the emperors went far beyond their immediate purpose. It amounted to the gradual growth of an imperial law, whose source was the emperor, which came to rank with the *ius honorarium* and eventually took its place.

The underlying theory which made this result possible was the principle, recognized from the time of Hadrian, at the latest, and expressed in the Perpetual Edict, that "constitutions" of the emperors had equal force with public laws, plebiscites, and *senatus consulta;* in other words, to use Gaius's expression, they obtained *legis vicem,* the "place of a law."[31] In consequence of this principle, constitutions were considered as binding directions for judges, even in cases other than the one in which they had first been obtained. Part of the work of an advocate in preparing his argument consisted in collecting imperial decisions favorable to his party; and constitutions were used in lawsuits in a manner very similar to that in which precedent is used under Anglo-American law,[32] From the point of view of the creation of new legal rules, the theory in question was the more important since it was combined with the other—likewise accepted by the classical jurists —that the *"princeps* was not bound by the laws";[33] that is to

[30] See, for example, A. A. Schiller, "Bureaucracy and the Roman Law," in *Seminar,* Vol. VII (1949), 46.

[31] Gai., *Instit.* I 5.

[32] The practice can be observed in the Egyptian papyri. It extended even to decisions by imperial officials, but it is unlikely that these were accorded official authority as binding precedents. This difference between the legal authority of imperial decisions and the merely actual—though fairly faithful, as it would seem—attention given in provincial practice to other precedents was ignored by Jolowicz in his otherwise very illuminating discussion, "Case Law in Roman Egypt."

[33] Ulpianus, *Dig.* 1.3.31.

say, he was free to deviate from principles expressed in sources of civil, praetorian, or imperial law.

In actual practice, it is true, the emperors down to Diocletian were not prone to do so but rather insisted on the strict observance of Roman law as laid down in statutes, edicts, and writings by legal authorities. This conservative attitude was of particular importance when Caracalla's extension, in A.D. 212, of Roman citizenship to all free inhabitants of the Empire (*constitutio Antoniniana*) confronted the emperors with the problem of enforcing Roman law among provincial populations which clung to their own traditions. Nevertheless, it was not infrequent that imperial interpretation gave the old law a new twist; and occasionally emperors simply ignored its provisions and followed their own ideas regarding what was the best solution to the problem under consideration. Any doubts concerning the validity of such decisions were dispelled by the principle just cited. A limited number of legal innovations during the Principate had their origin in imperial rescripts.

The importance of this imperial law increased in the same measure as the Principate took on an ever more openly monarchical character. In post-Hadrianic times, imperial constitutions aroused the interest of the jurists. Ulpianus and Paulus, in particular, paid much attention to them and cited them frequently. Paulus, in addition, wrote special works on decrees and sentences of the emperors; and another contemporary jurist, Papirius Iustus, published a collection of imperial constitutions. The number of rescripts known to us increases sharply from the time of Septimius Severus (A.D. 192–211), but this may be so because rescripts of this and succeeding emperors were recorded more carefully than those of earlier rulers. Our legal sources have preserved for us thousands of rescripts, chiefly from the late second and third centuries. Most of those preserved appear in Justinian's Code, but quite a few are also found in other legal sources and some have come down to us in inscriptions and papyri.

The mixture of republican and monarchical elements—which, at least theoretically, characterized the Principate to the end—is responsible for the fact that direct imperial influence on the progress of the law found expression chiefly in decisions of individual cases, while true legislative efforts of the emperors were in the main disguised as resolutions of the Senate. Besides, as long as classical jurisprudence flourished, the influence of the emperors had to compete with, and was probably overshadowed by, that of the jurists. For the jurisconsults, though of course more restricted than the emperors, had ample opportunity to bring new ideas into play through their interpretation of existing law.

The picture was changed under the Dominate. From Diocletian and, even more decidedly, from Constantine, direct imperial legislation came into use. Decisions rendered in individual cases lost much of their importance unless it was expressly declared that the principle stated should be generally observed.

This was more than a mere change of constitutional forms and governmental methods. It involved, from Constantine on, a new attitude toward the law itself. The emperors, clearly conceived as rulers of the world and vested with unlimited powers, felt less bound by Roman traditions than had either the jurists or the emperors of the Principate, who had still to some degree clung to the conception that the real Roman state was the city of Rome and the real sovereign the people of Rome. Even now, it is true, the law of the Empire remained, in theory and in fact, *Roman* law; and the officials of the imperial chancellery, guided in their legal thinking by the books of the classical authorities, could not help thinking in Roman legal terms.

But the institutions of Roman law had lost the authority which preceding periods had accorded them. The emperors were the masters of the law as they were the masters of the Empire. In consequence of this attitude, they did not hesitate to overrule time-honored conceptions and to introduce new doctrines and institutions, sometimes alien to the spirit of the old law, whenever they saw fit to do so in view of a changed situation or in order to open the gates to new spiritual forces, such as the teachings of the Christian religion which now became the religion of the whole Empire.

The question of how and to what extent this new approach actually altered the character of Roman law will be discussed in Chapter V, Section III. In any event, the new relationship between emperor and law reflected the changed status of the law itself. A tendency long apparent and gradually gaining momentum through centuries of slowly growing absolutism had finally achieved victory. The law had lost its quality of being an integral part of the life of the nation and had become a mere tool in the hands of authoritarian government. Under the constitutional conception of the Dominate, the government no longer administered the law of the Roman people: it now dictated the law. The old law—as well as new institutions—had become completely dependent on the absolute will of the ruler.

CHAPTER IV

LAWYERS AND LEGAL SCIENCE

I. PRELIMINARIES

THE MAGNIFICENT STRUCTURE of the mature Roman law could never have come into existence nor could Roman law have achieved its world-wide influence had it not been for a class of legal experts who, in counseling parties and advising magistrates and judges, developed from early times a special skill in appraising new situations produced by the increasing complexity of Roman life and in suggesting solutions consistent with the order of the legal system as a whole.

It was these men who actually stood behind the progress of both the *ius civile* and the *ius honorarium*, by finding new doctrines and by showing new ways of utilizing doctrines already recognized. From the time of the middle Republic, some of them prepared in literary form restatements of, and commentaries on, the legal system. Under the Principate, their activities culminated in that great, scientific treatment of the law which enabled Roman law, in a manner unique in ancient times, to combine consistency, theoretical refinement, and a high degree of practical elasticity, thus causing historians to call this period of Roman legal history the "classical period."

Historically, this classical science of law was the outstanding particular contribution of Rome to the cultural evolution of mankind. For the first time in the history of human thought, legal phenomena were approached in the spirit of true legal scholarship, which combines systematic analysis with constant attention to practical results. It was this attitude which not only attained for Roman law its place as the first of the leading legal systems of the world, but made the great Roman jurists of the Principate the inspiration to legal scholarship in succeeding centuries.

It is true that Greek philosophers and rhetoricians also had included questions of law in the range of their investigations. But their interest had been concerned with such problems as the nature of justice, the purpose and place of law in state and society, ethics and psychology, and the art of presenting a convincing forensic argument. Accordingly, discussion of legal matters had been only incidental with them. They had little interest in satisfactory and practical decisions of disputes within the order defined by a specific legal system. Thus their writings had little, if any, influence on the daily practice of the courts in the Greek cities and monarchies.

Roman jurists, on the contrary, for all their philosophical and rhetorical education, never showed more than a superficial interest in purely philosophical problems. The originality of their approach lay in their interest in, and intimate connection with, the practical application of Roman law as it was. Their efforts were directed not at building a purely theoretical jurisprudence, but at demonstrating from every possible angle the practical use to which the institutions of their law could be put.

Quite naturally, it took Roman jurisprudence centuries to reach the crest of its achievements. The main phases of this evolution, which were inseparably linked up with the social and political history of Rome, will be described in the following.

II. THE PONTIFICAL JURISPRUDENCE

The need of legal experts was felt early in Rome because the insistence of the primitive law on the strict observance of prescribed forms compelled the average Roman to seek the assistance of men familiar with those forms. This assistance came from the "college" of the *pontifices* (pontiffs), a board of priestly officials who maintained an archive in which descriptions of the various rites and phrases were kept on file. Since none but the *pontifices* themselves had access to this archive, *even* they were able to preserve a monopoly of legal advice. *in Cicero's day.*

In view of the early distinction between *ius* and *fas* (see above, page 50), the question arises of why it was a particular group of priests that enjoyed the privilege of performing this function. The Romans did not, like the Hebrews, believe in a divine ordinance of their laws. Nor were Roman priestly officials sacred persons elevated above the rest of the citizens by any special and exclusive relationship to the divine. They were men who received the honor of being in charge of the religious affairs of the state on account of their social rank, outstanding character, and services rendered to the community. Until 300 B.C., they were exclusively patrician; later they were members of the senatorial class. Accordingly, a recently advanced theory finds in the legal function of the *pontifices* no more from the beginning than a social prerogative inherent in their status as outstanding members of the patrician class; the pre-eminence in the old days of the law of family and succession—i.e., of matters touching the sphere of sacred law—is believed to account for the fact that the function belonged to a priestly body rather than to the patrician class as a whole.[1]

This explanation, however, does not appear very satisfactory when we consider that the most important portion of the legal advice given by the *pontifices* must have concerned the formulas to be recited in the *legis actiones*. It seems hardly deniable, therefore, that pontifical guidance in legal affairs was caused by the existence, in the archaic period, of a close link between legal and religious conceptions, although the nature of that link is a matter of conjecture. Some authorities have sought it in magic beliefs; the pontiffs, according to them, guarded the formulas, because only the exact words of a fixed

[1] F. Schulz, *History of Roman Legal Science*, 8.

93

speech acts common to both

phrase could produce a magic effect. However, this theory is subject to grave doubts; and formalism can be explained more simply by the ordeal character of primitive judicial procedure (see above, page 50). Priestly advice regarding the proper ways of invoking the gods and the conditions on which a favorable verdict of the gods would depend might well be in order.

By the time of the XII Tables, at the latest, more rational methods of dispensing justice had replaced the ordeal; and in historical times certainly no religious foundation of any kind existed for activities by the *pontifices* in the legal field. Roman conservatism—and the more aristocratic than religious character of republican priesthood—may account for their continuation. But as there was no longer any reason why these activities should be the exclusive concern of the priests, others began to take an interest in them.

One Gnaeus Flavius, a freedman of Appius Claudius, the famous censor of 312 B.C., is said to have published a collection of formulas to be recited in court actions (the *Ius civile Flavianum*). The Roman tradition has, as usual, embroidered this event with a great deal of romantic detail, and its actual circumstances are not known. If we are to believe what the Romans tell us about it, it would appear as an episode in the struggle of the classes. For we hear that Gnaeus Flavius was later rewarded by being elected tribune of the plebs and curule aedile; and that his *patronus,* Appius Claudius, though a member of one of the most noble patrician clans, was noted for his friendliness toward the common people and for his pro-plebeian measures. But our sources are most unreliable on this point, and the revolutionary character of the *Ius Flavianum,* if it existed at all, may well be doubted. In any event, its publication did not involve the disclosure of any holy secret; in all probability, many of the forms of action must have been common knowledge.

The *pontifices* laid the ground for the later development of a legal science. For they were more than mere keepers of half-secret formulas. When they supplied inquirers with the proper phrases to be recited in transactions and court actions, they not only taught them the words but also indicated that these would have the desired effect. They were thus in a position to enable magistrates and parties to cope with new situations by showing them that traditional formal acts and phrases could be made applicable to them, and sometimes perhaps by altering or supplementing the traditional words in order to make them suit the circumstances of the case.

In this way the pontiffs became responsible for the *interpretatio iuris* (see above, page 63 f). Theirs was not a mechanical activity but required knowledge and skill. When in the third century B.C. the function of advising people about the law slipped out of their hands, the law had already reached such a high degree of intellectual and technical elaboration that only experts were then able to carry on their work.

III. THE COMING OF A LEGAL PROFESSION

At first the disclosure of the contents of the pontifical archive was merely to permit men outside of the closed group of the *pontifices* to compete with them in offering legal advice. The character of the activity itself was not changed. It continued to consist in *cavere*—i.e., producing proper formulas and, when necessary, drafting new ones for use in court actions and business transactions[2]—and in *respondere* or "answering" —i.e., giving expert opinions (*responsa*), which parties might submit to praetors or aediles and judges, on the legal situation and kind of relief required.

The strict formalism and ever growing intricacy of the law made ready aid by the *iuris consultus* (he whose advice is sought on questions of law) indispensable, even after the forms themselves had become public knowledge. By the same token, they resulted in the formation of a distinct class of professional experts. To be sure, there was nothing formal or

[2] This type of activity is known as "cautelary jurisprudence."

fixed about this. Anybody might engage in the giving of legal advice, no special training or examinations were required, and the success of the jurisconsult depended entirely on the quality of his work. But it is clear that only specialists who through experience had gained knowledge and skill could succeed.

Thus a kind of informal legal instruction came into being. Young men would, in the manner of apprentices, attend the consultations of an outstanding jurisconsult and afterward discuss the cases with him for further information. It was probably not long after the disclosure of the pontifical records that this type of instruction began. An unreliable tradition credits Tiberius Coruncanius (253 B.C.), the first plebeian elected *pontifex maximus* (chief pontiff), with having been the first to give legal advice in the presence of listeners.

again the political theme

It is not easy for us to realize fully the importance of these legal specialists in republican Rome. Though practicing as private citizens with no official position, they enjoyed a prestige far greater than that of even the most respected lawyer in modern society. This fact was due to the social function performed by them. The Roman jurisconsult did not practice law in the manner we understand by this expression. He would not ordinarily try cases in court or aid parties in their pleading before magistrates and judges. He confined himself to giving advice on questions of law. Moreover, his advice was free. He did his work, not as a way of earning a living, but rather as a gentleman's hobby. It was this very circumstance which gave the legal profession its unusual standing.

The consultative activities of the lawyers were part of the leadership supplied to the people by the aristocracy and were of equal prestige with the holding of high political office. As a matter of fact, most of the men engaged in this work came from the senatorial class and followed the usual political career of this class. The few exceptions rose to, and shared the prestige of, this class. We hear, for example, that an outstanding jurist of the time of Cicero, Publius Alfenus Varus, who rose to the consulship in 39 B.C. had started life as a cobbler; this is probably a gross exaggeration, but it is indicative of the opportunities that were open to a gifted man who engaged in legal work. The leading men in the profession—and only these count from the standpoint of this discussion—fully justified the confidence placed in them. Integrity of character and soundness of advice were of course indispensable prerequisites of their authority. But we must keep in mind the thoroughly aristocratic character of the Roman society and state in order to comprehend the role these lawyers played in the history of Roman law.

The importance of this role can hardly be overstated. It was during their time that Rome rose to political and economic leadership in the world. The adaptation of Roman law to new conditions—in particular the building up of the *ius honorarium*—was chiefly their work. As has already been said, their activities consisted primarily in giving individuals the technical means to realize their economic aims and in informing them about the legal implications of given situations (*respondere*) in order that they might pursue their rights in court.

As most of the praetors and aediles were not trained jurists but mere politicians, they leaned heavily on the suggestions and opinions of the jurisconsults. The *responsa* (opinions) of the most outstanding jurisconsults enjoyed an authority which for all practical purposes was equal to that of the law itself. In addition to the more indirect influence exerted through their *responsa,* many lawyers also had a direct hand in shaping the principles enforced by the magistrates by sitting on the *consilium,* the advisory council with which, according to immemorial custom, each magistrate surrounded himself; and some of the leading jurists occupied the office of praetor themselves, thus finding a direct opportunity for putting their own new ideas into effect.

97

IV. THE BEGINNINGS OF SCIENTIFIC TREATMENT OF THE LAW

The earlier republican jurisconsults were practitioners pure and simple. Their concern was the individual case with which they were dealing. Much of their work was, of course, of lasting importance, especially in so far as it found expression in new transactions or new forms of action, or was laid down in the praetorian or aedilician edict. But such gains were made in response to momentary needs, not with any purpose of systematic legal reform in mind. Nor were these men interested in systematic presentation of the law or theoretical analysis of its concepts for the purpose of obtaining deeper insight into its structure and spirit. Such an undertaking might have attracted a Greek, but it could not appeal to the practical, down-to-earth mind of a Roman nobleman of the third or earlier second century B.C.

The reason these jurists did keep instinctively in line with the spirit of their system was their cautious conservatism, which prevented them from ever stepping outside of what they believed was covered by ancestral custom and established principles. This attitude may have slowed the rate of progress, but it helped preserve the logical coherence of the law—in spite of the great discretionary power of the magistrates, on the one hand, and the lack of any theoretical grasp of the system, on the other. It also contributed to the security and predictability of the law in that it made, as a whole, for a great uniformity in the opinions held by various legal authorities. Differences of opinion may safely be supposed to have existed between the more daring and progressive and the more cautious and conservative. But there is little doubt that such differences concerned details, not basic principles. We are forced to confine ourselves to this hypothetical statement, because unfortunately almost nothing of the actual work of those earliest jurists is known to us.

It is in line with the character of the early Roman legal

activity that there was no legal literature. This does not mean that its achievements were entirely committed to memory. Carefully worded formulas for transactions and court actions were kept in the pontifical archive probably from earliest times; so were important *responsa*. But for a whole century the only book that made any of this material accessible to persons not belonging to the esoteric group of the jurisconsults and their pupils was probably the *Ius Flavianum;* and this, too, was only a bare collection of fixed formulas to be recited in the course of court actions.

The second publication of legal material in literary form occurred when Sextus Aelius Paetus (nicknamed Catus, "the sagacious one"), consul in 198 B.C., issued a book which, like the *Ius Flavianum,* is not known under its original title but is cited by ancient authorities under the title *Ius Aelianum.* It too was a collection of forms of action, including many which had been added during the century after the publication of the *Ius Flavianum.* Almost half a century later, a similar collection of forms for sale transactions was compiled by Manius Manilius.

These works still reflected the old unsystematic type of "cautelary jurisprudence" (see above, page 95, n.2). But the time had come when Roman jurists felt the urge to obtain greater clarity by subjecting their law to more systematic treatment. The first attempt in this direction was made by Sextus Aelius in a book known under the title *Tripertita* (i.e., tripartite presentation of the law). This work, which is lost to us but which exerted considerable influence for several generations, is supposed to have given the text of the XII Tables, the results of their interpretation at the hands of *pontifices* and jurisconsults (the *interpretatio iuris*), and a collection of forms of action to cover the various situations envisaged by the XII Tables and their interpretation. The *Tripertita,* of a mixed character, marks the transition from the mere case methods of the older jurists to a new approach which may be termed scientific.

This new approach owed much to the influence of Greek literature, which, from the closing years of the third century B.C., was becoming known in Rome. From Greek philosophical and rhetorical writers, Roman legal experts learned the "dialectical" method and brought it to bear on their specific subject. This method was a mode of logical analysis that both distinguished the various concepts and united under common heads those sharing the same essential traits. No longer content with simply applying existing rules and forms to given situations or with inventing new forms that responded to new needs, the jurists began to seek the logical connections between their institutions by creating a set of theoretical concepts for purposes of definition and classification.

The Roman jurisconsults naturally needed time for the assimilation and full use of the new method. Unfortunately, the details of this intellectual process are unknown to us, since we possess very little information about the actual achievements of the jurists of the second century B.C., although many of them are known to us by name. For some time philosophical interests and traditional methods of dealing with legal problems seem to have been followed by the same men, but with little connection between them. The first who really succeeded in combining the two may have been the younger Quintus Mucius Scaevola (the *pontifex*) who, about 100 B.C., wrote a comprehensive treatise on the *ius civile,* in eighteen books,[3] in which he assembled related legal phenomena and principles under common headings, while at the same time distinguishing the various forms of appearance of these broader categories. For instance, he first defined the general characteristics of what was called possession and then described the various individual forms (*genera*) of possession found in the legal system. The method may have been further perfected in

---

[3] The expression "book," when used with reference to the arrangement of matter in ancient literature, means rolls of papyrus, the writing material commonly used in those times. Each such roll contained a text amounting to about thirty to fifty pages in ordinary modern print.

the next generation by Servius Sulpicius Rufus, who is credited by his close friend Cicero with having been the first to introduce the dialectical method into the law.

In determining the significance of this intellectual movement for the history of Roman law, the fact should be borne in mind that the adoption of Greek methods of scientific analysis did not lure the Roman jurists away from their traditional activities or from the case-by-case approach connected with them. Their interest and work remained practical. They did not use the dialectical method for its own sake, for the mere joy of indulging in theoretical analysis, but for the purpose of gaining a deeper understanding of the practical aspects of the law. It was precisely their combination of practical aims with their interest in systematic analysis which enabled the jurists of the last century of the Roman Republic to keep abreast of the problems posed by the rapidly growing Empire.

For the first time, Roman lawyers were really able to see their system as a whole. Familiarity with Greek logic and ethics made them more fully aware of the sociological function of legal institutions and, consequently, enabled them to look behind, and overcome, the rigid formalism of the old *ius civile*. This was the most progressive period in the whole history of Roman law, the time when most of the principles of the praetorian law were conceived and put into force. The realization of all the implications of both *ius civile* and *ius honorarium*—in other words, the erection of the great and intricate structure which *we* know as Roman law—was the work of the "classical" jurists of the imperial period. But the foundations of that structure were laid by the *veteres* (the ancient jurists), as they were called by their classical successors —that is to say, the jurisconsults of the second and first centuries B.C.

Unfortunately, only insignificant remnants of the writings of these legal scholars have been preserved, so that it is impossible to follow in detail the developments just described.

But in other respects their period is one of the best-known from contemporary sources, among which the writings and letters of Cicero take a high place. It was also a period when Roman culture in general reached its peak, and a period of growing individualism. Although the names of many earlier *pontifices* and jurisconsults are known, it is no accident that now for the first time Roman jurists emerge as distinct personalities. It will not be amiss to name here the more important ones among them.

From the middle of the second century B.C., we hear of Manius Manilius, Marcus Iunius Brutus, and Publius Mucius Scaevola. Hardly more than their names and, to some extent, their political careers are known, but it is said of them that they "founded the *ius civile*"—an expression which indicates the importance attributed by later Romans to their legal writings. In the next generation the two Quinti Mucii Scaevolae, cousin and son of Publius, excelled—the older known as the *augur* (a priestly office), the younger as the *pontifex*. Q. Mucius the *pontifex* was very influential. His writings, among them the eighteen books on the *ius civile* already mentioned, enjoyed great authority and were still commented on by legal writers of the second century A.D. He had several pupils, among them Gaius Aquilius Gallus, an important innovator and inventor of new forms of action and new types of transaction.

Even more important seems to have been Servius Sulpicius Rufus (consul in 51 B.C.), the author of the first commentary on the praetorian edict and of many other works. The generation of his pupils led over into the classical period. Noteworthy among them were Aulus Ofilius and Publius Alfenus Varus. Several of their *responsa* are still known, partly from extant fragments of their own writings and partly from quotations by classical writers. Alfenus's work was commented on in classical times. Well remembered also was their contemporary, Quintus Aelius Tubero, and the slightly older Aulus Cascellius and Gaius Trebatius Testa.

V. THE CLASSICAL PERIOD

1. GENERAL CHARACTERISTICS

The classical period lasted over two hundred years. Its inception coincided with the coming of the Principate, its end with the beginning of the collapse of the Principate around the middle of the third century A.D. It is the best-known period of Rome's legal history because a considerable part of its immense literary production, in contrast with that of the preceding epoch, has been preserved.

It is difficult to account for this difference in the fates of the two periods of jurisprudence, and only a hypothetical answer can be given. With the exception of Gaius's *Institutes* and a few isolated fragments of other classical writings, the surviving Roman legal literature consists of those excerpts from the works of the great jurists which postclassical compilers—especially the compilers of Justinian's Digest—deemed worthy of inclusion in their works. The circumstance that the compilation, by imperial order, contained all of the legal literature still required to be studied, explains the total loss to us of the original writings of the ancient jurists.

The question remains, however, of why the compilation itself almost entirely ignores the authors of the republican era. The explanation that much of the old literature was already lost in the sixth century A.D. rather begs the question, for the same explanation applies to the earlier classical literature and yet the Digest does preserve some excerpts from writers of the first century of the classical era. The title of "classical" has, of course, been conferred on the jurisprudence of the Principate by modern scholars, but it seems clear that even in Justinian's time it appeared to be a distinct phase of development, which had rendered obsolete the writings of the epoch preceding it. In all probability, such must have been the feeling even of the later classical authorities themselves, as is indicated by the term *veteres* which they employed when referring to their predecessors in the closing century of the republican era. They did not use the term with reference to the jurists of the earlier imperial period.

It would seem, then, that the chief reason for this was the impact of the great personality of Marcus Antistius Labeo, a contemporary of Augustus who ushered in the "classical" period. This great jurist, who is said to have composed no less than four hundred book-rolls, seems to have absorbed the whole of the juristic achievements of the preceding period and to have given, by the originality of his ideas, new impulses to those who succeeded him. Unfortunately, very little of Labeo's actual writings have survived, but his influence is felt all through the classical period. Some of his works were commented on by later jurists, and countless references to his opinions are found in classical literature.

As far as the general character and methods of work are concerned, there was no decisive break with the past, especially in the earlier classical jurisprudence, i.e., down to about the time of Emperors Trajan (A.D. 98–117) and Hadrian (A.D. 117–138). The jurisconsults continued to be practitioners, giving free *responsa* to interested parties. More theoretical activities—such as discussion of legal questions with other jurists and with young listeners—also were dominated by the practical interest in discovering the right decision for the concrete situation rather than by an interest in definition and analysis of doctrinal concepts.

Labeo and others also found opportunities to display their skill in discharging the duties of the praetorship. Like their predecessors, the jurists published the results of their practical work in books. Most of their literary production presented legal principles through a rich display of individual cases, showing what these principles meant in actual practical application. As a matter of fact, as compared with the jurists of the republican (preclassical) period, the approach of the classical scholars was even more distinctly practical. The influence

of Greek philosophical thinking and methods was less pronounced in them than in their teachers.

This, however, should not be understood as the expression
of a less scholarly attitude, but rather as an indication that
the main task of developing a conceptual apparatus was completed. The system as such was now fully known, and the jurists
could again concentrate on the further development of its
practical implications in all directions. It seems that this tendency had already appeared in the last generation of the preclassical jurisprudence. That the accomplishments of the dialectical approach had become the firm possession of Roman
jurisprudence is evident from those books of the later classical
period which, for the purposes of elementary legal instruction, present a systematic outline of institutions without much
reference to concrete cases; this type of literature is exemplified chiefly by the *Institutes* of Gaius.

At first, to be sure, legal instruction remained as it had
been in republican times; that is to say, it remained based on
an informal personal relationship between teacher and pupil,
the latter attending the consultations of the teacher and join-
ing him, together with other admirers, for discussion of legal
problems. During the first century A.D., these purely personal
relationships crystallized into two distinct schools, in which
for somewhat less than a century legal studies were centered.
The coming of the schools was perhaps prompted by a newly
emerging tendency of the jurists toward a more definite professionalization (see below, page 111).

The two schools were called the *Proculiani* and the *Sabiniani* or *Cassiani*. Roman tradition regarded Labeo as the
founder of the former school and his contemporary Gaius
Ateius Capito as the founder of the latter. More likely, as
indicated by the very names of the schools, the organization
of the schools should be attributed to three outstanding jurisconsults of the middle of the first century A.D.—Proculus,
Massurius Sabinus, and Gaius Cassius Longinus. It is, of

course, possible that these men were in turn connected, either directly or through their teachers, with Labeo and Capito and that this fact caused later writers to link the schools to the two leading jurists of the period of Augustus. In the case of Labeo, who is known to have been interested in discussing legal problems with younger men, this is in fact likely.

We possess no information concerning the organization and teaching methods of these schools. It is likely that they were not schools in the strict sense of the word, with organized classes and methodical instruction. More probably they were clubs of jurisconsults and their apprentices, who in the traditional way convened for informal discussion through which opinions were exchanged and the young men trained. For the latter purpose—which from the start may have been the chief motive for the establishment of these schools—a certain organization seems to have existed. Thus we hear of leading jurisconsults who succeeded each other as the heads of the two schools, while jurists were connected with either one or the other and were held together by bonds of personal loyalty. We also know of numerous differences of opinion between the schools.

Nevertheless, all attempts to attribute to these schools definite contrasting attitudes concerning basic principles of law or philosophy have failed. Their dissensions referred to questions of detail, and frequently representatives of one school sided with those of the other and opposed their own fellow members or predecessors. After the time of Hadrian, the two schools seem to have lost their importance and eventually ceased to function. The reason for this can perhaps be sought in certain changes which the status of the lawyers had undergone.

These changes were beginning to take full effect at the time of Hadrian, but their causes lay in the political conditions inherent in the Principate. The situation we find under Hadrian and his successors throughout the second and third centuries was therefore not the result of sudden developments but had been gradually shaping since the time of Augustus— in other words, since the outset of the "classical" period itself.

During the republican era, the authority of the jurisconsults had been rooted in the social and political leadership of the senatorial class of which they were part and parcel; toward the end of the era, lawyers of equestrian rank like Ofilius, Cascellius, and Trebatius did rise to prominence, but this does not decisively alter the basic fact. The outward conditions of the work of the jurists were not changed by the coming of the Principate. In accordance with Augustus's policy of preserving so far as possible the traditional forms of government, the judicial organization of the city of Rome continued to function. Praetors and aediles still issued edicts and retained a sovereign power over the granting or denying of trial. Along with the forms of administration of justice, the role of the jurist, intimately connected with it, survived into the new epoch. Now as before, jurists acted as advisers to private parties and, as members of their *consilia* (advisory councils), to magistrates and trial judges. Now as before, their authority was great and their counsel was willingly accepted.

None the less, the shifting of the political center of gravity from the Senate to the emperor was working a change in the foundations of the authority of the jurisconsults. More and more their authority tended to rest on different elements. These were the personal prestige of the individual jurist— always an important factor, but now moving into the foreground—and the backing of the emperor's own authority. Both these factors made themselves felt as early as the time of Augustus himself.

They were, so to speak, symbolized in the very persons of the two leading jurists of his reign. Labeo, a staunch conservative politically and a believer in republican ideals, withdrew from a political career after his praetorship and refused a consulship offered him by the emperor. He devoted himself to his legal work—not in any way hampered by Augustus, to be sure, but, at least politically, aloof from him. Capito, described as a far more pliable man, accepted the political change. His prestige was not so much based on his excellence as a legal scholar—in contrast with Labeo, he showed no originality and followed conventional lines—as on his connection with the emperor.

Augustus took a positive step toward putting imperial authority behind the jurisconsults' activities. He granted outstanding jurists—apparently on application—the *ius respondendi ex auctoritate principis,* i.e., the right to give opinions with the backing of imperial authority. The sources concerning this institution are not clear, and there is no agreement among scholars as to its import and purpose. It is certain that opinions given by a jurist thus privileged carried great weight with magistrates and judges. It is not certain, however, though possible, that this went so far as to render judicial agencies legally bound to follow the opinion of a privileged lawyer. The question is linked up with that of the purpose of the institution.

A recent theory,[4] which seems to have much in its favor, connects the introduction of the *ius respondendi*—considered as an exclusive right to hand down opinions binding on the magistrate or judge concerned with the case—with Augustus's aim of restoring and ensuring the political prevalence of the senatorial class. It is certainly a striking fact that during the first decades of the Principate the leading jurisconsults represented the senatorial nobility even more decidedly than during the last generation of the republican era. Men of equestrian rank were exceedingly rare among them in the first century; the first equestrian to receive the *ius respondendi* —not from Augustus, but from his successor, Tiberius—was Massurius Sabinus, a man of extraordinary prestige.

Whatever may be the correct view of the *ius respondendi,*

4 Kunkel, "Das Wesen des ius respondendi."

the institution foreshadowed the coming change in the social position of the Roman jurist. The bonds between jurisconsults and imperial government grew tighter as the monarchical and bureaucratic elements in the government were ever more strongly emphasized. From about the time of Emperor Vespasian (A.D. 69–79), we find outstanding jurists in high positions of the imperial administration. As an example, the career of Gaius Octavius Iavolenus Priscus may be cited. Of senatorial rank, he held at first some of the traditional magistracies, but from A.D. 70 he is found in important positions in the military and civil service. He served as commander of legions in Dalmatia, Moesia (Romania), and Africa, as *iuridicus* of Britain (an office connected with the imperial administration of justice), and as governor of the German province, of Syria, and of Africa. In A.D. 87 he was consul, by now a republican magistracy in name only. After having completed long years of service, chiefly in the provinces, he became a member of the imperial *consilium,* a position which he seems to have held to his death at an old age.

The reign of Hadrian (A.D. 117–138) was a turning point in the history of Roman law and jurisprudence. The law was beginning to emerge, to an ever increasing degree, as an imperial law. The old forms of administration of justice—characterized by the division of the lawsuit into a preparatory stage before the magistrate and a trial stage before the *iudex privatus* (see above, page 73)—continued to be used in the city of Rome. But more and more importance attached to the bureaucratic *extraordinaria cognitio* (see above, page 85) and to direct imperial intervention in pending lawsuits, chiefly in the form of rescripts (see above, page 86). In the provinces the new modes of dispensing justice prevailed absolutely. Most important of all, the creation of new law became an imperial prerogative; this was the time when the Edict was issued in its final and perpetual form.

The men who did the actual work for the emperors came from among the leading jurisconsults. Salvius Iulianus, Iavolenus's great pupil, was the editor of the final Edict. Jurists were among the members of the imperial *consilium,* which Hadrian organized as a sort of supreme council of state. From about the same time, we find eminent legal scholars in those parts of the imperial administration which, in the name of the emperor, discharged the judicial functions of the government.

Thus the Roman jurist was gradually being transformed from a member of the ruling class in an aristocratic republic into a servant of authoritarian government. It should not be forgotten, however, that we have so far referred to only one aspect of the role of the jurisconsult in imperial Rome. For he never ceased to function in his traditional capacity as an independent practicing consultant and as a friend and adviser to magistrates. Actually, in the world-wide expanse of the Empire, the importance of his consultative role was increased rather than diminished. It was, in the main, the experiences gathered and the opinions formed in this type of work which were published in literary form and provided the foundation for the scientific achievements of classical Roman jurisprudence.

The interaction of all these various conditions and the old and new interests of jurists reacted upon their place and significance in Roman society. Their intimate connection with the senatorial aristocracy was gradually severed. Jurisconsults came increasingly from families outside of that class—and not all of them from rich or highly placed families. Massurius Sabinus, for instance, was in his younger years a man of very moderate means who had to be supported by his pupils; it was only at the age of fifty that he reached equestrian rank. If in the first century Sabinus was still an exception, however, this changed in later times. Many jurists of the later classical period—that is to say, after Hadrian—remained equestrians throughout their lives. In the second and third centuries many jurists were sons of the upper classes of Roman citizens living in the provinces. Thus Iulianus was born in Africa, Domitius Ulpianus in Tyre in Syria; Syria or Africa may also have been the homeland of Aemilius Papinianus. Others were not even of Roman nationality, although they were Roman citizens; for instance, Callistratus and perhaps Claudius Tryphoninus were apparently both Greeks.

Consequently, the source of the jurisconsults' authority was no longer, as it had been in republican times, the political preponderance of their class. It was based now on their professional prestige, enhanced by their connection with the imperial government. The jurists became a distinct professional class and felt themselves as such. Evidence for this is the fact that in their writings they frequently cited the opinions of their colleagues, expressing agreement or dissent, but never paid the slightest attention to legal views expressed by writers outside their own circle. They even cultivated a characteristic Latin style of their own. As was observed before, the formation of the two schools of *Proculiani* and *Sabiniani* also may have been an indication of a growing professional consciousness among the jurists, which created a feeling of solidarity and exclusiveness.

The characterization of these jurists as a distinct professional group requires some qualification, however. Their group did not include all those who were engaged in legal work. In particular, the jurists kept aloof from, and looked down upon, the *advocati* or *causidici*—i.e., those who made a living by taking cases and pleading them before the courts. This was the occupation of the professional orators who had acquired some, though rather superficial, legal education; for they did not study the law for its own sake but only to the extent necessary to present a good argument. The jurist, apart from his work in high offices in the service of the emperor, confined himself to the giving of *responsa;* more so, since the "cautelary" practice—i.e., the drafting of wills and business documents—had also become the function of men considerably lower in education and rank.

Furthermore, the group of scholars was confined to the city of Rome by the ties of tradition which linked the jurisconsults to their republican predecessors and to the particular forms of procedure still in use in the capital, and also by their close connection with the highest agencies of the central imperial government. In the small towns of Italy and in the provinces, there were, of course, legal experts of all sorts, from high imperial officials and learned men giving *responsa* for use in local courts[5] down to mere scribes of documents (*tabelliones*). There were also—from about the end of the second century A.D.—law schools in the provinces which trained young men for positions in the civil service and for the legal profession. But the great men in the capital did not consider the provincial jurists as their equals and paid no attention to them. The only possibly provincial jurist whose works were utilized by Justinian's compilers, the mysterious Gaius, is never quoted by any of the other classical authors.

Thus the classical jurists were still a very aristocratic group, although the foundations of their distinction had been changed since the republican period. They still gave their advice free of charge. They spoke as men who, by the highest authority of the Empire and by the judgment of their own colleagues, were recognized as maintaining the old tradition of Roman jurisprudence.

Not all of the men belonging in this group, of course, were engaged in all of its activities. Some never held any office but

[5] At least one *responsum* by a provincial jurist is verbally known. It was rendered in A.D. 138 by Ulpius Dionysodorus, a *nomikós* (lawyer) in Egypt, and concerned a problem of local (Greco-Egyptian) marriage law. Ulpius, who is not otherwise known, must have been a man of considerable local importance. Of Greek nationality, he possessed Roman citizenship, and as late as A.D. 181 his opinion was still known and cited as an authoritative precedent by one Dionysia of Oxyrhynchus in Upper Egypt in a lawsuit she had against her father. See B. P. Grenfell and A. S. Hunt, *The Oxyrhynchus Papyri*, Vol. II, No. 237, Col. VIII, lines 3–7.

were content with giving *responsa,* with teaching, and with writing. With respect to the post-Hadrianic period, we know of some who were solely teachers and writers. This may have been the direct result of the increasing professionalization which necessarily accompanied the growing ties between jurisprudence and imperial service and which may have made the previous loose teaching methods insufficient. Perhaps the disappearance of the two old schools is connected with this development. At any rate, there are signs that teaching became more systematic, involving lectures and class disputations. The *Institutes* type of literature, represented by Gaius's book, suggests the character of this teaching on the more elementary level.

Such was the general historical background of classical legal science. It is also the clue to certain of its peculiarities.

The law which these scholars applied to their *responsa* and presented in their books was the old *ius civile* and *ius honorarium* of the city of Rome. This law they strove to preserve pure and undistorted, while at the same time developing it by seeking out the most hidden possibilities of putting its institutions and doctrines to satisfactory practical use. They took little cognizance of the law of other nations. Foreign habits imported into Rome, such as the custom of expressing business transactions in written documents, were made to fit into the conceptual framework of the Roman legal system, if they could not be simply ignored. The same attitude the jurists maintained with respect to legal ideas and customs developed by Romans living outside the city—even with respect to irregular decisions sometimes given in imperial rescripts. This independence they maintained in spite of the fact that they recognized as an imperial prerogative the right of the *princeps* to deviate from the ordinary law.

Their theory and practice received their direction from the way of thinking inherent in the traditional procedural system within which they worked. Certain institutions—particularly in connection with the law concerning wills—which owed their existence to imperial initiative and were, even in the city of Rome, handled by special courts of the *extraordinaria cognitio*—were taken into consideration. But the effects of this form of procedure on the general law of the provinces, where it was the sole method of administering justice, lay outside the interest of the classical jurists, except for some of the later scholars who wrote special monographs on these matters. It is remarkable that even these treated the subject separately and, so to speak, not as part of Roman law in the strictest sense.

All this made for a strongly conservative attitude of the jurists, notwithstanding their open-mindedness towards all the phenomena of social and economic life. They were conservative in their choice of legal means to solve the problems posed by these phenomena. It was this conservatism which made them distinguish strictly between *ius civile* and *ius honorarium,* a distinction formally kept alive by the continued use of republican forms of judicial procedure but no longer of great practical value after the *ius honorarium* had been definitely stated in the Perpetual Edict.

The jurists were conservative also in their social and ethical attitudes. They clung to the standards of the Roman upper class, reared in traditional Roman ideals and in the doctrines of Stoic philosophy. These standards—such as *pietas* (i.e., respect for ancestral traditions in religion and life), *humanitas* (i.e., respect for human dignity), respect for authority, a keen sense for the dignity of the Roman family, and others—can be felt all through the work of the classical scholars, although they were too reserved and too well trained as lawyers ever to indulge in abstract discussion of ethical precepts or to allow such precepts to interfere with the operation of legal principles.

It is true that this conservatism, coupled with an almost complete lack of interest in, and understanding for, the problems of historical evolution, resulted in a certain doctrinairism and haughty disregard for legal concepts grown outside of, or incompatible with, the Roman legal system as understood by the jurists themselves. Therefore, what we learn from the remnants of their writings is really only the law of the city of Rome. In theory, this was also the law of the whole Empire. But papyrus documents and inscriptions show us that the law which was actually observed in the Empire was different in some respects—even if we think only of Roman law as administered by Roman officials in the provinces and forget about the native laws which everywhere remained in force, often administered by native officials, alongside the imperial law.

A somewhat less rigid attitude might have borne rich fruit in sound legal reform. Social developments which were taking place in the provinces—particularly, the emergence of the colonate—called for the attention of legal authorities. Provincial practice had, within the institutional framework of local laws, invented legal techniques which could have been utilized for Roman law if the authorities in the capital had condescended to pay any heed to them. For instance, the habit, prevalent in the Greek East, of documenting obligations in written form had given provincial lawyers the idea of drafting certain clauses in the documents in such a way as to give them a practical effect not dissimilar to that of modern negotiable instruments. All this and more was missed by the classical jurisconsults.

On the other hand, it was precisely the conservative attitude of the lawyers which kept Roman law so remarkably free from alien influences and inorganic admixtures and which was therefore largely responsible for the clarity of its structure. Furthermore, when we find a certain doctrinairism in the approach of the classical authorities, we must emphasize all the more that this doctrinairism did not extend to the handling of their own system. Equipped with a comprehensive knowledge of their system, they conceived it as a set of principles devised to make possible the just solution of the problems posed by the clash of conflicting interests. They kept strictly to the doctrines of their law, but rarely did they show misunderstanding of the sociological import of its rules or an unreasonable clinging to lifeless concepts. As a matter of fact, it cannot be denied that the disdain of classical scholars for pure theory was so great that sometimes their doctrinal grasp of legal situations did not measure up to their intuitive feeling for the right decision. None the less, it was the combination, unique in ancient times and never surpassed since, of a sure instinct for the necessities of life with the conscious application of firm principles which has given the accomplishments of these lawyers their eternal value.

One more characteristic trait which contributed to the success of classical Roman jurisprudence should be mentioned. It is again a result of the conservative attitude of the lawyers. The Romans knew no case law in the sense in which this term is understood in Anglo-American law. We may pass over the doubtful question as to whether magistrates and judges were bound to follow the opinions of certain jurisconsults given in cases other than the one before them; it is certain only that views held unanimously by the authorities—and perhaps only by those possessing the *ius respondendi*—were accorded the force of principles of the *ius civile*.

In any event, the jurists themselves did not feel obliged to accept each other's opinions. Controversies abound in the sources, and we should know more of them if Justinian's compilers had not tried to eliminate them as far as possible in their excerpts from classical legal literature. Nevertheless, these controversies referred to details. There is a remarkable uniformity all through classical law as far as the principal attitudes and methods of approach are concerned. It goes too far indeed to call, as has been done, the classical jurists merely "interchangeable quantities"; for even the comparatively small part of classical literature that has survived allows us to recognize distinct differences between the jurists' personalities and style and to trace important innovations to individual scholars. But in most questions there was unanimity. Successive generations of jurists as a whole accepted the decisions given by their predecessors and confined themselves to adding new ideas which could be fitted into the whole without making obsolete what had been done before.

Needless to say, some jurists contributed more and others less, but none of them really deviated from the set pattern. Two reasons may be stated for this fact. One was the conservative sense of the jurists and their typically Roman belief in authority and tradition. The other was the fact that—at least after Hadrian—the institutional framework of Roman law was completed, apart from occasional legislation by the Senate and some innovations introduced by imperial rescript. The task of the jurists no longer consisted, as had that of their republican predecessors, in building up the praetorian law but was concerned primarily in interpreting and perfecting the existing system. The impressive unity of classical literature is not the least of the qualities which have had their share in producing the timeless authority of Roman law.

2. INDIVIDUAL JURISTS

The group of Roman lawyers who were responsible for the classical jurisprudence was always small at any particular time. Nevertheless, in the course of two and one-half centuries, their total reached a considerable number, and a good many of them, probably the majority, are known to us. Of some we know only names, others can be distinguished somewhat more, and with a few we can form a real picture of their work, either from fragments of their own writings or from quotations of their opinions in the writings of other jurists—sometimes from both sources combined. Here, only the most important among them will be presented. (In the discussion that follows their full names will be given as far as possible, with that name italicized by which they are commonly referred to.)

Reference has already been made to two men of the time of Augustus, the great Marcus Antistius *Labeo* and the insignificant Gaius Ateius *Capito*. In the period following them, jurists were connected with either the Proculian or the Sabinian school. The most important among the former were Proculus, a respondent and author of a collection of *responsa;* Publius Iuventius *Celsus,* who succeeded his father, also named Celsus, as president of the school; and Lucius *Neratius* Priscus. Neratius, a contemporary of Trajan and Hadrian, is the last one mentioned in connection with the Proculian school. The most important of these men seems to have been Celsus the son; unfortunately, very little of his writings is still extant, although he is often quoted by later jurists.

The most prominent names of the Sabinian school are Massurius *Sabinus;* his successor, Gaius *Cassius* Longinus; Gaius Octavius Tidius Tossianus *Iavolenus* Priscus, already mentioned; and Lucius Octavius Cornelius Publius Salvius *Iulianus* Aemilianus, the greatest of them all and probably the most eminent jurist since Labeo. Massurius *Sabinus,* who held no office and was only a respondent, teacher, and writer, won particular fame by a systematic presentation of the *ius civile* in three books, which gained extraordinary influence and was commented upon by several later classical jurists.

Iulianus, the final editor of the Perpetual Edict, was a universal genius in the legal field. In the works which he composed, in addition to his manifold practical activities as an imperial official and councilor and as a respondent, he covered in great detail the whole field of the law. Being an original thinker of great force and clarity, he spoke the final word in many of the controversies among legal scholars, often siding with his contemporary Neratius and other authorities of the Proculian school. No other classical jurist seems to have been quoted by later writers as often as Iulianus, and his influence must have been immense. For this reason, we still know a good deal of Iulianus's opinions in spite of the circumstance that most of his own literary production is lost. A good many of his decisions are, furthermore, known from the fragments of a work by his pupil, Sextus Caecilius *Africanus,* which in the main was a report on legal cases discussed by Iulianus and on the solutions suggested by him. Thus we are fortunately still able to observe how Iulianus illuminated numerous problems which had so far remained obscure.

During the remainder of the second century A.D., jurisprudence moved on in the elevated sphere to which Iulianus and his perhaps equally gifted rival, Celsus the son, had lifted it. The most outstanding representative of the two generations after Iulianus seems to have been Ulpius *Marcellus,* member of the *consilium* of Antoninus Pius (A.D. 138–161) and Marcus Aurelius (A.D. 161–180), a jurist remarkable for the originality of his ideas. He, too, enjoyed great influence. Among his contemporaries, Lucius Volusius *Maecianus* and *Venuleius* Saturninus deserve credit for their books on special subjects. Maecianus seems to have been a pupil of Iulianus's; Venuleius also probably belonged to the Sabinian school. An acute jurist of great authority, remarkable for the fact that he was frequently consulted by persons living in the Greek parts of the Empire, was the somewhat younger Quintus Cervidius *Scaevola.*

Two more men of this period deserve mention, not so much because of the importance of their original contribution to the progress of legal science as on account of their activities as writers and teachers. One of them is Sextus *Pomponius,* a writer of great knowledge and productivity but little originality. In his voluminous works he gathered the whole of the achievements of classical jurisprudence up to his time and presented it in great detail, using the common method of giving cases and their decisions. Although he took most of his materials from the writings of earlier and contemporary scholars, he showed independent judgment in selecting what seemed to him the best of conflicting views. Being somewhat more theoretically-minded than most of his colleagues, he also wrote a short outline of the history of Roman law.

In the same class—though less profound than Pomponius—was Gaius, more or less his contemporary. There is a mystery about Gaius. We cannot even be certain that we know his name, for the name Gaius was a common Roman *praenomen* and in the imperial period it was also used as a *nomen gentile* (see above, page 23). In the case of the jurist, it is impossible to say in which sense the name was used. It has been suggested that he was a teacher of law in one of the provinces of the eastern half of the Empire. This is possible but cannot be proven. In any event, he was almost certainly a Roman citizen, had probably studied in Rome, and was thoroughly familiar with Roman law as practiced and taught by the authorities of the capital.

In contrast with Pomponius, who was highly respected and frequently quoted by classical writers, Gaius was apparently ignored completely by them. His authority, nevertheless, was all the greater with the so-called postclassical jurists; Justinian affectionately called him "our Gaius." This fame Gaius earned by the simplicity and lucidity of his style, which made his books ideal for the desk of the ordinary lawyer and judge and for the school. It was particularly one of his works which became the favorite piece of classical legal literature in later times. This was a brief and easy introduction to law for beginners, entitled *Institutiones* (*Institutes*) and composed in four books about A.D. 161. A lucky accident has given us this book more or less in its original form. In 1816, the historian B. G. Niebuhr found an almost complete manuscript of the *Institutes* in the library of Verona; several smaller fragments have also since been unearthed in Egypt. Gaius's *Institutes* is the only specimen of classical legal writing that has come down to us in anything approaching its original length and form.[6]

The beginning of the third century A.D. saw the last of the truly great figures of the classical period. This was Aemilius *Papinianus,* imperial official and councilor, respondent, writer, and perhaps teacher of law. In A.D. 212, he was put to death by Emperor Caracalla because he had criticized the outrageous murder by Caracalla of his brother and coemperor, Geta. Papinianus, a good portion of whose production is still extant, excelled by his deep insight, the clarity of his presentation of case and decision, and the subtlety—sometimes indeed approaching obscurity—of his reasoning. Scholars of antiquity and of the Middle Ages—as well as many modern scholars—have considered him the greatest of all the classical jurisconsults.

After Papinianus the classical period rapidly approached its end. The great jurisprudence had almost spent its force. The time had come to reap its fruits in huge commentaries on "Sabinus"—i.e., presentations of the *ius civile* following the system used by Sabinus in his brief outline—and on the *Edict,* as well as in monographic treatments of special subjects. Two generations earlier Pomponius had already undertaken this. Now it was done again by two assistants of Papinianus's, Domitius *Ulpianus* and Iulius *Paulus* (a pupil of Scaevola's). Each of them wrote, in addition to more specialized works, two great commentaries—one on Sabinus and one on the Edict.

6 The *Institutes* have been edited many times. A recent edition with an English translation is that by F. de Zulueta, *The Institutes of Gaius.*

The manuscript of Verona, to be sure, is not really a book published by Gaius himself or by one of his pupils on the basis of lecture notes (the latter is the opinion of Schulz, *History of Roman Legal Science,* 142). As the author hopes to point out in detail elsewhere, our text of the *Institutes* owes its existence to an editor of the later classical period (early third century A.D.) who adapted Gaius's work to the needs of his time through partly abridging it and through incorporating some marginal glosses containing comments by contemporary expounders. The book, which under the title of *Institutes* survived to the times of Justinian and was most successful all through the postclassical period, was only one of several efforts to reissue the original in modernized form. Fragments of two more versions, roughly contemporary to the *Institutes,* which reached Justinian's period under the title *Res cottidianae sive aurea (Daily Matters or Golden Sayings),* are found in Justinian's Digest and Institutes.

The works of the two jurists show much similarity in both form and contents. Both of them were thoroughly learned men and excellent jurists, not geniuses like Papinianus but not mere compilers either. They were independent thinkers using their own judgment, and since they were also engaged in practical activities, as high officials and as respondents, they were in a position to contribute from their own experience. Of the two, Paulus was the more profound and original. Since there was no Scaevola or Papinianus to follow them, Ulpianus's and Paulus's commentaries came to be considered as final statements of *ius civile* and *ius honorarium* and thus became the standard works of the postclassical period. A very large part of Justinian's Digest consists of fragments taken from these four commentaries. Showing Roman law as it was after two centuries of incessant and intensive development by a group of outstanding jurists, Paulus's and Ulpianus's commentaries are therefore our primary sources for classical law.

Ulpianus and Paulus, however, were not the last of those considered as classical jurists. Until the middle of the third century, legal scholars continued to function in the classical manner, although no longer quite in the grand style of the past. The last jurist considered classical was Herennius *Modestinus,* a pupil of Ulpianus's.

3. CLASSICAL LEGAL LITERATURE

It was already observed that we possess only a small part of the legal literature of the classical period. Its original size was very large. Gaius's *Institutes* are almost completely extant, though only in a postclassical edition in which parts of the original work were omitted and probably some passages altered or added. Of other classical literature we have only fragments. A number of them are found in some compilations of the fourth century A.D., but most of what is preserved is found in Justinian's Digest. Justinian tells us that the men who prepared the Digest took into consideration more than two thousand "books"—with about three million lines—and that they condensed this to about 150,000 lines. In view of the fact that all of the old literature was no longer available even to Justinian's compilers, we must conclude that less than 5 per cent of it has survived. Even what we have, is in many cases not the original text; for, as will be explained in the next chapter, many fragments were abridged, added to, or otherwise corrupted in the almost three centuries between the end of the classical period and Justinian, as well as by Justinian's own compilers. Moreover, the greater part of the excerpts assembled in the Digest was taken from works of the last two generations of the classical period, chiefly from Ulpianus and Paulus. None the less, enough has survived to provide a very detailed view of the classical law and also to indicate clearly the types of literary works produced, and the methods of presentation employed, by the classical scholars.

The primarily practical approach of classical jurists explains their reluctance to become involved in theoretical discussion. They simply illustrated the rule under consideration through cases showing it in actual operation, usually without entering upon any discussion of purely doctrinal problems. Actually, their dislike for theoretical argument went so far that the writers usually hinted at the reasons for their decisions rather than fully explaining them. When they did give reasons they found them in the individual circumstances of the case rather than in the purely logical results deriving from general principles. Frequently, when the reason seemed to be clear to any person equipped with common sense and a knowledge of the legal system, they refrained entirely from expressing it. In this way they developed a unique ability to point out with a minimum of words the relevant features of a case, so that the decision followed almost as a matter of course. All this was done in a very simple and unadorned yet pleasant style. The jurists employed, of course, a certain amount of technical terminology, but this consisted of easily understandable expressions of daily life.

Most of classical legal literature was written in this manner. In fact, even the preclassical authors of the last century B.C. were masters of the method of presenting the point under discussion by simply assembling a number of pertinent cases. The method remained the same down to Modestinus. This produced, of course, much repetition and a somewhat tiring uniformity, but it contributed also to that unity which was so characteristic of classical jurisprudence. The only exceptions were some books written for the purpose of quick information and, in post-Hadrianic times, for use as textbooks in the classroom. These were systematic surveys of the legal system, usually brief. Massurius Sabinus's three books on the *ius civile* and, in the later period, various works entitled *Institutiones,* exemplified by Gaius's treatise, belong to this group.

Those works which were based on the method of compiling cases fall among several well-defined types. There were, on the one hand, the great systematic commentaries on the *ius civile* and on the Edict. Those on the *ius civile* usually followed the system of one of the surveys written by outstanding authorities of the earlier period, such as Quintus Mucius, Sabinus, and Cassius. The author of the first commentary on the Edict was Servius Sulpicius, Cicero's friend, and many others followed in the classical era. Among others, Labeo and Gaius commented on the Edict, Gaius writing one commentary on the urban Edict and another on the *edictum provinciale*.

These earlier works were later superseded by the great standard works of Pomponius, Ulpianus, and Paulus. Similar in character to the commentaries on the Edict were those on the XII Tables—Labeo and Gaius wrote on them—and on other individual statutes or parts of the Edict. The latter kind formed the bridge to the group of monographic treatises on special subjects, presently to be mentioned. The commentary type of literature was of great importance for ordinary practitioners outside the group of the classical scholars in Rome. In postclassical times, many of these works were reissued in modernized form. Several fragments of such works have been found among the Egyptian papyri.

Of a more technical character—and therefore more subtle in their approach—were a number of works in which jurists dealt with more complicated problems that had occurred to them in practice and teaching. Here more difficult cases were analyzed, sometimes with a rather full discussion of the pros and cons of the decision and with side glances at related situations. Works of this type usually followed a free arrangement of matter, with little regard to any system. Collections of *responsa,* which several jurisconsults issued, and a number of works, often entitled *quaestiones* (questions) or *disputationes* (disputations), represent this group. *Quaestiones* and *disputationes* were largely based on actual discussions held by the authors with friends and advanced disciples. To some extent they dealt with fictitious cases made up for the purpose of inquiring into special problems. Papinianus's *Quaestiones* is perhaps the most important specimen of this type of literature.

Of a related type were works called *digesta* (arrangements). They covered in a somewhat more systematic way the whole of the legal system, but without the purpose of commenting on every institution of the *ius civile* and *ius honorarium.* They were also of a more specialized and scientific character than the commentaries. The most important among these works was the *Digesta* of Iulianus in no less than ninety books. A work known under the title *Digesta* by Scaevola was probably a collection of decisions by this jurist made by some postclassical compiler.

Not infrequently works belonging to this category were annotated by later classical scholars. Thus Iavolenus wrote notes on Labeo, Iulianus on a certain Urseius Ferocius, Paulus on Neratius, and Marcellus on Iulianus. There were other publications of the same type. It is probably correct that such *notae* were not merely attached on the margin of a copy of the work commented upon, but had the form of "lemmatic commentaries." That is to say, they were issued separately, each *nota* being introduced by a brief indication (*lemma*) of the statement to which it referred.[7]

Finally the monographic literature should be mentioned. In works of varying size jurists commented on individual statutes, special institutions, or problems involved in the jurisdiction of certain officials. Some of them were more of the scientific type, while others—especially those on special jurisdictions—were handbooks devised to aid the officials concerned in their practical work. These works dealt particularly, though not exclusively, with problems of the *extraordinaria cognitio* and of criminal and administrative law. Literature of this type became rather abundant toward the end of the classical period. Ulpianus was especially active in this field.

[7] See Schulz, *History of Roman Legal Science*, 185.

CHAPTER V

THE POSTCLASSICAL PERIOD

I. THE COMING OF A NEW JURISPRUDENCE

THE LONG SUCCESSION of classical scholars reached its end with Modestinus, about the middle of the third century A.D. After Modestinus, there apparently was no other Roman jurisconsult who continued the classical tradition of giving *responsa* and who maintained the professional and personal prestige accorded to the classical jurists. Doubtless Modestinus was the last to publish the results of his legal activities in the typical manner of the classical lawyers.

Scholars have always been baffled by this seemingly sudden collapse of a great tradition. It is likely that there was no one reason, but rather a combination of reasons, to account for the decline of classical jurisprudence.

Some of these may perhaps be found in the conditions and inherent character of classical jurisprudence itself. The final fixation of the praetorian Edict had ended the development of the *ius honorarium*. Legal progress, of course, did not come to an end, for new institutions sprang from imperial sources by way of senatorial legislation or through rescript. It is certainly true that imperial legislative and judicial activities were widely determined by the great jurists in the imperial service. But the jurisconsults acted here in their official capacity; there was no room for a *responsum* where an imperial rescript decided the issue. Certainly the authority of the jurists was still great enough that their advice was sought by many. But the conservative attitude of the jurists and their self-imposed restriction to the law of the city of Rome as it had come down from republican times left comparatively little room for individual ingenuity.

This limitation was bound to have a detrimental effect when, after Hadrian, the advisory practice of the jurist was in the main confined to the interpretation of the closed system of the Edict. Creative minds, like Marcellus, Scaevola, or Papinianus, were still able to make remarkable contributions. After Papinianus, however, classical jurisprudence was approaching the limit of its fertility; and this danger grew worse after Paulus and Ulpianus, through their great commentaries, had comprehensively stated the whole of the classical achievement in such a way as to make it easily accessible to all. New impulses and progress within the confines of traditional interests and methods would have required another Papinianus, and a man of such stature did not appear.

Yet these circumstances alone are not sufficient to explain the drying up of the source of classical jurisprudence. Not only had imperial competition in the second and earlier third centuries failed to reduce the importance of the consultative practice of the jurisconsults, but the disappearance of this practice actually coincided with a marked decrease in the flow of imperial rescripts—at least this conclusion seems to follow from the scarcity in our source materials of rescripts from the period between A.D. 245 and 285, and it is what we should expect in a period of general confusion.

Individual originality, on the other hand, had never been the ambition of classical lawyers, and their kind of activity might have lasted if general conditions had not at the same time erected further barriers to its continuance. For it was the time when the Empire collapsed and a half-century of civil wars ensued. This epoch, with its political insecurity and social and economic dislocations, was simply not propitious for the work of aristocratic scholars who depended on their connection with established political authority and on the social prestige and financial independence derived from it.

However, it is a mistake to think—as is frequently done— that the decline of classical jurisprudence was tantamount to a collapse of legal culture in general. In spite of all political troubles, imperial government, run by the professional bureaucracy, was never suspended; nor did those agencies in Rome and in the provinces which were in charge of the administration of justice cease to function. The offices, especially those of the central agencies in Rome, were staffed with trained jurists. Legal instruction and the knowledge of classical literature were preserved. In the beginning many of the officials in the capital were doubtless men who had studied with the latest classical scholars themselves. These men, steeped in the classical tradition, continued to work in the classical spirit. It is for this reason that those imperial rescripts which we possess from the second half of the third century and, in greater quantity, from the reign of Diocletian reveal a thorough familiarity with the classical law and the ability to handle it.

To be sure, the social position of the lawyers and thereby the character of their work had changed, so that we are entitled to date a new period of Roman legal history from this point. The new period is commonly referred to by the rather colorless term of postclassical. The new men no longer worked as individuals, as members of an honored profession and representatives of a great tradition, and as practitioners and scholars at the same time, with all the self-confidence, ambition, and prestige involved in such a status. They were mere officials, anonymous career men who simply prepared the decisions and decrees to be issued in the name of the emperor. Their outlook was narrower. They were in no position to propose new solutions as their own, and—with few exceptions—they no longer published the fruits of their work and experience in books under their own names. This remained so, when under Diocletian and Constantine the Empire was reconstituted and more stable political conditions and a certain prosperity returned. The political climate of the absolute monarchy, the loss of relative importance suffered by the city of Rome, and the replacement of the republican forms of judicial administration by imperial courts—all these stood in the way of a revival of classical jurisprudence.

Responsibility for legal progress was shifted from the practicing jurists to the imperial chancellery. The process of transformation, which had begun with the reforms of Hadrian, was complete when, from the time of Constantine (A.D. 307–337), legislation became the chief concern of the chancellery. Below the top level, where the laws were made, there were now—apart from teachers of law—only the courts staffed with imperial officials and the advocates, who followed in the footsteps of the old orators rather than of the classical jurists. The law was now imperial law pure and simple, and this period of Roman legal history—covering the three hundred years from the end of the classical era to Justinian—has been aptly described by a recent writer as the "bureaucratic period."[1] The difference between Rome and the provinces, still so important in classical times, was leveled off with respect to the law, as it was with respect to general political institutions.

There was now—at least theoretically and from the standpoint of the imperial government—only one law, the Roman law as administered by the emperor for the whole Empire; just as there were, since the *Constitutio Antoniniana* of A.D. 212 (See above, page 88), practically only Roman citizens among the free inhabitants of the Empire. Similarly the sharp difference between the jurists in the capital and those in the provinces was now wiped out, although, of course, the ablest of the legal experts were still in the capital—Constantinople, from A.D. 330—and connected with the imperial government. But these men were mere officials like the others and no longer a separate class as were the classical jurists.

As a whole, the postclassical period compares unfavorably

[1] Schulz, *op. cit.,* 262 ff

with the classical period. Legal science suffered a sharp decline from which it never fully recovered in ancient times, the probable reasons for which will be discussed in the following section. As a consequence, literary production in the legal field sank to the level of mere editing, abridging, and compiling of classical writings. The unity and stability of Roman law was lost. Imperial legislation became whimsical and vacillating and often lacked clarity. The simplicity and brevity of the classical style gave way—in imperial statutes of the fourth, fifth, and sixth centuries—to rhetorical and bombastic verbosity. There was no longer the same subtle scholarship and disciplined adherence to strictly legal argument.

Instead we often find an inclination to base arguments on emotion and the substitution of a vague feeling of justice for clear juristic thinking. Deprived of the guidance formerly provided by the great scholars, many jurists all over the Empire were no longer able to maintain even mediocre standards. The law frequently underwent a process of barbaric simplification, particularly in the western half of the Empire, where from the fifth century less civilized peoples gained the upper hand.

Nevertheless, the extremely low opinion of the postclassical era which many scholars have formed on account of these defects does not seem to be justified. We have already observed that knowledge of the Roman legal system and ability to handle it persisted all through the third century. Statutes enacted by emperors of the fourth and fifth centuries also reveal familiarity by the councilors of the imperial chancellery with the doctrines of classical law. Postclassical legislation, furthermore, reflects the serious and often successful effort to adjust the law to changed social conditions. Even apart from the evidence of imperial constitutions, indications are not lacking of intense and rather intelligent studies of classical literature during the first two or three generations following the decline of classical jurisprudence. In the East, legal scholarship reached again a respectable level in the fifth century, although it was not comparable to that of the classical jurists. Under Justinian the successful attempt was made to restate in modernized form the whole of the legal achievement of the Romans.

The difficulty in ascertaining the actual state of affairs is often great, because much of the evidence is hidden in the excerpts from classical literature and imperial constitutions assembled in Justinian's Digest and Code and in postclassical compilations made prior to Justinian. Many of these texts have not reached us in their original form. They are frequently enlarged by "scholia" or "glosses"—that is to say, comments, brief recapitulations, or casual annotations, which were jotted down by postclassical readers in the margins of copies of classical works, or were, perhaps, even laid down in separate commentaries on such works. Some of these were later incorporated into the texts themselves by later editors or compilers. Other editors also changed classical texts through abridging or omitting portions of the original. Sometimes spurious passages completely replaced the original passage. Whole classical works circulated and were utilized by the compilers in abridged form, and there were works which circulated under the names of classical scholars but were really postclassical anthologies of classical material. Justinian's compilers themselves adapted classical texts to their own needs and to the law of their own time by means of changes, additions, abridgments, and omissions.

Unfortunately, there is seldom any direct indication in our sources as to what part of the text is genuine and what part owes its existence or present form to postclassical revision. It is possible, however, to detect "interpolations"—this is the technical expression used by scholars for any kind of addition to classical texts—as well as omissions or abridgments. They may reveal themselves through deviation from classical principles, for instance (though often without intent and knowledge of those who were responsible, since as a rule postclassical editors had no intention of altering the law). Typical signs of postclassical authorship are also inconsistencies in thought or peculiarities of style or vocabulary which exclude the classical jurist as the author of the passage in question. Obviously the results of critical analysis of the sources are often conjectural and controversial. But concerning the principal question of whether a comparatively large amount of postclassical tampering with classical literature did or did not take place, Romanists have long been almost unanimous in the affirmative answer. There is, however, much doubt regarding the nature, cause, and time of alterations, and of their legal import. Research into these questions is in full flux. In particular, efforts to determine the exact phase of development to which spurious passages should be attributed—i.e., whether they belong to the earlier or later postclassical period or to Justinian—have just begun.

As a consequence of this uncertainty, the evalution of the postclassical period is a matter of disagreement among scholars of Roman law. Controversies exist about the forms and ways in which classical literature survived to the age of Justinian, the character and role of postclassical legal science, the manner in which classical literature was utilized by Justinian's compilers, whether and to what extent non-Roman concepts and institutions superseded the true Roman law, and the impact of Christian ethics. In the following sections the attempt will be made to describe the various factors of evolution that played their part in the postclassical era and to appraise their effect. But the reader should bear in mind that at the present state of our knowledge many of the statements made will necessarily be tentative.

II. LEGAL SCIENCE AND LITERATURE

The type of legal writing developed by the classical jurists —together with the jurists themselves—disappeared and could never be revived. It was too intimately connected with their practice of giving *responsa* to survive this practice. It is conceivable that the place of classical jurisprudence might have been taken by a more theoretical jurisprudence, and apparently some preconditions for such a development did exist in the third century A.D. Under the later Principate, for instance, there existed law schools for the training of the rank-and-file jurists who wished to enter upon a career in the imperial civil service. A school at Berytus (Beyrouth) in Syria, which came to great fame in the fifth century, is known to have existed in A.D. 239, and its beginnings were perhaps as early as the latter part of the second century. There was also a law school in Rome, and others may have existed elsewhere.

These schools survived the decline of classical jurisprudence and cultivated a scholarly approach to the law through extensive studying of, and commenting on, classical writings, the latter done largely by adducing further materials gathered from other classical works. There is, for instance, in the fragments of the two great commentaries by Ulpianus—and perhaps of other works of the same author—evidence that a chain of abridged quotations from Julianus's *Digesta* was systematically compiled on the margins of a copy of Ulpianus's works by an unknown scholar, probably of the late third century.[2] Moreover, a certain tendency towards thinking in theoretically conceived legal categories, which is noticeable in imperial constitutions of the third century and of the time of Diocletian, indicates that the early postclassical law school was able to some extent to present the law in terms of a scientific system of concepts. In view of the classical *Institutes* type of literature, on which postclassical teaching was based, this is what should be expected.

In spite of such possible starting points, no truly scientific jurisprudence developed. It seems hardly sufficient, however,

---

[2] The evidence is presented in the author's paper "Zur Ueberlieferungs-geschichte von Ulpian's *libri ad Sabinum*," in *Festschrift Fritz Schulz*, Vol. II (Weimar, 1951), 145–71.

to explain this fact—as many legal historians have done—by merely pointing to the cultural decline which accompanied the political and economic crisis of the second half of the third century. A decline did take place but it was by no means a complete collapse; suffice it to mention the outstanding philosopher, Plotinus, who lived in Rome at the same time as the latest classical jurists, or Cyprian, bishop of Carthage and great writer on Christian topics, and other eminent Fathers of the Church of the third and fourth centuries. The reasons a new type of important legal writing did not emerge should rather be sought primarily in the conditions of jurisprudence itself.

On the one hand, the very attitude of the classical jurists— i.e., their lack of interest in purely theoretical questions—had prevented them from fitting the results of their deep knowledge of the workings of the legal system into a framework of scientific concepts and thus from preparing the ground on which a new type of legal scholar, capable of succeeding them, might build. The *Institutes* type of literature was too elementary to provide such a basis. On the other hand, the legal theorists who made teaching their profession had, with a few exceptions such as Pomponius, never belonged to the group of leading authorities, for true legal talent found better opportunities in the imperial service. It is obvious that those who in the third century engaged in legal teaching were at best mediocre jurists, capable of gathering and somewhat generalizing, for the purpose of presentation in the classroom, classical doctrines, but too dependent on the classical authorities to create an original jurisprudence of their own. Rome never produced a John Austin.

Thus the political, sociological, and intellectual situation in which legal experts found themselves in the third and fourth centuries forced creative scholarship to a virtual standstill. It is therefore not surprising that literary production in the legal field reached a low ebb in both quantity and quality. What was relatively best in it consisted of brief manuals for use as guides to officials and judges of the *extraordinaria cognitio*. Fragments of such manuals have been preserved in Justinian's Digest under the names of Arcadius Charisius and Hermogenianus, of the late third or fourth century. These modest little works were at least independent achievements, and this is why the names of their authors remained known. Arcadius Charisius and Hermogenianus were the only authors of the postclassical era whose works were utilized by the compilers of Justinian's Digest. This seems to indicate that they were outstanding among their contemporaries.

As a matter of fact, these conclusions are borne out by what we know of other legal publications of the time. They were not—nor did they pretend to be—original accomplishments. Most of these publications, usually anonymous, merely served the purpose of facilitating access to those sources which, in addition to imperial statutes, were considered in school and courtroom as authoritative statements of law—primarily the rescripts of former emperors and the writings of the great jurists of the past. This was an urgent task indeed. All over the Empire, Roman law as laid down by emperors and classical jurisconsults was now supposed to be the law applied by the imperial courts. Poor library facilities in the provinces and the immense mass of legal material made convenient means of information a vital necessity for practitioners, teachers, and students of law. The problem was solved in the only way known to the lawyers of this period, lacking originality and possessed of a boundless reverence for the old authorities; that is to say, by compiling, abridging, and revising the statements of their great predecessors.

Imperial constitutions—issued by emperors from Hadrian to Diocletian—became available to the public through two collections published in the closing years of the third century. These were the *Codex Gregorianus* and its supplement, the *Codex Hermogenianus*. Their authors, Gregorius and Hermogenianus, were in all probability legally trained officials connected with the imperial chancellery; perhaps those are right who identify this Hermogenianus with the author of the same name, fragments of whose works appear in the Digest. To the two Codes their authors contributed only through their selection and arrangement of materials. They simply reproduced the answers given by emperors to inquiries addressed to them, indicating in each case the names of the emperor and the inquirer and the date of the rescript. Both works are lost to us, but some of their contents are known from other works in which they are quoted. Later they were also exploited by the compilers of Justinian's Code, but it is not possible for us to determine which of the constitutions assembled there were taken over from the Gregorian and Hermogenian Codes.

About the same time—or perhaps somewhat earlier—two works appeared which are known as *Pauli Sententiarum ad filium libri quinque* (Five Books of Sentences, dedicated to his son) and as *Ulpiani Regularum liber singularis* (Rules of Law in one book). The former is known from extensive fragments incorporated in a codification of Roman law made in A.D. 506 by the Visigoth king Alaric II for the Romans of his realm in Spain, as well as from a number of excerpts found in Justinian's Digest. The so-called *Regulae* of Ulpianus still exist in the form of an *epitome* (abridgment) in a manuscript of the Vatican Library in Rome.

For many centuries both works were accepted as classical, but modern research has demonstrated that this is not so. The *Sentences* is now considered to be a brief presentation of Roman law extracted from the writings of Paulus (and possibly other classical writers) by an unknown author of the latter part of the third century, probably in one of the western provinces of the Empire.[3] The *liber singularis*—likewise a repre-

[3] This was shown by E. Levy, "Paulus und der Sentenzenverfasser," in *Z. Sav. St.*, Vol. L (1930), 272–94. For an analysis of the work, see Levy, *Pauli Sententiae. A Palingenesia of the Opening Titles as a Specimen of Research in West Roman Vulgar Law.*

sentative product of legal scholarship in the late third and early fourth centuries—was, according to the prevalent opinion among modern Romanists, not even compiled from the works of Ulpianus but was based on Gaius's *Institutes*.[4] How it came to be connected with the name of Ulpianus is not explained.

It is not unlikely that the two works were typical of a form of literature which was common in the early postclassical period. Modern critical research has caused Romanists to doubt the authenticity of many of the ostensibly classical works, excerpts of which were incorporated in Justinian's Digest. It is believed that at the time of Justinian a number of works were found in the libraries which were ascribed to classical authors, and accepted as such by Justinian's compilers, but which were actually productions of the postclassical period. It is not likely that the suspicion is justified in all cases in which it has been voiced. In several instances, however, it has much in its favor, and in at least one case the postclassical origin of a seemingly classical work has been proven. There are a number of fragments in the Digest taken from a work entitled "six books of *responsa*," the author of which is supposed to be Cervidius Scaevola. It has been shown[5] that the six books were never written by Scaevola but were a postclassical abridgment of another work, attributed to the same author and entitled "Digest in sixty books." The latter work was a collection of *responsa* of the jurist (possibly itself a compilation made by some unknown person from Scaevola's private records after the jurist's death).

The tendency of this type of literature is clear. It was devised to make access to the opinions of the great authorities easier. This is why the names of those who composed these works were forgotten, if indeed they were ever revealed. The

4 Schulz, *History of Roman Legal Science*, 181.

5 F. Schulz, "Ueberlieferungsgeschichte der Responsa des Cervidius Scaevola," in *Symbolae Friburgenses in honorem Ottonis Lenel*, 143–244.

person of the compiler of such a book was unimportant; what mattered was the name of the classical authority whose legal views were set forth in it. In this respect all these productions followed the same plan, although their character varied. Some of the compilers showed a higher degree of originality than others. Paulus's *Sentences,* for example, is an attempt at a free presentation of Roman law based on decisions found in writings by Paulus, with perhaps some admixture taken from other classical authors. On the contrary, the ambition of the compiler of Scaevola's *responsa* does not seem to have reached beyond reproducing in abridged form part of the decisions assembled in the larger work. There is little doubt that there existed more of this type of literature and that a good deal of it was utilized by Justinian's compilers. For the time being, however, no more detailed statement can be made since research into these problems is still in its beginning stages.

The spurious origin of these works was probably soon forgotten, if it was ever known at all to any considerable number of contemporary lawyers. It is therefore not surprising to find that in Justinian's time they were considered as classical literature. Some of the books in question even attained great prestige. In particular, Paulus's *Sentences*—recommended already in a statute of Constantine's—became a book of authority, chiefly in the western parts of the Empire. Here legal and general education suffered an especially serious decline in the stormy age of the Migration of Nations; and such elementary and short statements as the *Sentences* were all the lawyers of the barbaric kingdoms in the West were able to comprehend and had any use for. The *Sentences* exerted great influence on legislation issued by Germanic kings. In southern France it was studied far into the Middle Ages.

Closely related to the activity just described was another practice in which legal scholars of the fourth, and perhaps also of the fifth, century engaged. It was, of course, not exclusively compilations and abridgments that were read by the lawyers of the time. Much of the genuine classical literature remained in circulation. The demand for it probably arose primarily in the law schools, but it may be assumed that some of it, especially the great commentaries by Paulus and Ulpianus and monographic works dealing with special jurisdictions, found their way to the desks of many a judge or advocate. This must have caused a permanent demand for new copies. It is likely that these were made, either privately or by bookdealers, as the need arose.

In some cases, however, it was not merely new copies of the original which appeared on the market—presenting the classical text altered, if at all, only an account of mistakes made by copyists—but real revised editions of the old works made by contemporary jurists. An external circumstance may have provided an additional inducement to undertake such a task. The years around A.D. 300 happened to be the time when ancient book production abandoned the traditional form of the scroll and adopted that of the *codex*, i.e., the bound book as we know it. The need of reissuing old books in the new manner would have made jurists more aware of their own want of what they may have considered a more up-to-date text.[6]

Evidence for such an edition, probably published between 310 and 320, exists for Ulpianus's commentary on the Edict,[7] which appears soon to have replaced completely the original and to have remained in use, in the main unaltered, down to the time of Justinian. Ulpianus's books on Sabinus were also reissued in a similar manner. The same may be expected of other classical works, but definite statements must await the results of further research.

6 Cf. F. Wieacker, "Lebensläufe klassischer Schriften in nachklassischer Zeit," in *Z. Sav. St.*, Vol. LXVII (1950), 387–95.

7 The evidence can be found in the author's article on "Ulpian XVIII *ad Edictum* in Collatio and Digest and the Problem of Postclassical Editions of Classical Works," in *Scritti in onore di Contardo Ferrini pubblicati in occasione della sua beatificazione*, IV, 64–90.

Utterly sterile though this whole secondhand literature was, it did reflect an application of intelligence on the part of those who produced it. They sometimes tried to at least adapt the classical works under their hands to changed conditions. For instance, the author of Paulus's *Sentences* wrote for an audience of provincial practitioners. Accordingly, he picked from the writings of his authority those matters which were of real interest to his readers, leaving other subjects aside. His statements, brief recapitulations of what the classical author had said in *responsa* or other utterances, were worded to make them applicable to the procedure of the *cognitio extraordinaria,* which alone would be intelligible to his audience. He therefore remolded some of the passages in which the views of Paulus had assumed the existence of the republican-classical forms of civil procedure.

It can be shown also that the editor of Ulpianus's commentary on the Edict worked from a copy of the original which contained marginal glosses by one or more readers. Part of these he saw fit to work into the text as though they had actually been written by the classical jurist. In other cases, he omitted passages found in the original text because he apparently considered them superfluous or useless for his purpose. Occasionally he replaced them by others of his own making, and sometimes he even added to the classical text.

These and other methods can be understood when we realize that ancient times did not have as much respect for the individuality of an author as modern times have. The tampering certainly did not, from our point of view, improve the text, but it must be admitted that from the standpoint of the lawyers of the time the old books did need modernization. This the editor of Ulpianus's work sought to achieve; in addition he may have hoped to make things more intelligible than they seemed to him in the original text (in this he frequently failed indeed); and, finally, it is conceivable that he even tried now and then to show a little originality, which, however—in the timid manner of those anonymous lawyers of that period —he hid under the name of the classical celebrity.

This brief description of the methods of two of the post-classical authors may suggest the character of that kind of literary activity in general. As for detail, we must of course expect considerable variety from work to work. For example, the editor of Ulpianus's *libri ad Sabinum* followed a program far less ambitious than that of his approximately contemporary colleague, the editor of the *libri ad edictum*.[8] He simply copied a manuscript of the original, which contained two or more chains of marginal scholia as well as some casual glosses, in such a way as to write everything—text, scholia, and glosses—in a continuous column, fitting marginal material into the text wherever he found it. He did not care if the interpolation of a marginal remark destroyed the cohesion of Ulpianus's presentation, although it is not impossible that he marked, as such, passages fitted by him into the text. His own contribution was confined to a few words occasionally needed to establish connections; he may also be responsible for a few omissions.

There was still another type of literature which consisted of compilations of assorted excerpts from classical writings. It was essentially related to the Gregorian and Hermogenian Codes which were similar collections of imperial constitutions; and the same literary technique was employed in the fifth and sixth centuries in bringing forth the great codifications, as will be seen.

There are two works to be mentioned in this connection. One is a voluminous collection of fragments taken from works of Papinianus, Paulus, and Ulpianus; several imperial constitutions are also included. The compiler of the collection—as well as the title and purpose of his work—is unknown; its time is controversial, estimates ranging from the early to the

---

8 See the author's paper "Zur Ueberlieferungsgeschichte von Ulpian's *libri ad Sabinum*."

late fourth century. Only part of this compilation has been preserved, in a single manuscript of the Vatican Library; it is therefore known as the "Vatican Fragments."

The other book bears the title of *Mosaicarum et Romanarum Legum Collatio (Comparison between Mosaic and Roman Laws)*. This extremely poor piece of work is subdivided into titles, each of which begins with a quotation from the law of Moses followed by quotations from literary and imperial sources of Roman law. These quotations are supposed to prove—although they do not always do so—that biblical and Roman law were in agreement. According to the opinion now prevalent among scholars, the *Collatio* was composed early in the fourth century by a Jew, for the purpose of defending the Jewish law against attacks launched against it by Romans; others believe that the author was a Christian of the late fourth or early fifth century, possibly St. Ambrose. No absolutely convincing arguments have so far been advanced for either hypothesis, but it seems that the former is preferable, at least as far as the question of the time of the compilation is concerned.

The various forms of literary activity in the field of law all show one thing very clearly: namely, the extent to which the postclassical period remained under the spell of classical jurisprudence. The only force productive of legal ideas was imperial legislation. Whatever legal science existed contented itself with the study of the old authorities, who came to be looked upon with an almost religious awe. Practitioners and judges, unless otherwise directed by specific imperial statutes, relied on the old books or on the new books which were supposed to give them the gist of the old law in condensed form. The classical jurists also dominated legal instruction.

In one of the statutes introducing Justinian's codification (*constitutio "Omnem"*), the emperor describes in detail the plan of legal studies followed during his time in the law schools of the Eastern Empire. We learn that legal studies consisted entirely in reading classical books and imperial constitutions, and for each of the four or five years required for graduation, the works to be studied were rigidly prescribed. The strict adherence to a hard and fast plan was probably a more recent development, but the underlying principle of basing legal instruction on a perusal of classical literature had certainly been followed all through the postclassical period. This alone can account for the important role the use of classical authorities played in judicial proceedings of that time.

The degree to which the ideal of a full education in classical law was realized varied, of course, from time to time and from place to place. In early postclassical times—i.e., in the late third and early fourth centuries—a considerable amount of scholarly interest in the law seems to have existed in the West, in all probability centering chiefly in the law school of Rome. The assumption that most, if not all, of the literary activities described took place in the West may very well be correct. This aftermath of classical jurisprudence apparently reached its end under Constantine, when Constantinople became the seat of the government—and thereby the meeting place of the best legal minds—and when the East began generally to overshadow the West. Legal culture in the West took a sharp downward trend, which was aggravated by the confusion and decline of general culture caused by the barbaric invasions.

In the fifth century we find nothing but decadence and disintegration of Roman law in all parts of the West, although the results were not equally catastrophic in all places. Thus scientific treatment of Roman law never ceased completely in southern France. There a school of Roman law flourished in the early Middle Ages. It was here, in the city of Autun, that a commentary on Gaius was composed, probably in the fifth century; this commentary is known to us as the "Gaius of Autun."

Another testimony to a modest amount of legal culture is

what its Renaissance editor called the "Consultation of some old jurisconsult," a little book written somewhere in the West in the fifth or sixth century. It is really a schoolbook, reflecting a schoolroom discussion of some selected problems. All the anonymous author does is to state the questions and to cite pertinent passages collected from the Gregorian, Hermogenian, and Theodosian Codes and from Paulus's *Sentences*.

Elsewhere in the West, however, legal education does not seem to have gone beyond elementary information about the main institutions of Roman law, adapted somewhat to changed conditions. This at least is the impression to be gathered from the fact that Visigothic Spain in the fifth and sixth centuries did not even read such simple books as Gaius's *Institutes* but contented itself with a poor abridgment of the work. Thus knowledge of the law sank disastrously low. The appalling amount of legal misinformation found in the writings of St. Isidore of Seville in the sixth to seventh centuries allows us to form a picture of the sad condition in which legal knowledge was at that time; the more so, since Isidore was certainly a man in full possession of all the education and scholarship of his time and country.

A more favorable picture is presented by the Greek East. It is true that here, too, the knowledge of classical literature by the average legal expert was most incomplete. Credit for the fact that the East avoided a general decay of jurisprudence, such as occurred in the West, is due two of the eastern law schools, the ancient Berytus and, from not later than 425, Constantinople. At first private institutions, the schools were brought into ever closer connection with the imperial government during the course of the fourth and fifth centuries. Salaries for law professors were apparently paid by the government after 425. Later in the fifth century certificates of attendance of law courses at one of the official schools of the Empire—either Rome, Constantinople, or Berytus—were required of those who wished to practice before the court of the *praefectus praetorio,* the highest court of the Empire. At some time—perhaps when the schools began to be official institutions—the courses offered by them were fitted into a definite curriculum which had to be followed by the students (see above, page 143f.).

At the two outstanding places of legal learning, Berytus and Constantinople, the study of the old authors gave rise in the fifth century to a new type of truly scientific jurisprudence. The revival of legal learning apparently was in the main confined to the two places named. This at least seems to be the conclusion called for by the following circumstances: that the names of several scholars of these two schools are still known, while no name of any professor of any other law school has survived; and that Justinian allowed only these two schools to carry on under the new plan of instruction introduced by him in connection with the enactment of the Digest.

In their time the professors of the two great Byzantine schools—the "teachers of the universe," as they were admiringly called—enjoyed a tremendous prestige. There is no better proof for this than the fact that Justinian entrusted them with carrying out his plans for the final codification of the whole law. The first in the line of distinguished scholars at Berytus was perhaps Cyrillus, in the early years of the fifth century. A younger contemporary of Cyrillus may have been Patricius, now recognized as the most outstanding among the men of Berytus. Other noted jurists of the fifth century were Demosthenes, Eudoxius, Amblichus, and Leontius.[9] It is known that these men wrote commentaries on imperial rescripts and statutes, as well as on a few works of classical scholars. Nothing of their work has been preserved, but some of it is known from quotations by Justinian's contemporaries, whose works were in part transmitted along with the *Basilica.*

The Byzantine legal science, as we call it, was not, to be sure, the creative and practical kind of jurisprudence the clas-

[9] About scholars of the time of Justinian, see below, page 179.

146

sical period had known. The representatives of this new legal science were teachers, not practitioners. Their ambition was not to produce new legal ideas but to obtain a real knowledge of what the classical jurists had left to posterity and to explain the doctrinal contents of classical decisions. There is, moreover, no doubt that Byzantine legal science was characterized by an utter lack of originality and productivity. In the discovery of doctrinal concepts underlying the practical work of the classical jurists, it can at best be credited with a very modest beginning.

However, this did make it a forerunner of the medieval and modern science of Roman law. Furthermore, whatever its flaws, Byzantine science did succeed in getting back genuine familiarity with the whole of the classical achievement. Its efforts bore rich fruit. Their new insight into the workings of the old law enabled men coming from these schools to improve on the technique of imperial legislation, so that the statutes of Justinian and his immediate predecessors differ favorably, in clarity of both thought and style, from those of the fourth and early fifth centuries. Last but not least, Byzantine legal science was capable of crowning its work by producing that comprehensive compilation and condensation of the law which is known as Justinian's *Corpus Iuris*.

This is about all, however, that can be stated without becoming involved in the violent disputes raging among legal historians concerning Byzantine legal science. The exact amount of its importance and of its influence on the evolution of postclassical law has long been a matter of sharp controversy, as will be seen shortly. This uncertainty is due to the fact that, while we do know something of the methods and accomplishments of Byzantine scholars of the era of Justinian and after, we possess only scanty information about their achievements in the period before Justinian.

Of literary productions still extant which may have originated in Berytus or at least reflected its influence, only two are worth mentioning here. One is a presentation of institutions of civil and imperial Roman law, now referred to by the misleading title of the "Syro-Roman Lawbook"; its Greek original is lost but several translations into Syriac, Arabic, and Armenian are extant. The other is part of an explanatory commentary on Ulpianus's books on Sabinus; it exists in only one manuscript which was found in the monastery of Mt. Sinai and is therefore called the "Sinai Fragments."

More revealing of the character of Byzantine science—though more difficult to ascertain—are direct utterances, attributable to Byzantine scholars but found in the form of interpolations in the fragments of classical literature assembled in Justinian's Digest. The existence of such bits of Byzantine jurisprudence may be considered as established, although their identification is almost always hypothetical and often very uncertain, especially since it is as yet unknown in what form such Byzantine comments had originally been set down. They may have been marginal notes in the copies of classical books in the compilers' library. They may also have been separate publications in the manner of the Sinai Fragments. In these two cases it would have been the compilers who fitted them into the texts.

There is also some indication, however, that the compilers used several classical works, in editions made in the late postclassical period, in which Byzantine scholia were already incorporated in the text and probably regarded as classical by the compilers. It is likely that Byzantine utterances came to the compilers in all of these forms. Romanists are faced with the task of ascertaining the origin and transmission of glosses, since this is frequently a condition on which correct appraisal depends. The difficulty of the task is increased by the fact that as yet no certain criteria have been discovered for even distinguishing interpolations originating in Byzantine legal science from those belonging to earlier phases of postclassical annotations of classical texts.

Despite the element of doubt which is usually inescapable in attempts to identify Byzantine contributions, enough is known to allow at least a general characterization. Interpolations and other surviving remnants show the scholarship of these professors and also their unoriginal and schoolmaster-like, pedantic, approach. They tried to explain the classical decisions, sometimes to show doctrinal principles underlying them or practical consequences that might be derived from them; they called attention to parallel passages; but they set forth no independent theories of their own.

III. GENERAL TRENDS OF POSTCLASSICAL LEGAL DEVELOPMENT

In considering the course of postclassical legal evolution, one has to bear in mind the fact that only imperial legislation was in a position to exert an immediate influence on the formation of law. In consequence of this, the whole Empire, united under one government with absolute powers, was supposed to live under one imperial law. Within Roman law, the distinction between *ius civile* and *ius honorarium* lost its importance. In the Empire the law as set forth in imperial statutes and as administered by imperial courts took precedence over the local laws of the provinces, although the latter retained some importance. After the emergence of separate Eastern and Western Empires, which came with the partition of the Empire between the sons of Theodosius the Great in A.D. 395, the uniform imperial law split into two branches.

However, as long as the Western Empire existed, the two branches grew mainly along parallel lines, since many laws were enacted jointly by Eastern and Western emperors; while other laws, first enacted in the East, were soon adopted by Western emperors. A few statutes issued by Western emperors independently were short-lived and of no great importance. The theoretical reunion of the whole Empire under one head —after the deposition of the last West-Roman emperor, Romulus Augustulus, in A.D. 476—involved, though again only theoretically, the reunion of the two branches of imperial law. The considerable discrepancy between the law observed in the East and that of the West, which actually developed from not later than the fifth century, was due to forces working beneath and outside the imperial legislation.

The imposition of a uniform imperial law through imperial administration of justice and statute did not have the effect of forcing Roman law pure and simple upon the peoples of the Empire. It is true indeed that emperors from Caracalla to Diocletian did try to do just this; for such a policy was the natural consequence of Caracalla's *Constitutio Antoniniana* which extended Roman citizenship to all free inhabitants of the Empire. In particular, Diocletian conceived his restoration of the Roman Empire as involving not only the re-establishment of firm government, but also the restoration to the greatest possible extent of true Roman ways. Hence his persecution of the Christians; and hence also his attempt to enforce all over the Empire Roman law in the form worked out by emperors of the Principate and by classical jurists. Hundreds of Diocletian's rescripts, preserved in Justinian's Code, reflect his opposition to provincial customs conflicting with rules of Roman law.

With Diocletian's successor, however, came a complete reversal of policy. Constantine, in line with his shifting of the political center of the Empire to the East and with his championing of Christianity, also opened the gates of Roman law to foreign influences. His legislation is marked by the adoption into the imperial law of institutions originating in the usages of Greek and near-Eastern peoples, as well as by the introduction of principles derived from the precepts of Christian ethics.

Constantine's innovating radicalism was not equally shared by all of his successors, and it seems that the vacilations which characterize the legislative activities of fourth-

and fifth-century emperors were in part owing to their changing attitudes toward Christian and other non-Roman influences. All in all, however, it has to be said that during the whole period from Constantine to Justinian the imperial law felt a strong impact of Christian and Eastern ideas and customs.

Such influences can be found at many points of the legal system, a few of which may be mentioned here. The Christian concept of the indissolubility of marriage, though not incorporated outright into the law, was the driving force behind enactments by Constantine and some of his successors which, by providing severe penalties, aimed indirectly at curtailing the freedom of spouses to declare a divorce. A feature entirely alien to old Roman law and copied from customs of the near East was the "marital gift" to be made by the groom to his bride in order to secure her against destitution after his death or after an unprovoked divorce. Concepts developed in the traditions and social conditions of Greek cities also found their way into the imperial law concerning illegitimate children. The custom of the Hellenistic East of embodying obligations in written instruments was fitted into the imperial law and virtually replaced the old Roman institution of the oral *stipulatio*.

This brief enumeration could easily be enlarged. However, it should be remarked that the exact extent of such influences is still a subject of intense research and of lively controversy, although most of these problems pertain to detail only.

Behind them, however, looms a question of paramount importance—in fact the crucial question of the whole history of postclassical Roman law. Was this law really still what it pretended to be, namely, *Roman* law? Or was it—as many legal historians claim—a mixture of Roman, Greek, Near Eastern, and Christian elements, based on doctrinal concepts which breathed the spirit of Greeks or Hellenized orientals and were totally alien to the classical Roman spirit? In other words, was the legal system which emerges from Justinian's *Corpus Iuris* really Roman law or largely a product of non-Roman thinking?

This question involves more than just the adoption into imperial law, by imperial statutes, of foreign institutions or of ideas derived from Christian ethics. There is no doubt that such adoption took place; the disputes among scholars concern only its extent. But were these adoptions merely external additions or were they part of a deep transformation of the Roman law which began at the law schools of the East and thence spread to the imperial chancellery and to all other agencies administering the law of the Empire?

When the presence of a large number of interpolations was first discovered in the remnants of classical literature assembled in Justinian's Digest, it was assumed that all of these were inserted by the compilers of the Digest and that all of them served the purpose of modifying the classical law, with the result that deep differences were found between the law of the classical jurists and that of Justinian. Then, when the importance of the Byzantine legal science was realized about a generation ago, it became a habit of many Romanists to attribute most of these supposed changes to the professors of Berytus, and since these were Greeks or perhaps Hellenized Semites (Berytus was a Syrian city), to explain the changes by the theory that they were due to an influx of Eastern (Greek or Semitic) legal concepts and of theories formed in Greek philosophical and rhetorical schools.

It was not long, however, before this interpretation was vigorously attacked by the famous Italian Romanist, Salvatore Riccobono. Riccobono does not deny that many of the ostensibly classical texts in the Digest are corrupt, nor does he deny that some of these corruptions were caused by the desire of postclassical revisers—or, as Riccobono would still probably prefer to say, in the majority of cases,[10] of Justinian's

10 Recently, however, Riccobono has acknowledged the existence of early

compilers—to adapt the texts to changes of the law brought about by imperial legislation or by the impact of Christian ideas. Most of the textual changes, however, Riccobono would explain as "formal"—that is to say, as made merely in order to eliminate from the texts discussions and phrases pertaining to the difference between *ius honorarium* and *ius civile,* which had become meaningless. Riccobono believes that most of the innovations and modernizations attributed by his opponents to the Byzantines had already been made by the classical jurists, chiefly in their interpretation of the praetorian Edict, which gave them an opportunity to overcome the more rigid concepts of the old *ius civile.* Accordingly, Riccobono emphatically insists on the genuinely Roman character of the legal principles displayed in Justinian's compilation. He denies any influence of Eastern concepts or institutions—and this means to him, any importance of Byzantine science—save for such alien elements as were introduced by express legislative fiat of the emperors.[11]

The argument between Riccobono and his opponents is still one of the most important among the many disputes of Romanists. A full discussion of the problem is impossible here, since it would require a detailed investigation of the history of individual legal institutions and doctrines. However, a few suggestions can be given of the direction in which a solution to the very complex problem may lie.

postclassical glosses. See his paper "Sul fr. 32 D.XV, 1: Ulpianus II Disputationum," in *Studi in onore di Siro Solazzi,* 590–93.

11 Riccobono has briefly stated his views in "Outlines of the Evolution of Roman Law," in *University of Pennsylvania Law Review,* Vol. LXXIV (1925), 1–19. His main writings on the subject are: *Dal diritto romano classico al diritto moderno,* in *Annali del Seminario Giuridico della R. Università di Palermo,* Vols. III–IV (Palermo, 1917); "Fusione del ius civile e del ius praetorium in unico ordinamento," in *Archiv für Rechtsphilosophie,* Vol. XXVI (1922), 501–22; and "Fasi e fattori dell'evoluzione del diritto romano," in *Mélanges Georges Cornil,* I, 237–381. Representative of the opponents of Riccobono is Emilio Albertario; for a comprehensive statement of his views, see his *Introduzione storica allo studio del diritto romano giustinianeo,* I, 81–133 (Chapter IV: *"I fattori della evoluzione del diritto romano postclassico e la formazione del diritto romano giustinianeo"*).

It would seem that the truth lies somewhere between the views of Riccobono and those of his more radical opponents. It is probably correct that the vast majority of interpolations and other alterations and corruptions of classical texts in the Digest should be ascribed to early postclassical and Byzantine tampering with classical writings or to comments on statements found in those writings. But the abridgers and later editors of the early postclassical period—as well as the scholars of Berytus—were characterized by a lack of originality and by their reverence for classical authority, as has been explained above. These factors alone were sufficient to prevent them, as a rule, from deliberately altering the law stated in their sources.

Even more important, however, is the fact that these men were neither authorized nor psychologically prepared to make or suggest changes in the law. They were living in the stifling atmosphere of an absolute—we may well say totalitarian—monarchy which jealously monopolized the making of new law, even as regards details, and which did not encourage any independent professional influence or original interpretation of the existing law in the manner of the classical jurisconsults. As a matter of fact, it can be shown that those abridgers and editors almost never deviated intentionally from what the classical authors had said, except when they were forced to adapt the text to actual changes brought about by imperial legislation or by the administration of justice in the *extraordinaria cognitio*.

Similarly, those Byzantine writers of comments who explained or elaborated on statements made by a classical authority clearly had no other purpose in most instances and did not dream of contradicting the classical jurist. It seems safe to say that throughout the postclassical period the authority of the classical jurists remained unchallenged and their solutions accepted as uncontradictable revelations of judicial wisdom.

Nevertheless, the legal conceptions which emerge from

the fragments assembled in the Digest are not quite those of classical law, with adaptations for new forms of procedure and for changes by imperial legislation. Though almost always unintentional, some real changes did come about through the work of postclassical jurists in the time before Justinian. Mistakes in abridging were inevitable. Comments, often written by ignorant and thoughtless glossators, were fitted into the text by incompetent postclassical editors of classical works. These comments had the effect of distorting the text so that succeeding generations, including Justinian's own, took what they read for classical doctrine and therefore for sacred truth. Even more serious were mistakes made by Byzantine scholars who, while trying to explain the classical text or to elaborate on it, were apt to give it a twist not envisaged by the classical author, by erroneously imputing to him doctrinal theories not conceived by him or by drawing practical conclusions not intended by him. Last but not least, dogmatic generalization, applied by classical jurists rarely and with great caution, was a popular device with the theoretically minded Byzantines and was likewise a source of unintentional distortion of the meaning of classical decisions.

It cannot therefore be denied that we find in the Digest a number of views and doctrines attributable to postclassical legal scholarship and certainly completely alien to any classical jurist. To this extent Riccobono's opponents are certainly on the right track. Nevertheless, the danger of exaggeration is not always avoided by them. In particular, two points should be taken into account in appraising those undoubtedly postclassical contributions (which, incidentally, do not always deserve the scorn that many Romanists confer on everything connected with postclassical jurisprudence).

First, these contributions consist mainly in mere scholastic theories proposed by men who did not conceive them as their own free inventions but who believed that they were only following through hints or suggestions found in their classical authorities. Thus, when the practical consequences of such theories actually deviate from what a classical jurist would have decided, the reason must be sought in the pedantic and dogmatic attitude which characterized those Byzantine book-worms and which deprived them of the practical realism and the open-minded flexibility that were so typical of classical lawyers. But it remains true that the ultimate root of such postclassical theory always lay in some classical precedent.

Second, it is hardly ever possible to trace postclassical theories back to Greek or other non-Roman legal doctrines or practices. It may be quite correct that those professors who taught law in the Byzantine schools were men who, being Greek by descent or at least by culture, had gone through the whole course of the usual Greek philosophical and rhetorical education. It is very likely indeed that they owed to this Greek background their inclination to theorize and systematize (it is hardly accidental that in the Western, i.e., purely Latin, law schools the interest seems to have been much more on the practical side, with little understanding for the doctrinal import of legal rules).[12] But this appears to be all that can be claimed for Greek influences on the scholars of Berytus and Constantinople. The thinking, as such, of these professors moved, for all we can see, along strictly Roman lines—it moved, that is, along the lines of the classical books whose study and interpretation was the life work of these scholars. Even those theoretical categories which were actually alien to the classical jurists can be shown to be the fruits of their effort to extract and systematize the doctrinal contents of classical decisions.

What is true for the professors must be true also for the pupils—that is to say, for the official jurists, trained in the law schools, who drafted the imperial statutes. Knowledge of clas-

[12] It is interesting to note a parallel phenomenon in contemporary theological literature. Eastern church writers were chiefly concerned with questions of theological dogma, while Western writers interested themselves primarily in questions of the practical impact of Christian ethics.

sical legal literature is quite evident in these statutes, and the doctrinal concepts underlying the enactments are obviously derived from this knowledge. This is the light in which the adoption into the imperial law of Christian, Greek, or Near Eastern institutions or doctrines should be viewed. Such adoption did not mean that the chancellery succumbed to foreign ways of thinking, but only that the practical value of some alien institutions or doctrines was acknowledged and that the need was felt for giving recognition to deeply rooted customs of non-Roman populations and to urgent demands of Christian ethical teaching.

A close study of such enactments reveals that the jurists of the chancellery actually showed little understanding for the real doctrinal import of non-Roman institutions and rather strove to integrate them into the Roman legal system, which alone was known to, and understood by, the authors of the statutes.[13] This aim was successfully achieved. In practice, as in theory, Roman law remained essentially Roman.

The scientific basis which the law possessed in the East was absent in the western half of the Empire. Political and economic collapse, a retrogressive tendency in general education which accompanied it, and the influence of more primitive concepts held by the young nations which established themselves in the western provinces, all contributed to the barbarization of Roman law. In the West, too, its Roman character was preserved. But while in the East, Roman law showed a tendency to become lost in scholastic dogmatism and unrealistic theorizing, it took the opposite course in the West. Here it lost all subtlety and was stripped to a bare skeleton by unsophisticated jurists with little knowledge, and even the little that was left of it was sometimes misunderstood by the lawyers of the time.

[13] For an example, see the author's article on "Doctrinal Trends in Postclassical Roman Marriage Law," in *Z. Sav. St.*, Vol. LXVII (1950), 261–319.

CHAPTER VI

CODIFICATION

I. THE DIFFUSENESS OF LEGAL MATERIALS

ONE OF THE MOST PRESSING PROBLEMS confronting the postclassical era was the vastness of the materials comprising the law it had inherited. The problem was made more urgent by the timidity of judges in an age of absolutism, who sought no original solutions but relied so far as possible on established authority. The task of making the materials available was, as we saw, undertaken at first by individual scholars. The constitutions of the emperors of the Principate were collected in the Gregorian and Hermogenian Codes, while access to the opinions of classical authorities was made easier by up-to-date editions, abridgments, and compilations.

We may assume that efforts of this kind brought some relief. But the success achieved in preserving knowledge of the classical law and in making it available for use was far from complete. There is little doubt that there were, in the fourth and fifth centuries, some very able jurists, chiefly in the top agencies of the imperial government. But the rank and file of what passed as legal experts in the Empire apparently was of an appallingly low quality. Theodosius II, emperor of the Eastern Empire, and Valentinian III, emperor of the Western Empire, complain in the year 438: "Often has our Grace wondered what cause has brought it about that, in the face of so many proposed prizes by which arts and studies are nourished, those are so few and so rare who are in full possession of a knowledge of the civil law, and that, with so much grievous paleness from nocturnal work, hardly one or the other has received the firmness of perfect learning."[1]

The legal history of the fifth and sixth centuries is marked by successive attempts on the part of the imperial government to remedy this situation. The highhanded methods used to achieve the goal are characteristic of both the absolutistic form of government and the utterly dependent attitude and blind submission to authority on the part of the jurists of that time.

II. THE "LAW OF CITATIONS"

The vast amount of classical literature not only made it impossible for the average legal expert to familiarize himself with it but also presented a further difficulty. Judges who were expected to follow established authority must often have felt at a loss when they found themselves confronted with the numerous controversies which existed among classical scholars, all of whom were in principle considered as infallible oracles. Here the government at first attempted to help by arbitrarily and mechanically fixing the degree of authority to be accorded the old books.

Constantine took the first steps in this direction. From him, we possess two constitutions concerning the authority of classical writings. One of these—*Cod. Theod.* 1. 4. 1, issued between A.D. 321 and 324—declares certain works "abolished": this expression in itself throws an interesting light on the attitude of the age of absolutism toward classical literature. The works selected for this treatment were notes by Ulpianus and Paulus on Papinianus. The other constitution of Constantine —*Cod. Theod.* 1. 4. 2, of about A.D. 327—expressly confirmed the validity of the whole of Paulus's literary work, including the *Sentences*. What occasioned the latter constitution is unknown. As regards the former, the emperor himself tells us his motives: his desire "to eradicate the perpetual controversies of the learned men" and his aim to maintain the reputation of

[1] *Novella Theodosii* 1 *pr.*

Papinianus, since Ulpianus and Paulus, "while aiming at the praise of the genius [i.e., of Papinianus], did not want so much to correct him as to deprecate him."

The two ordinances should be understood in the light of a custom which had developed in postclassical judicial practice. This consisted in the reading in court of classical opinions pertinent to the legal question at issue. Judges were supposed to follow a unanimous opinion of the authorities, but to make their own choice in case of disagreement. Even this restricted discretion of the judges must have proved unsatisfactory, however, for Theodosius II and Valentinian III saw fit in 426 to regulate the use in court of classical precedents through what modern scholars have called their "Law of Citations."[2]

In this peculiar statute the emperors proclaimed as authoritative the writings of four of the latest classical scholars, namely, Papinianus, Paulus, Ulpianus, and Modestinus, and in addition those of Gaius. The opinions of earlier jurists quoted by the five principal authors might also be heeded, provided the quotations could be verified from the original books. In case of dissension among the authorities, the judge was to follow the majority, and in case of a tie, the opinion shared by Papinianus. If no utterance of Papinianus's could be found and if the others were tied, the judge was directed to use his own judgment in selecting the best of the solutions proposed.

It must be admitted that the Law of Citations provided a partial solution to the problem created by the unwieldy mass of legal materials and by the poor library conditions which we may assume to have prevailed everywhere in the Empire outside of a few centers of learning. It may also have improved the chances for uniformity and predictability of judicial sentences. On the other hand, it bears witness to the degree to which judges had lost the right and—as we probably must add

2 *Cod. Theod.* 1.4.3.

—the ability to form an independent judgment. As a matter of fact, the harsh criticism of contemporary jurists, which the same emperors pronounced twelve years later (see above, page 158f.), makes us wonder if the presumptions on which they founded their law of 426 were still too optimistic as regards the average lawyer of their time.

III. THE *CODEX THEODOSIANUS*

The effects of the Law of Citations must have proved unsatisfactory or else it may have been intended from the first as a provisional measure, in preparation for a larger undertaking. For less than two and one-half years later, Theodosius appointed a commission of distinguished lawyers—high officials and scholars—and charged them with the task of compiling a code, to be systematically arranged and to contain all the imperial laws issued since Constantine that were still in force, as well as a collection of legal principles derived from the Gregorian and Hermogenian Codes and from classical literature. The project was not carried out, for reasons not now known, but a second commission, appointed in 435, did complete in 438 a compilation which fulfilled the first of the two assignments.

This monumental work, called the *Codex Theodosianus,* was given the force of law in the Eastern Empire and replaced, as of January 1, 439, all the individual imperial laws enacted since Constantine. Substantially, however, most of these remained in force, but in the form given them in the new Code and by virtue of their re-enactment in this Code. Valentinian shortly afterwards issued the *Codex Theodosianus* separately for the Western Empire.[3]

A large portion of the *Codex Theodosianus* has been pre-

---

3 T. Mommsen and P. M. Meyer, *Theodosiani libri XVI cum constitutionibus Sirmondianis et leges Novellae ad Theodosianum pertinentes.* Meyer's volume contains the post-Theodosian *Novellae.*

served. It consists of sixteen books, subdivided into "titles"—
i.e., chapters—which contain the whole of the imperial legislation considered as still valid; in other words, it presents a comprehensive statement of the then existing law, but not a reform of the legal order. It deals with matters of constitutional
law, administrative law, ecclesiastical law, procedural law,
criminal law, and private law. The former enactments were
copied literally, though sometimes possibly with some changes
and editing to bring them up to date and to reconcile them
with other provisions of the Code. Only those portions of
statutes which had a bearing on the subjects treated were rendered in each title, so that some laws were broken up and
their parts distributed over several titles; of others only certain passages were taken over and the rest omitted. Within
each title the fragments were arranged chronologically. Fortunately for us, from the standpoint of historical research,
Theodosius decided to give due credit to those emperors who
had first enacted the several statutes. Therefore each fragment incorporated in the Code was carefully identified by giving the name of the emperor who had issued the particular
statute and by indicating the exact date of issue.

IV. JUSTINIAN'S LEGISLATION

1. PRELIMINARIES

The *Codex Theodosianus* was a remarkable achievement,
but it did not solve the difficulties with which the lawyers of
the time were struggling. The principal problem remained:
that of finding a way to revive and make effectively usable the
treasures of judicial experience and wisdom lying in the classical writings and in imperial rescripts of the classical period.
The need of a comprehensive restatement of the law that was
hidden in the classical sources had been felt as early as Theodosius II, and some steps toward satisfying the demand had
been taken then but without result. Early in the sixth century

the task was again undertaken—this time in the West—and brought nearer fulfilment, though with insufficient means and poor success (see below, Section V). But a century after the enactment of the *Codex Theodosianus*, a happy union of propitious conditions—personal, political, and cultural— made it possible to carry out on a larger scale the project envisaged by Theodosius.

On April 1, 527, a vigorous man ascended the throne in Constantinople in the person of Flavius Iustinianus (527– 565). Immediately upon his accession, Justinian set out to put in effect an ambitious plan: the restoration of the whole Roman Empire under one emperor, one church, and one law. In pursuance of this plan, he engaged in military action which resulted in the reconquest, from their Germanic rulers, of North Africa, Italy, and part of southern Spain. He undertook the building of St. Sophia in Constantinople as the greatest church of Christendom and as a symbol of the unity of Empire and church. Finally, he carried through a complete codification of Roman law.

The latter undertaking proved to be his greatest and most enduring success. The achievement was possible because its intellectual foundations had been prepared by decades of intense study of classical sources at the two principal Byzantine law schools of Berytus and Constantinople. Under the personal guidance of the emperor and under the immediate direction of Tribonianus, his *quaestor sacri palatii* (see above, page 47), several legislative commissions, largely composed of professors of the two schools, completed within less than seven years—from 528 to 534—what jurists since the Renaissance have become accustomed to call the *Corpus Iuris Civilis* (Body of Civil Law). Subsequent special legislation by Justinian further built up and amended the system laid down in the codification.

2. THE CODIFICATION

The purpose of the codification was twofold: to serve as an authoritative statement, with legally binding force, of the whole of Roman law; and as the one and only text to be studied in the schools. It was to replace and did replace all former statements of law, both in literature and in legislation. It was to be the only source of law in the whole Empire. In this way Justinian hoped to make the law uniform throughout the Empire and to displace the diffuse mass of legal materials that had caused so much confusion.

The *Corpus Iuris* consists of three parts:[4] (1) a brief introductory survey of the whole system in four books, called the Institutes; (2) a collection in fifty books of excerpts from classical literature, called the Digest (*Digesta;* Latin for "systematic arrangement") or Pandects (*Pandectae;* Greek for "books containing everything"); and (3) a collection in twelve books of imperial constitutions, called the Code (*Codex Iustinianus*). In the following discussion the three parts will be described in accordance with the actual course of the codification; that is to say, in an order opposite to that in which they are listed above.

A. THE CODE. The *Codex Theodosianus* had remained the basis of the imperial law down to Justinian. However, it had long ceased to be up-to-date, since—beginning with Theodosius himself—many statutes had been issued by the emperors, and the law had undergone some changes.[5] Moreover, as we saw earlier, the Theodosian Code recorded only the imperial

[4] The standard edition of the *Corpus Iuris* is P. Krueger's *Corpus Iuris Civilis, editio stereotypica.* The first volume contains the Institutes and the Digest, and the second volume contains the Code. The edition of the Digest is based on Mommsen's critical edition, *Digesta Iustiniani Augusti.* Another convenient edition of the Digest, likewise based mainly on Mommsen's text, is the two volume *Digesta Iustiniani Augusti* by P. Bonfante, C. Fadda, C. Ferrini, S. Riccobono, and V. Scialoja.

[5] See above, page 161, note 3.

statutes from the time of Constantine and not any rescripts or other decrees by earlier emperors.

In 528, Justinian ordered the compilation of a new code which was to contain the whole of the imperial law—i.e., both constitutions (rescripts and others) of pre-Constantinian emperors and statutes issued since Constantine. It was to be assembled by drawing on the Gregorian, Hermogenian, and Theodosian Codes, the post-Theodosian laws, and Justinian's own laws enacted up to that time; all this was to be arranged in systematic order in books and titles, and the statutes (or parts of them) selected for incorporation in the new code were —by textual changes, if necessary—to be made to correspond with the actual state of the law at the moment of its promulgation.

The compilers worked with remarkable speed, and the fruit of their efforts, the (first) *Codex Iustinianus,* was published after little more than a year, on April 7, 529, and given legal force on April 16 of the same year. It replaced and invalidated all sources of imperial law issued prior to the day of its publication and not included in it.

However, imperial legislation did not rest with this. Immediately following the promulgation of the Code, Justinian issued a number of new decrees aimed at settling many moot points of law. Part of these were, in 530 or 531, assembled in a special collection known as the *Quinquaginta Decisiones* (Fifty Decisions). This collection has not been preserved.

These amendments of the Code—as well as the work on Digest and Institutes, which was completed with amazing rapidity—rendered it obsolete within five years. A revision was necessary and was promulgated on November 16, 534, as the conclusion of Justinian's legislative activities aimed at codification of the law. The new Code, known as the *Codex Iustinianus repetitae praelectionis* (Justinian's Code of the resumed reading), is what we actually have, the first Code being lost save for a brief fragment of a survey of its contents and two fragments (one doubtful) of its text, all on papyrus found in Egypt.

The general pattern of composition followed in Justinian's Code is the same as in the Theodosian Code, although the former differs considerably from the latter in content. The two Codes differ in their arrangement, in the materials included, and in the degree of changes made in earlier enactments.

B. THE DIGEST OR PANDECTS. This is the most important part of the *Corpus Iuris*. The commission for its compilation was appointed on December 15, 530, and completed its work within three years, so that the Digest could be made public on December 16, 533, with legal force as of December 30 of the same year. It consists of thousands of excerpts from works by (or attributed to) legal writers of the first century B.C. to the fourth century A.D.—in other words, mainly of the classical period. The earliest author used is Quintus Mucius Scaevola, the *pontifex*; and the latest writers are Arcadius Charisius and Hermogenianus. The majority of the books drawn upon came from the later classical period; Ulpianus alone furnished about one-third of the whole, Paulus one-sixth. Altogether, the compilers claimed to have examined more than two thousand books with more than three million lines and to have condensed these to about 150,000 lines.

The matter is presented in fifty books, each of which—with three exceptions—is subdivided into titles. As in the Code, the arrangement of matter follows more or less the system of the praetorian Edict. The titles differ very much in length. Each title contains a number of fragments gathered from widely scattered places, the test for inclusion being the judgment of the compilers as to whether the passage had a bearing on the subject treated in the title, not the context in which the original author had made the statement.

Every fragment is carefully identified by the name of its author, the title of the original work, and the number of the book in which it was found. Thus the fragments convey the impression of being copied literally from the original works, although in actual fact the contrary is often the case, not only on account of postclassical tampering with the classical texts, but also on account of interpolations, cancellations, and other alterations made by the compilers themselves.

No source tells us what circumstances and methods enabled the compilers to complete their gigantic work within the brief space of three years. But modern analytical research has endeavored to find answers to this question. According to one hypothesis, Justinian's compilers were not forced to start from scratch but were in possession of a "Pre-Digest," i.e., one or more private compilations, made by Byzantine scholars, which, done in a similar manner, had prepared the ground. In its original and more radical version, in which it assumed the existence of a complete compilation that needed only to be perfected, this theory has been refuted. Neither has a less radical theory, recently advanced,[6] which claims the existence of several partial anthologies of classical materials studied in the classroom, as yet been corroborated by decisive proof.

But another theory, not necessarily incompatible with that of the "Pre-Digest," has thrown considerable light on the procedure of compilation. It rests on a discovery made in 1820 by a German Romanist named Friedrich Bluhme.[7] Bluhme noticed that, title by title, most of the fragments of classical works assembled in the Digest are systematically arranged in three groups. They are attached either to excerpts from commentaries on Sabinus or on the Edict, or to excerpts

6 V. Arangio-Ruiz, "Precedenti scolastici del Digesto," in *Conferenze per il XIV centenario delle Pandette (15 dicembre 530–15 dicembre 1930)*, 296–328.

7 "Die Ordnung der Fragmente in den Pandektentiteln," in *Zeitschrift für geschichtliche Rechtswissenschaft*, XIV, 257–472.

from the *Responsa* and *Quaestiones* of Papinianus. Accordingly, he was able to assign the bulk of the classical works drawn upon for the Digest to what he called the "Sabinus-mass," the "Edict-mass," or the "Papinianus-mass," respectively. In addition, some works not belonging to any of these "masses" were classified by him under the name of "Appendix-mass." Subsequent research has also brought out the fact that the three main groups correspond to the materials read during the first, second, and third year of legal studies at the schools of Berytus and Constantinople.

It is usually assumed that the compilers split up into several work groups, each of which sifted one of the four "masses" and submitted the passages it deemed worthy of inclusion in the Digest to the plenary commission, which made the final selection and co-ordination. However, a more satisfactory explanation of the compilers' procedure may be the recent hypothesis that the various titles of the Digest were assigned to individual members of the commission who from their teaching were familiar with the respective subjects. These members are supposed to have prepared the first drafts by using their classroom materials, as well as by utilizing some additional books not studied in the classroom (the "Appendix-mass").[8]

Along with the promulgation of the Digest, Justinian decreed a new curriculum of legal studies based on the compilation. Thus in both classroom and courtroom the Digest was substituted for the old books. Even references to the old books were expressly forbidden. Thus the Law of Citations, which had still been reproduced in the Code of 529, became obsolete and was omitted in the Code of 534. The Digest is now almost our only source of information about classical law.

C. The Institutes. As it was justly felt that a successful study of the Digest required a previous introduction to the

---

[8] F. Wieacker, "Die Struktur der Sabinusmasse," in *Z. Sav St.*, Vol. LV (1935), 292–308; and *Vom römischen Recht*, 184 ff.

main elements of the legal system, another special commission was charged with working out a brief text which would serve this purpose. This text, the Institutes, was published on November 21, 533, and went into force, simultaneously with the Digest, on December 31, 533. It was likewise a compilation, its sources being the *Institutes* of Gaius and several other books of similar character which had been used in elementary teaching. However, unlike the Digest, the Institutes do not indicate the origin of their parts but offer a coherent text, skillfully woven from copied passages and from the additions made by the compilers in adapting the text to the actual state of the law of their time.

3. THE *Novellae*

Justinian's legislative activities did not come to a stop after the codification was completed. Soon after the promulgation of the second Code, Justinian began to issue a long series of further statutes which have become known under the name of *Novellae* ("Novels"; best rendered by "amendments"). The emperor's plan to gather the results of this additional legislation in another codification was not carried out, but many of his *Novellae*—as well as a few issued by his two successors, Justin II (565–578) and Tiberius II (578–582)—have been preserved in a private collection.[9] Most of Justinian's *Novellae* are also known from Latin translations.[10] One of the Latin collections—called the *Epitome Iuliani*—was probably made in Justinian's own time for the purpose of introducing the *Novellae* in reconquered Italy; the other—called the *Authenticum* (not always reliable)—was the work of medieval scholars.

[9] The commonly used modern edition of Justinian's *Novellae* is that by R. Schoell and G. Kroll in the third volume of Krueger's *Corpus Iuris Civilis, editio stereotypica*.

[10] In contrast with the *Corpus Iuris*, which was issued in Latin, the language of its sources, most of the *Novellae* were promulgated in Greek, the language spoken in the Byzantine Empire. Some were issued in both languages.

The greater part of this legislation was concerned with Justinian's administrative measures and reforms or served to implement the emperor's church policies. However, to some extent the need of additional legislation arose from the nature of the great codification itself. The Digest and Code, in their almost impenetrable vastness, often have the effect of concealing rather than precisely setting forth the principles of the law. Moreover, the decisions assembled in them were centuries old. While not incompatible with certain new principles which owed their existence to postclassical legislation (Justinian's own contribution playing an especially conspicuous role in it), the Digest and Code did not disclose these principles either; and even when expressed in statutes or interpolations, such principles were frequently scattered over various titles and were hard to discover. Moreover, the very work of compilation had given the emperor and his advisers conclusions of their own on a number of legal problems.

These reasons account for the occurrence among the *Novellae* of a number of statutes which clarify questions of private law already treated in the two great compilations. They do so chiefly by assembling and recapitulating earlier scattered enactments, but also by removing doubts that had remained and, to a limited degree, by introducing new rules. Some of these *Novellae*—such as one on marriages (*Novella* 22), one regulating the status of illegitimate children (*Novella* 89), and one concerning successions (*Novella* 118)—are in fact partial recodifications. These acts must therefore be considered as supplements to the great codification; most of them were issued in the years immediately following the codification, i.e., between 535 and 539.

4. THE GENERAL CHARACTER OF JUSTINIAN'S LEGISLATION

From its very beginning, the aim of Justinian's legislation was more ambitious than that of Theodosius's codification had been. Theodosius had intended to give judges and attorneys a convenient statement of the institutions and concepts, accumulated in centuries of legal evolution, that were still valid. Justinian also undertook the same project, but on a much larger scale. His plan included both a revival of the great classical tradition and a certain amount of reform and clarification, the need of which was realized as the close examination of the old sources and their comparison with more recent laws proceeded.

The first of these purposes was served by the two great compilations, especially the Digest. These compilations, while condemning to oblivion most of the actual production of earlier scholars and legislators, nevertheless brought to light and to renewed vitality much that had been buried in countless books read by a few but completely closed to most lawyers.

The aim of legal reform was in the first place achieved by direct legislation. But occasionally the compilers also used the Code or Digest to introduce innovations. They were able to do this by means of the power expressly given them by the emperor to make changes, through interpolations and other alterations, whenever this was deemed necessary to bring the old writings or imperial constitutions into agreement with current doctrinal trends or new institutions.

The extent of such highhanded treatment of old texts by the compilers is not as great as it was believed to be a generation ago (and is still believed by some Romanists). For as we now know, many of the textual corruptions found in the Digest belong to periods prior to Justinian. But it is an even greater mistake to deny the existence of interpolations, as is still sometimes done; the more so, since Justinian himself, in one of the acts by which he bestowed legal force on the compilation (*constitutio "Tanta"* 10), testifies to their existence.

When we consider Justinian's legislation as a whole, we are thus struck by the fact that it reflects the attempt to satisfy two conflicting desires. One is what has been aptly called Justinian's "archaistic tendency"[11]—that is to say, a conscious effort to keep alive or even bring back from oblivion time-honored doctrines and concepts, not because they had any foundation in actual institutions or legal customs practiced in the Empire, but because they had been worked out by the revered authorities of the remote past. It was a tendency which was characterized by a deep respect for the historical simply because it was historical, but which lacked understanding of the intimate relationship between historical phenomena and the passing conditions to which they are linked and which justify them. It is symbolized by the retention of the Latin language, and it resulted in the preservation of old distinctions and of an old terminology, the terms sometimes being used in an entirely different sense which had none but a purely external resemblance to the original meaning.

At the same time, however, we find the desire to establish a legal system which would really meet the practical needs of the time. This desire found expression in the elimination from the old texts of references to forms of transaction and court procedure which had been rooted in the social and political conditions of the city of Rome but had become meaningless in the changed environment of the bureaucratically governed World Empire. It also found expression in vigorous efforts by legislative fiat to lay down new principles and to cut through obsolete ways of thinking and through confusing controversies.

Both tendencies are apparent in all parts of Justinian's legislative work, although of course the chief interest of the compilation, especially in the case of the Digest, is rather focused on the past, while that of the original legislation is rather focused on the present. It is for this reason that Jus-

11 F. Pringsheim, "Die archaistische Tendenz Justinians," in *Studi in Onore di Pietro Bonfante*, I, 549–87. Pringsheim's theory has not remained unchallenged, however: see chiefly S. Riccobono, "La verità sulle pretese tendenze arcaiche di Giustiniano," in *Conferenze per il XIV centenario delle Pandette*, 237–84.

tinian's statutes—especially the *Novellae*, which were made when the emperor and his advisers were no longer under the immediate spell of the classical literature—breathe a spirit which is markedly different from that of the Digest. The old doctrinal concepts, it is true, continued to dominate the minds of the draftsmen. But often they had become an empty shell, and the actual provisions resulted from the religious, ethical, or economic needs of the day and were hardly compatible with traditional theory.

In view of what has already been said, it need not be emphasized that all this was not without precedent. Tribonianus and his staff combined in their legislative activities the classicistic and theoretical attitude of the scholars of Berytus and Constantinople and the practical aims of the postclassical imperial chancellery. They had for their objective the welding together of the achievements of both into one official body of law. Thanks to their well-organized and co-ordinated effort, however, they met with such success that Justinian's age stands out as one of the most distinguished periods in all legal history. After centuries of groping scholarship and frequently haphazard and vacillating legislation, Roman law was once more conceived and understood as an integrated system. Justinian's codification and subsequent legislation, which brought to a conclusion a millennium of Roman legal history, were also the culmination of the postclassical era.

Nevertheless, we must not overrate the practical effect of the codification—particularly, of its pivotal part, the Digest—in its own time. The Digest was meant to be both a schoolbook and a positive law with the force of an imperial statute. But in its vastness it was still too much for the rank-and-file lawyer to master, and in its classicist spirit too remote from the real legal thinking of the age to have a decisive impact on the practical work of the courts. "It is," so a noted Romanist has said, "a world-historic paradox of rare pointedness that the most influential codification of all times was not in real force at any time."[12]

V. WESTERN CODIFICATIONS

From the standpoint of political theory and of scientific tradition, Justinian's legislation was the medium through which the law of the Roman people and Empire found its final expression. However, under the political conditions of the time, it could not be introduced in all the lands claimed by the Empire, but only in those areas which were under Justinian's own effective control—i.e., in the Eastern Empire and in the western territories reconquered by Justinian.

After the partition of the Empire by Theodosius I in 395 A.D., East and West had partly become separated as regards their legal development, as well as in other respects. The severance had become more definite after 476 when the last West Roman emperor had been deposed and the last shred of actual imperial control over the Germanic rulers in the former Western Empire had disappeared. Thus we find that even earlier than Justinian some of the Germanic kings attempted to find solutions to the problem, described above, posed by the diffuseness of legal materials. Here, too, the method chosen was codification. The idea had been in the air since the *Codex Theodosianus*. Yet the attempts made in the Western Empire must not be considered as forerunners of Justinian's codification, but rather as the final points of a branch development of Roman legal history.

Three almost simultaneous acts of legislation are known from Germanic kingdoms that had arisen on the soil of the former Western Empire. They were compilations like Justinian's codification, but done more crudely, from far fewer and less significant sources, and without the legal finesse and the scientific spirit of the Byzantine emperor's great accom-

---

[12] E. Levy, "Westen und Osten in der nachklassischen Entwicklung des römischen Rechts," in *Z. Sav. St.*, Vol. XLIX (1949), 240 n.

plishment. This statement, however, should not be taken as a purely negative criticism. For the much more simple enactments of the Germanic kingdoms had the advantage of being more in line with the actual needs of the time, of being within the intellectual grasp of the average lawyer, and thus of meeting more fully the practical problem with which the latter was confronted.

The most elaborate, but also least original, of these enactments was the *Lex Romana Visigothorum* (Roman Law of the Visigoths), issued by the West Gothic king, Alaric II, in 506; it is also referred to as the *Breviarium Alarici* (Alaric's Breviary). It consists of excerpts from the Theodosian Code and from Paulus's *Sentences,* of post-Theodosian *Novellae,* of an abridgment of Gaius's *Institutes* (nowadays referred to as the "Westgothic Gaius"), of some fragments of the Gregorian and Hermogenian Codes, and of one fragment from the *Responsa* of Papinianus. All these sources were included one after the other, without any attempt at systematic arrangement of the subjects treated. In addition, the *Breviarium* contains an "Interpretation," accompanying the various sources (except Gaius), which repeats in abridged or paraphrased form the contents of the individual statutes or paragraphs and sometimes notes parallel passages; it probably was compiled from earlier private treatises.

The other two legislative achievements were the *Lex Romana Burgundionum* (Roman Law of the Burgundians; in southeastern France), probably issued by King Gundobad (died in 506); and the *Edictum Theodorici,* promulgated before 508 by Theodoric the Great, the king of the eastern Goths in northern Italy. They were compiled from more or less the same sources as the *Breviarium,* but the matter was condensed into independently drafted codes subdivided into articles. Theodoric's Edict, in particular, was very brief.

All three of these works codified Roman law. The Visigoth and Burgundian codifications laid down the law for the Roman populations of their respective kingdoms, while the Germanic immigrants continued to live under their own laws. Theodoric's Edict, on the contrary, laid down the law for both groups, in accordance with Theodoric's policy of promoting a fusion of the two national elements.

CHAPTER VII

ROMAN LAW IN
MEDIEVAL AND MODERN TIMES

I. PRELIMINARIES

J USTINIAN'S REIGN was the terminal point of the history of
the Roman Empire and law in antiquity. Once more—and
for the last time—the greater part of the former Empire
was united in the hands of a Roman emperor. Likewise for
the last time, the attempt was made to enforce the old law, in
its original Latin language, as the law of the whole Empire.
However, this new political and legal unity did not last long.
Most of the reconquered western areas were lost again soon
after Justinian's death, and the separation of the Greek East
and the Latin West became permanent.

Roman law did, however, remain in force in both East
and West. But in both halves of the former Empire it assumed a different character and developed separately along
divergent lines. In the Byzantine Empire—where central imperial government persisted and Justinian's codification and
subsequent legislation remained in force, and where legal instruction and scientific treatment of the law maintained a comparatively high level—Roman law in the form laid down by
Justinian survived in the main. In the West, Roman institutions, known chiefly from such sources as the Theodosian
Code and Paulus's *Sentences,* continued in use among the Roman elements of the population, and Roman forms of legal
thinking largely dominated legislative and judicial activities
of ecclesiastical authorities. But lacking the support of uni-

form direction by a central imperial government and of a scientifically trained class of legal experts, Roman law here frequently suffered further barbarization and corruption by admixtures derived from the customs and conceptions of those Germanic peoples who became the dominant element in these lands. Here Roman law nearly ceased to be a living force. The great resurrection which it experienced centuries later—after a complete copy of the Digest had been discovered[1]—and which made possible the tremendous impact it had on Western civilization was a purely scholarly achievement that had, at least at first, little to do with the actual law of the time.

The history of Roman law, in so far as it was the law of Rome, had run its course with Justinian's codification. But this codification enabled Roman law—no longer the law of one nation or even one empire, but an independent intellectual force—to exert that world-wide influence which singled it out from all other legal systems in the history of mankind. This chapter will deal briefly with the ways in which the law of the Romans, in the shape it had received from Justinian, attained its world-historic importance.

II. BYZANTINE LAW

Justianian's codification was the work of professors, and it was intended to be not only the actual law of the Empire but a textbook for legal studies in the universities. It is therefore not surprising to find that the same professors busied themselves with preparing the material for practical use in school and courtroom. Many remnants of the work of the scholars of Justinian's generation have been preserved in the form of scholia later added to the *Basilica;* for most of these scholia were excerpts from the writings of the men who, immediately after the publication of the great codification, had spent a great deal of effort in making it understandable to their contemporaries.

[1] Concerning the impact of the discovery, see below, page 186f.

The first and most important task of these scholars resulted from the fact that the very language of the codification presented a serious handicap to their students. Much of their work was therefore simply to translate into Greek passages from the Digest and Code. In addition they wrote brief résumés in Greek of such passages and collected parallel utterances found in other parts of the codification. Occasionally they did a modest amount of original work by elaborating and explaining classical statements reproduced in the *Corpus Iuris*. While one can observe certain differences in the interests and methods of the personalities engaged in these activities, the basic features of this type of literature are always the same.

The names of several of these authors—such as Stephanus, Dorotheus, Cyrillus, Isidorus, Theodorus, and Anatolius—are still known. But one of the most active of these was a man whose name is lost and who is cited only as Anonymous or Enantiophanes. The latter name is derived from the title of one of his works: *Peri enantiophanôn*, a Greek phrase meaning "about what seems to be contradictory." In this work he tried to demonstrate that seemingly contradictory passages in the Digest can be reconciled with each other. Theophilus, who had been one of the compilers of Justinian's Institutes, also seems to be the author of a Greek paraphrase of this work; his book is a free translation of the original with some additions. Of other works, one of the best was Thalelaeus's commentary on the Code.

These scholars of the period of Justinian were typical representatives of the Byzantine legal science which had been flourishing for several generations. The remarks made concerning this school of legal thought (see above, page 146 f.) are applicable to Justinian's contemporaries as well. Therefore, original thinking is not what should be expected of them. However, it must be said that some of them might have done better work had they not been prevented from expressing the best of their abilities. For twice—in a constitution of 530 *(const. "Deo auctore")*, by which he commissioned the compilers of the Digest, and in one of 533 *(const. "Tanta"* [Latin version] or *"Dedoken"* [Greek version]), by which he promulgated the complete work—Justinian forbade all comments on the Digest unless they were kept within narrow limits defined by the emperor; contraventions were threatened with harsh punishment. The motive for this strange measure was the emperor's fear that what he believed was hard-won clarity about the law might again be confused by a flood of conflicting opinions of scholars.

The wording of the ban differs, not only between the two enactments, but even—though to a lesser degree—between the Greek and Latin versions of the decree of 533. In all cases the meaning is quite obscure. Most Romanists understand the provision to mean an absolute ban on all kinds of comments on any part of the compilation, save for literal translation into Greek, brief résumés, and indication of parallel passages. According to a recent suggestion, however, the ban prohibited only comments on the Digest pointing out contradictions, the purpose being to prevent polemics among expositors.[2]

This suggestion, as a matter of fact, would agree fully with the character of extant remnants of early postcodification legal literature. The conclusion that the Byzantine scholars understood the ban in this way is perhaps more correct than the conclusion which most modern observers felt compelled to draw, that Justinian's own collaborators more or less brazenly defied the emperor's command, but did not suffer the severe consequences such behavior should have entailed. None the less, whatever its exact implication may have been, it is cer-

[2] A. Berger, "The Emperor Justinian's Ban upon Commentaries to the Digest," in *Quarterly Bulletin of the Polish Institute of Arts and Sciences in America*, Vol. III (1945), 656–96; this article is reprinted in revised and enlarged form in the 1948 *BIDR Supplement Post Bellum*, 124–69. Most recently the question was again discussed by F. Pringsheim, "Justinian's Prohibition of Commentaries to the Digest," in *Revue Internationale des Droits de l'Antiquité*, Vol. V (1950), 383–415. Pringsheim concurs as to Berger's main theory but suggests modifications as to the exact meaning of the ban.

tain that the ban was apt to stifle most independent and original interpretation of the Digest by contemporary jurists.

At any rate, the ban apparently was soon forgotten, for it is evident that later Byzantine legal literature was no longer affected by it. Scientific treatment of the law never completely ceased in the Byzantine Empire till its final liquidation in 1453, and at times it reached quite respectable levels. A number of works on legal subjects are known, both of a monographic and of a more general character. Justinian's Roman law remained the basis of these treatises, although account was taken of some changes undergone by the system in the course of the centuries, as well as of some additions to it.

As can be expected in an absolute monarchy, further substantial changes came through the operation of legislation. Imperial legislation in the form of *Novellae* continued and reached considerable dimensions under some emperors, particularly during the reign of Leo the Isaurian (717–741) and Basilius (867–886). This legislation dealt with specific problems created by changing social and economic conditions. For instance, an important statute laid down new rules governing maritime law; another regulated the growing feudalization of the Empire.

The need for new legislation arose also, from the circumstance that Justinian's codification never became in fact the sole source of law in the Byzantine Empire. Written in a language that was foreign in the Empire and embodying institutions and conceptions created in the remote past by a foreign nation, it was much too far above the grasp of the people and of the average lawyer to uproot the traditional legal customs and ideas of a predominantly Greek population. An attempt to solve the conflict was made in the eighth century by Emperor Leo the Isaurian who, after a period of decline, succeeded in restoring the power of the Empire under strong government. He issued a kind of new and briefer codification in Greek, called the *Ecloga* (*Selection*), which endeavored to adapt the imperial law to usages actually observed by the inhabitants of the Empire.

The purpose of the *Ecloga* was not so much to replace the law of Justinian's codification as to make it more understandable, both in language and spirit, to those who were charged with administering it. New efforts in this direction were made a century and one-half later under Basilius and his son, Leo the Wise (886–911). The former issued two new condensed systems, based on Justinian's codification, entitled *Procheiron* (*Manual*) and *Epanagoge* (*Introduction*). But it was under his son that the plan of a great new codification was carried out, a restatement which followed Justinian's codification and *Novellae* but modernized the legal system by eliminating matters which had become obsolete in the meantime.

This work, known as the *Basilica* (*Imperial Law*), consists of sixty books, subdivided into titles, which reproduced Justinian's lawbooks in the form of Greek abridgments. Institutes (in Theophilus's version), Digest, Code, and *Novellae* were worked into one whole, and the sequence of titles was somewhat different from that in Justinian's books, but compared with the old collections, the contents were little changed. Somewhat later, scholia were added, chiefly compiled from the writings of the contemporaries of Justinian.

During the centuries following the publication of the *Basilica*, there appeared other condensations of Roman law, prepared by private scholars. Noteworthy among them is the *Hexabiblos* (simply meaning "Six-book-edition") by Constantine Harmenopoulos, published in 1345. The *Hexabiblos* was recognized as an official source of law in Greece (both under Turkish rule and even after its liberation in 1821) until a modern civil code was enacted in 1940.

As in the West after the fall of the Roman Empire, in the East after the fall of the Byzantine Empire Roman law survived and exerted its influence on the evolution of the law in countries formerly within the orbit of Byzantine civilization.

We have mentioned its continued validity in Greece in the form it had received in the *Hexabiblos*. But the radiation of Byzantine civilization brought Roman law—though not in pure form—to other nations as well, chiefly to the Slavic nations of the Balkans and to Romania. Even Russian law felt its impact in some degree.

III. THE TRIUMPH OF ROMAN LAW IN MEDIEVAL WESTERN EUROPE

1. THE DECAY OF ROMAN LAW AND ITS REVIVAL IN ITALY

It is one of the paradoxes of history that Justinian's achievement was destined to play its greatest role in Western Europe, where it was never officially introduced or where its most important part, the Digest, remained for many centuries virtually unknown. Italy was the only occidental country to feel the direct impact of the Byzantine emperor's legislation, which had been formally introduced there in 554. But it was only the Institutes, Code, and *Novellae* that gained practical significance; and even these lost their immediate authority in the northern parts of the country, which soon after Justinian's reconquest were again wrested from Byzantine rule by the Langobards (Lombards).

Nevertheless, it was in the lands of the West that the law of the classical Roman jurists was rediscovered. In the centuries following A.D. 1100, it was scientifically analyzed, adapted to the needs of the time, and again made an active force in the life of the people. The movement—the result of revived scholarship, general attitudes, and political conditions—began in Italy and spread thence to Spain, France, and Germany, and even influenced England and countries of northern and eastern Europe. It was these propitious conditions which made Roman law a great intellectual force and gave it the reputation of being the *ratio scripta*—the "written reason" and final word on matters of law.

The condition of Roman law also reflected, however, the deep depression through which general culture in Western Europe had in the meantime to pass. It is true that neither the knowledge, the teaching, nor the practical application of Roman law ever ceased completely in occidental countries during the early Middle Ages. Some instruction in Roman law was given in monastery and cathedral schools, although it was subordinate to the teaching of rhetoric and did not rise above a very elementary level. The church "lived Roman law." The secular law, too, kept a certain amount of Roman institutions and concepts alive. Legislative efforts of the time reflected Roman influence either directly through copying from Roman sources or indirectly through preserving Roman ideas in their provisions. Documents and wills drawn up by notaries indicate a survival in many places of Roman terminology and formalities.

In Spain the Romans of the Visigoth kingdom continued to live under Alaric's *Breviarium* (see above, page 175), although its importance was reduced when, late in the sixth century, King Leovigildus enacted laws aimed at bringing about a merger of the Roman and Germanic elements of the population. Eventually the *Breviarium* was officially abolished, probably through the *Liber Iudiciorum* (*Book of Judicial Actions*) (also known under its Spanish title, *Fuero Juzgo*), a comprehensive codification issued by King Reccesvind in 654. But not only are these laws to some extent based on the *Breviarium,* but in some parts of the realm Alaric's code remained in use as a subsidiary source of law. Similarly other sources included in the *Breviarium,* chiefly Paulus's *Sentences,* enjoyed a certain amount of authority in southern France and in some countries north of the Alps.

Yet the overall picture of Roman law in those centuries is one of progressive decay. The scanty literature of the period consisted chiefly of abstracts from older works, short glosses affixed to such works (such as the so-called Turin Gloss of the

Institutes), short codes, and collections of patterns for documents. This literature shows us an increasing quantity of misconceptions, a complete lack of originality or ability to carry through doctrinal analysis, a further barbarization of institutions, and a greater mixture with elements of Germanic origin. However, from the standpoint of the historian of Roman law, the efforts of those centuries of decline are important, because they preserved the memory of, and respect for, Roman law until the revival of legal studies.

This revival came toward the close of the eleventh century as part of a general recovery of European civilization. A new Empire—comprising Germany, Burgundy, and the northern half of Italy—had come into existence; the kingdom of France was consolidating itself; the reconquest of Spain, lost to the Moors in the eighth century, had begun; and well-organized Norman kingdoms were being formed in South Italy and in England. The church, inspired by the ideas emanating from the monastery of Cluny in France, was emerging from the spiritual abyss into which it had fallen and under the leadership of Pope Gregory VII was rising to political power. The economic life of Western Europe, which had sunk after the collapse of the Roman Empire to a very primitive level, was again tending toward urban forms and intensified international commerce; especially in North Italy were powerful and prosperous cities evolving.

All this was accompanied by a new upward trend of culture, which, among other manifestations, showed itself in the great achievements of Romanesque architecture and in the beginnings of scholastic philosophy in the persons of Anselm of Canterbury and of Abélard in Paris. Among the intellectuals, a keen interest in the great ancient past sprang up, which has caused historians to speak of a "Renaissance of the twelfth century."

It was in keeping with the general trends of the period that legal studies also were filled with new life. We find in the second half of the eleventh century law schools in Provence and in the North Italy cities of Pavia and Ravenna. Historians are divided as to whether these schools were newly founded at that time or were old establishments reaching back into late antiquity. At any rate, in the eleventh century these schools were reaching a level not attained before. In all three centers, principles gathered from Roman sources supplied the basis for discussions by learned men. In Pavia, Roman law was studied in combination with, and in subordination to, Lombard law.[3] Ravenna, which for centuries had remained under Byzantine rule, had to some degree preserved the tradition of the law of Justinian. Similarly, the scholars of southern France were benefited by an uninterrupted tradition of Roman law in that region.

However, all this was still within very modest limits. For although there is no doubt that progress was made in the eleventh century in acquiring knowledge of Roman institutions and in grasping their true spirit, these schools were still far from obtaining a real insight into the whole of the Roman legal system. One of the chief reasons for their shortcomings was the fact that the main text of the Digest was unknown to them, though passages from it were quoted. How much of it was available to scholars we do not know. Certainly they undertook no systematic study of the Digest as a whole.

It was therefore an epochal event when a complete manuscript of the Digest was found in Pisa, late in the eleventh century.[4] Luckily the time was propitious for the utilization of

[3] The Lombard kingdom had been annexed by Charlemagne, but even after its incorporation in the Frankish Empire the country had retained its law, chiefly Germanic.

[4] The manuscript was later brought to Florence, where it is kept in the Laurentian Library and is known under the name of *Florentina*. It was made as early as about A.D. 600. Apart from some short fragments found recently in Egypt, it is the only manuscript of the Digest that has survived from early times; all other manuscripts were copied either from the *Florentina* or from copies of it. Modern editions of the Digest are based on the *Florentina*.

such a find. A painstaking study of the text was at once begun by Irnerius, a professor of grammar in Bologna. Irnerius—who died in or after 1125—made the exploration and explanation of the Digest, as well as of the other parts of Justinian's legislative work, his lifework. He and his school, comprised of students from all the countries of Europe, recreated the science of Roman law, which has continued to this day.

Irnerius had many pupils, some of whom continued his work of teaching and research in Bologna and transmitted their knowledge and methods to succeeding generations. Most famous among Irnerius's own pupils were the "Four Doctors" —Martinus, Bulgarus, Iacobus, and Hugo. Eminent representatives of the school in the later twelfth and in the thirteenth century included the very influential Azo, and Accursius, the author of a comprehensive work which restated the grand total of the results reached by the school.

The school of Bologna is known under the name of "Glossators." This name is derived from the method they employed —a common one among scholars of the period and in fact the only practicable means for assimilating the gigantic mass of material with which they were confronted. This method consisted in writing short comments on the texts, passage by passage, in marginal glosses. Employing the general pattern of scholastic reasoning, they extracted the legal principles underlying the decisions on which they commented. They did this by interpreting each of the several passages as such, by collecting parallel passages from other parts of the *Corpus Iuris,* and by seeking to harmonize what appeared as contradictory statements. On the basis of results obtained in this explanatory work, they developed two further types of treatment. These were the so-called *Summae*—i.e., more comprehensive statements of the system or parts of it (the units treated in this way were the titles of Digest or Code)—and "Distinctions"—i.e., explanations of legal concepts attained by analyzing a general concept into its subcategories and then proceeding to ever more subtle definitions until all the implications of the concept had been developed.

A century and one-half of intense work enabled the Glossators to attain, for the first time in Western Europe, a thorough familiarity with the whole of Justinian's legislative achievements. Their work laid the ground for a theoretical understanding of the *Corpus Iuris* and for practical application of the legal ideas stored in it. They deeply influenced the legal thinking of all succeeding centuries; and some of their theories have become the lasting possession of legal science in all countries of Civil law and have found their way into modern codifications.

Being true medieval men, the Glossators were not motivated by any historical interest in Roman law. To their mind, Justinian's codification embodied the law of their own time; for they adhered to the theory that the Holy Roman Empire was the successor of the old Roman Empire, so that the law of the Byzantine emperor was conceived as the imperial law of their own period. Nevertheless, the *Corpus Iuris*—which was the almost exclusive concern of the Glossators (they did pay some attention to legislative acts of emperors of the Hohenstaufen dynasty)—was not the real law of their time anywhere.

The law actually in force was largely based on native, i.e., chiefly Germanic, conceptions; in Italy it was a mixture of often degenerated Roman and of Lombard institutions. Canon law—i.e., the law of the Catholic church—was essentially Roman in spirit and followed the patterns of the late Roman law with regard to part of its institutions, such as court procedure; yet it was not the same as the legal system laid down in the *Corpus Iuris*. All this remained outside the orbit of the Glossators' interest. So did the rich crop of statutory law that in their own time was growing in many Italian cities, even though the teachings of the Glossators themselves found expression in these statutes. The attitude of the Glossators was not even changed by the fact that the professors of Bologna, through their own opinions on specific questions of law and through their graduates who went out into chancelleries and court-rooms of all Western Europe, exerted considerable influence on the development of the living law. The attitude of the Glossators was purely academic and their interest concentrated on only what they deemed worthy of scientific treatment.

In the long run, the approach of the Glossators inevitably proved insufficient. About the middle of the thirteenth century, the eclipse of the Bolognese school came, after the *Glossa Ordinaria* of Accursius had stated its results in an encyclopedic compilation of glosses. The school lost its dominant position, although its approach continued for a long time to be taught at Bologna. The place of the scholars of Bologna as the leading authorities on Roman law was taken by other men, who relied on the methods and achievements of the Glossators but approached their task from a different angle and with different problems in mind. The leading men of this school were Italians, too; the most renowned place of their activities was Perugia. Bartolus de Saxoferrato and Baldus de Ubaldis, both of the fourteenth century, were the outstanding authorities among those representing the new type of legal scholarship.

The new school began in the thirteenth century, reached its peak in the fourteenth century, and continued into the fifteenth century. It is known as the school of the "Postglossators" or "Commentators." The latter name, nowadays more commonly used than the former,[5] is derived from the fact that these men no longer contented themselves with interpreting the *Corpus Iuris* directly and in isolation. They wrote coherent treatises, or "commentaries," on specific topics and they took an important step forward by combining Roman law with the statutory law of Italian cities and with canon law. In this manner they succeeded both in adapting Roman law to

[5] The other name, which has a somewhat derogatory implication and characterizes those jurists of the later Middle Ages as mere epigones of the Glossators, was chosen by Savigny, who did not yet fully appreciate their importance.

the actual practical needs of their time and in giving the contemporary law a scientific basis through theoretical concepts derived from Roman law.

The breadth of their interests enabled some of the Commentators to make truly original contributions and to set forth new theories which would have been unattainable from the narrower standpoint of the Glossators. To name a few examples, they founded the sciences of commercial law and of criminal law, and they laid the ground for what became the European theory of conflict of laws. The work of the Commentators is unthinkable without the previous achievement of the Glossators, but to the Italian Romanistic science of the fourteenth century—if judged as a whole and in its most outstanding representatives—goes the credit of being the real founders of modern legal science.

2. THE DIFFUSION OF THE SCIENCE OF ROMAN LAW IN EUROPE

It was not long before the new science of Roman law as inaugurated by the Glossators in Bologna spread out into other countries, first of western and then also of central and eastern Europe. Chairs of Roman law were established in the universities which came into being everywhere: in France, England, and Spain from the twelfth century; and in the Netherlands, Bohemia, Germany, and Poland from the fourteenth century. Here men trained in the methods of the Glossators—such as Placentinus in Montpellier or Vacarius in Oxford—and of the Commentators taught the law of Justinian's *Corpus Iuris*. The only other legal system that aroused academic interest was canon law, the sister-system of Roman law.[6]

There were several reasons to account for this rapid spread

[6] Hence the degree of *Iuris Utriusque Doctor* (J.U.D.), "doctor of both laws," which is still awarded by European universities. At the time this degree had a real meaning, the two laws were Canon and Roman law.

of Roman law studies. Where some form of Roman law had survived—such as in the "lands of written law" (*pays de droit écrit*) in southern France—the *Corpus Iuris* helped to explain institutions actually in effect. Furthermore, the law of the *Corpus Iuris* was a highly developed system providing solutions for many difficult legal questions and was conveniently assembled in one great codification. In contrast with this, the local laws were undeveloped and differed from region to region, and often from community to community. Many had never been put to writing and were thus inaccessible to scientific treatment and academic teaching.

But these were not the only or most important causes of the dominant position of Roman law. The twelfth and thirteenth centuries saw the appearance of comprehensive statements of legal rules followed locally—and in some cases even regionally or nationally—in Spain, France, Germany, and England. Some of these were made by men versed in Roman law who deliberately endeavored to bring their systems into the greatest possible agreement with the *Corpus Iuris* and its interpretation by the Glossators. Yet the universities paid no heed to these systems.

The ultimate explanation for the priority of Roman law can probably be found in the political and psychological conditions of the Middle Ages. Medieval men believed in a single, universal empire of all Christendom, and Roman law was the law of this empire. For the empire, so they thought, had once existed under the Christian emperors Constantine and Justinian, and it had been renewed by Charlemagne. It was this theory which justified the efforts of the Glossators, who, accordingly, were staunch supporters of the imperial cause in the political struggles of the twelfth century, when the cities of Lombardy resisted the claims of Frederic Barbarossa.

The reality of the Middle Ages, of course, fell short of the ideal; for the new Empire which, after the collapse of the Carolingian Empire, had arisen in the tenth century under

Otto the Great comprised only Germany, Burgundy, and parts of Italy. Moreover, the kings of the Iberian peninsula, of France, England, Scotland, the Scandinavian countries, and Poland never recognized the supremacy of the German-Roman emperor. Nor can it be said that all the emperors based their claims for supremacy in Germany and Italy on the conception of the universal empire, although the imperial idea did in part determine the policies of Frederic Barbarossa (1152–90) and his son, Henry VI (1190–97), the two emperors during whose reign the school of Bologna reached the peak of its fame.

None the less, the theory that Justinian's *Corpus Iuris* embodied the universal law of Christendom was—not always without difficulty—accepted outside the boundaries of the actual Empire. This will be understood when we realize that the conception of the empire was not exclusively, and perhaps not primarily, political in character. It included the idea of the cultural unity of all Christendom. Rome, considered as the imperial city where Christ's vicar had established His church, was the center of this ideal universal community. This "cultural idea of Rome" ("*kulturelle Romidee*"), as it has aptly been called,[7] even more than the political idea of Rome, created in medieval thinkers, imbued with reverence for established authority, the belief that the law of the Roman Empire, as stated in the imperial codification, was the revelation of legal truth and therefore above all the customs by which men actually lived.

Thus cultural and political motives, both springing from the same source, combined to assign to Roman law its unique role in medieval life. A theory invented by French jurists significantly reveals the attitude of the time. To enable the French king to put forth his monarchical claims, which found support in statements made in the Digest, they asserted that in France the king was emperor and thus entitled to enforce the imperial law.

3. THE RECEPTION OF ROMAN LAW

Thus from the outset, the cultural and political signifi-cance of Rome gave the study of Roman law an importance far greater than that of a purely academic concern with a body of more highly developed historical legal doctrine. As a matter of fact, the victory of Roman law in medieval Europe did not remain confined to the realm of theory. The revival of studies of Roman law proved to be the stimulus for, and the instru-ment of, one of the most remarkable phenomena of European history. This is the so-called "reception" of Roman law, that is to say, the penetration of Roman principles and institutions into the actual legal life of Europe.

It is impossible here to give a full account of the very di-versified and complicated details comprised under the term of "reception," many of which are still insufficiently explored or matters of dispute among historians. But to convey an ap-proximate view of the importance of the reception, it will be sufficient to outline briefly its general course and some of its motives and media in the principal countries.

The reception was not planned and was nowhere complete. It was a complex process of gradual infiltration through the action of university trained judges, lawyers, and draftsmen of legal documents; through opinions based on Roman law, ren-dered by professors of Roman law for the use of judges or parties in specific lawsuits; and through the work of learned men who undertook to draft statutes or to compile compre-hensive statements of legal principles for the use of judges and attorneys. It took different forms and worked with a vary-ing intensity in the several countries, but few countries re-mained entirely untouched by it. Its effects ranged from the assimilation in England of a few Roman modes of legal think-ing to the adoption of many specific rules and of a whole ap-paratus of Romanistic conceptions in Germany.

There is another important fact which must be stated at

[7] Koschaker, *Europa und das römische Recht,* 45 f., 79.

the outset. The reception took effect everywhere through the medium of learned men who had received their instruction in the universities and who saw Roman law with the eyes of their teachers. Consequently, such doctrines of Roman law as achieved practical recognition were not drawn directly from the *Corpus Iuris* but from the works of the Glossators and Commentators, with the meanings accumulated through medieval exposition. Nowhere was it really Justinian's law that dominated the legal life of Europe, but a law which, though ultimately derived from Roman sources, had gone through a process of adaptation to the attitudes and conditions of a new time. The proverb coined in the seventeenth century in Germany—*"Quidquid non adgnoscit Glossa, non adgnoscit curia"* ("Whatever the Gloss does not recognize, the court does not recognize")—aptly expresses the approach of the reception.

Much of the influence of the jurists was doubtless due to the fact that the law which they pleaded before the courts and which they applied in their decisions enjoyed the reputation of being *ratio scripta*. But nowhere did the reception proceed without resistance, a resistance which often was very strong indeed. The absolute authority theoretically accorded to Roman law, the persuasive force inherent in a sophisticated system competing with an amorphous mass of simple traditions, and the intellectual superiority of the Romanistically trained jurist to the unlearned folk-judge—these are reasons why the resistance was overcome in so many places. These circumstances seem to explain, for instance, the ineffectiveness of a ban placed on all pleadings not based on local customs or general laws of his kingdom by James I of Aragon (1213–76). They also played a powerful part—to name another important example—in bringing about the extraordinary success of Roman law in Germany.

Still, neither the theoretical authority nor the intellectual superiority of Roman law could have conquered the lands of

Western and Central Europe, had not a further factor paved the road for them. This factor was of a political nature. In the Empire, as well as in the independent kingdoms of Western Europe, the later Middle Ages were dominated by the struggle of the rulers to establish full sovereignty against the centrifugal tendencies of the feudal nobility. Roman law profited in several respects by the efforts of rulers to establish central authority.

Rulers were prone to take a friendly attitude toward Roman law because it provided them with powerful arguments in support of their claims to political supremacy. In classical and postclassical times, Roman law had been the legal order of a centrally-governed authoritarian monarchy. The assertions of imperial authority found in several statements by Roman jurists (see above, page 87) were a welcome support to those who strove to establish their own full sovereignty. The example of France is very instructive in this respect.

Here political antagonism toward the Empire had in the beginning produced a strong sentiment against Roman law. In 1219, Pope Honorius III forbade its teaching at the University of Paris; the measure was in part caused by the rivalry of canon and Roman law, but it is probably correctly assumed that the French crown also had a hand in bringing it about.[8] Later, however, its usefulness for the purposes of the crown was felt to be greater than its possible harmfulness. French jurists, as we saw, found a way of making its application in France possible while avoiding the danger that this might be construed as implying a recognition of any claims made by the Empire. It is also significant that Roman law studies, which, under the impact of humanist ideas, took a strong upward trend in sixteenth-century England, met with decided sympathy on the part of Henry VIII, who aided them by the establishment of new professorships (the *regii professores*) at Oxford and Cambridge.

[8] Koschaker, *ibid.*, 76, refers to further literature.

It is true that the importance of these phenomena should not be overemphasized. It has been shown that legal arguments drawn from Roman sources played only a secondary role in the gradual establishment of centralized monarchical government, which was primarily the result of an increasing concentration of power in the hands of rulers and of their success in drawing to themselves governmental functions formerly left to the feudal nobility. Nor should the fact be forgotten that the political use of Roman law arguments did not necessarily involve the application of this law in private litigation. Nevertheless, the introduction of Roman law into the political struggles implied its recognition as a valid legal system. Moreover, more centralized government brought with it conditions, machinery, and personnel which, by their own weight, made for the penetration of Romanistic doctrines into daily legal practice, even though the rulers seldom deliberately promoted, and sometimes even sought to obstruct, this development.

The consolidation of royal power required a more rational approach to government and administration of justice, and the need could be filled best by trained jurists. In the same measure that royal courts and administrative institutions were competing with or replacing feudal courts in various countries, legally trained officials were being substituted for feudal councilors. Thus, with the infiltration of Romanist concepts and the direct application of specific rules of Roman law, the influence of graduates of Bologna and other universities was growing.

Furthermore, in the thirteenth century, there was hardly a European country which could boast a national common law. The innumerable local laws showed great diversity, most of them were primitive in both form and substance, and many were not even recorded. As most of them were based on Germanic conceptions, the variety often pertained to detail rather than to underlying principle; but their actual inaccessibility in many cases and the circumstance that law students were trained only in Roman and canon law and were usually ignorant or contemptuous of local laws tended to conceal this fact from the legal experts.

There were, it is true, compilations of laws observed in certain regions or even countries. Eike von Repgow's *Sachsenspiegel* (*Mirror of the Saxons,* a description of legal customs and institutions observed in parts of North Germany), of the earlier thirteenth century, or Beaumanoir's *Coutumes de Beauvaisis* (*Customs of Beauvaisis,* in northern France), of the latter part of the same century, exemplify the former category. The *Fuero Real* (*Royal Lawbook*) of King Alfonso the Wise of Castile (about 1255), a work of at least half-official character, represents the latter category. These compilations and others of the same kind certainly had considerable practical importance.

None the less, it was only Roman law that could truly raise the claim of being common to all, and it was only Roman law that could supply rules needed to fill the innumerable gaps found in statements of national law. Wherever royal judges were supposed to apply the laws of the kingdom—but could not find them in statements of national law—Roman law naturally offered itself as the source on which to draw.

To be sure, there was one major exception: England. There the reception of Roman law was checked. But the way in which this was achieved actually furnishes a negative confirmation of what was just stated. In twelfth-century England, the general situation was not basically different from that on the Continent. The law was founded on customs and differed from county to county and even in smaller subdivisions. Scholarly interest in Roman law existed. In fact, it dated back to Lanfranc, chancellor of William the Conqueror and archbishop of Canterbury, who came from the pre-Glossator school of Pavia. In the thirteenth century it was represented by Vacarius in Oxford.

But the early establishment of a well-ordered system of royal courts under Henry II (1154–89) made possible the beginning of a unification and, soon, comprehensive statements of the national law, by Glanvil in the twelfth and by Bracton in the thirteenth century. This, combined with the rise of a legal profession trained in the national law and proud of it, gave sufficient strength to English law to withstand the intrusion of Roman ideas. The habit of recording judicial decisions, begun at the end of the thirteenth century under Edward I, gave further aid. Roman concepts were by no means completely barred, however; Bracton dwelt on some of them and in typically medieval fashion, did so without even feeling them as something foreign. But such concepts were not allowed to interfere with the growth of English law on the foundations which had been laid by English courts from the days of Henry II.

Elsewhere Roman law was more successful. Castile, which also saw the early rise of a strong monarchy, received about 1260 a sort of codification of Roman law in the so-called *Siete Partidas* (Seven Parts) of King Alfonso the Wise. The *Partidas* was, with some modifications, largely a reproduction in Spanish of the *Corpus Iuris*. The work was accorded great authority and exerted great influence on the doctrine and practice of medieval Spain, notwithstanding the fact that it was not given the full force of a royal law. In Germany, somewhat later, Roman law obtained so strong a position that there the expression "common law" came to denote Roman law.

Resistance to the introduction of Roman ways arose primarily from the desire of local forces to preserve their ancient privileges and traditions against the centralizing and levelling tendencies inherent in the new type of state that was coming. It was therefore particularly strong among the feudal aristocracy. Thus Spanish *Cortes,* in both Aragon and Castile, launched protest after protest against the application by royal judges of Roman rules and Romanist doctrines; and their attitude was typical of that of the estates everywhere. But the nobility was not alone in its opposition. Self-governing cities clung to their own laws; the Romanization of municipal laws, which did occur in Italy and, somewhat later, in Germany, had nothing to do with any trend toward centralized, bureaucratic government (see below, page 203). Switzerland was hardly touched by Roman law because the Confederation had won its virtual independence before the reception got under way in Germany.

Hence, much of the opposition to Roman law should be considered as part of the resistance with which rulers every-where met in striving to establish their sovereignty. This circumstance explains an important limitation of the sphere in which Roman law was applicable. Nowhere, with the exception of England, did the nascent national state possess the strength necessary to substitute its own laws for local jurisdictions, whether these were still exercised by local communities in the old Germanic forms of administration of justice, by the courts of feudal lords, or by those of chartered cities. Only on the highest level not reached by local jurisdiction was justice dispensed by the judges of the rulers. Except for cases involving feudal law, these applied the common law of the land.

But it stands to reason that under such conditions local customs and statutes prevailed wherever they provided rules to guide the judges. This, in fact, was the case not only on the local level, but also—partly on account of the widely accepted principle of the "personality" of laws—when cases were brought before the central courts themselves. Here lay the reason why everywhere Roman law had only subsidiary validity—that is to say, the reason why it found application only if and in so far as local laws or laws pertaining to certain classes (such as merchants, peasants, Jews, and so on) supplied no sufficient basis for a decision. This doctrine governed, for instance, the *Siete Partidas* of Castile, the codification which served Spanish judges and attorneys as a half-official source of rules for situations not covered by the local charters (*fueros*) or the *Fuero Real*. In the *Ordenamiento* of Alcalá of 1348, this principle was even expressly stated. Similarly, the law primarily used in northern France was that found in local and regional *coutumes* (customs).

It was for the same reason that Germany came into the orbit of Roman law later than the countries of the West; for German emperors, in contrast to the Spanish, French, and English kings, had failed to establish their authority as strong, central rulers against the opposition of the great vassals, and the Tribunal of the Imperial Court (*Reichshofgericht*) had proved unable to function as a true supreme court. It was as late as 1495 that, in the course of an attempted reform of the Empire, a more effective supreme court, the Imperial Chamber Court (*Reichskammergericht*), was established. This court was directed to dispense justice according to "the Empire's common laws"—i.e., Roman law—unless the existence of overriding local customs or statutory provisions could be proved.

It is, nevertheless, not as paradoxical as it may seem at first sight that the same political conditions which at first delayed the reception of Roman law in Germany were, in the time after 1500, highly instrumental in bringing about the result that Germany was to feel the impact of Roman law more strongly than any other country. For the age of the Reformation witnessed in Germany the duplication of the process of monarchical consolidation which the western countries had undergone somewhat earlier—with the important difference, however, that in Germany this process did not unfold on the national but on the territorial level. The rulers of the larger territories, originally vassals of the emperor, were reaching the first stages of territorial sovereignty. Centralized administration and princely tribunals came into being in Austria, Saxony, Brandenburg, Bavaria, and many other states. With them came university trained officials and judges and, in essentially the same manner as in the later Middle Ages in western European countries, Roman law.

The patterns of organization and procedure which the territorial courts largely took over from the Imperial Chamber Court—as well as the fact that the official theory behind the establishment of that court had frankly proclaimed Roman law as the common law of the Empire—now aided and accelerated the process of Romanization. Only the areas of the so-called Saxon law—i.e., those parts of North Germany in which the *Sachsenspiegel* had attained the rank of an authoritative lawbook—were able to some extent to withstand the impact of Romanization. Even here Roman law served to fill gaps found in the *Sachsenspiegel*, and provisions of the *Sachsenspiegel* were construed in accordance with Romanist doctrine.

Thus we see that the rise of absolutism on the European continent was, as a whole, a development favoring the reception of Roman law. It is true, however, that there were exceptions to the rule. Sometimes the monarchy sought to achieve its aims by backing national law with its authority. We have mentioned the attempt, more or less futile, of King James I of Aragon to ban arguments based on Roman law from the courts of his kingdom. Alfonso the Wise caused the compilation of the *Siete Partidas,* but also that of the *Fuero Real.* The codification of the *Coutumes* of northern France, a movement which filled the sixteenth century and deeply influenced the further development of French law, was accomplished under the orders and authority of the royal government but through resolutions passed by the local estates; and local traditions, needs, and wishes were loyally respected.

Moreover, absolutism was apt to set limits to the extent of the reception. Government-made statutory law might check common law with the same ease as it could set aside local law. The *Constitutio Joachimica* of 1527, a statute of Elector Joachim I of Brandenburg, concerning successions and other matters of private law, is an example. It expressly recognized Roman law, but preserved the principles traditionally observed in the March of Brandenburg with regard to the mutual succession of husband and wife.

While the reception of Roman law in the later Middle Ages can be understood only if seen against the background of the political conditions and tendencies of the period, these conditions and tendencies alone are not sufficient to explain the phenomenon. The emergence of the new state certainly stimulated the spread of Romanism in many instances. Even more important, however, was the part played by the emerging political order in setting the stage for a movement motivated and promoted by other social and intellectual forces. Increased trade was calling for refined legal techniques which local laws were unable to supply. The works of the Glossators and, even more so, those of the more practical minded Commentators provided answers to the questions that arose. The more complex economic intercourse grew, the more the need for trained jurists was felt; and everywhere, except in England, the jurists of the fourteenth, fifteenth, and sixteenth centuries were "Bartolists."

Finally, there was the purely intellectual aspect of the reception; this, as a matter of fact, was perhaps the most potent among the several factors responsible for it. Romanist legal education could not fail to work by its own force in the direction of a penetration of Roman institutions and Romanist forms of thinking into the legal systems which existed in the various countries and regions of Europe. The Renaissance with its admiration for ancient civilization added further strong impulses. It was, in fact, the combination of propitious political conditions, as described above, with the humanistic interest in Roman ways that accounts for the rapidity and thoroughness of the reception in sixteenth-century Germany.

The effects of the new familiarity with Roman law began to show early. As early as the twelfth century, Aragonese writers of legal documents inserted clauses based on Roman law. Roman institutions and discussions based on Roman law crept into local codifications and into the books which some of the learned men of the thirteenth century wrote about the legal customs of their homelands. A typical example is Beau· manoir. He never quotes the *Corpus Iuris;* but not only does he consider Roman law as an ultimate subsidiary source of law in France but his knowledge of Roman law is apparent. Even Bracton succumbed to this influence in some degree; so did the *Fuero Real* and other Spanish codifications of national law. The *Sachsenspiegel* is remarkably free of Roman influence, but other similar statements, made in Germany a little later, are not.

Of a similar type, but even more far-reaching was the influence of Roman law on local legislation. It was especially strong in the period of the Glossators and Commentators in Italy, where statutes enacted by cities were drafted by graduates of Bologna and other universities, who sought to combine local traditions with the doctrines worked out by their teachers. Again in the years around 1500, some German cities produced "reformations" of their municipal laws—i.e., restatements and partial reforms of the legal customs followed by their citizens. As the authors of those "reformations" were usually learned men who had studied in Italian, French, or German universities where Roman law was being taught along the lines laid down by the Commentators, much of the contents of these statements had a more or less purely Roman character. Some Roman influence is also noticeable in French *coutumes* codified in the sixteenth century.

In many places the courts—both local and national or territorial—formed an avenue of entrance for Roman ideas. For it became a habit, although not one without exception, to staff courts with learned men, just as advocates pleading before the courts were often university trained men or had at least a smattering of Roman law. These learned judges and advocates brought Roman forms of judicial procedure and frequently based their arguments and decisions on Roman principles. The direct influence of the legal faculties in the universities on judicial decisions of specific cases has already been mentioned (see above, page 193). The practice of obtaining such opinions was especially widespread in medieval Italy and again in Germany in the period after the Reformation. There it became one of the features of common (i.e., Roman) law judicial procedure. Difficult questions were referred to a faculty of law, and the opinion rendered was considered binding on the court that had requested it.

The reception of Roman law in Europe was a many-sided phenomenon, and only a few of its aspects can be presented here. The various political, social, and intellectual forces active in it sometimes combined, but sometimes opposed, one another. Roman law met with stronger resistance here and with weaker resistance there: the reception was not a uniform process. It sprang from different motives, took different forms, and led to different results from country to country, from region to region, and often even from locality to locality.

Nowhere was it the conscious adoption of the whole or of parts of an imported legal system. It was a trend and a movement. It consisted in the appropriation of a certain approach in interpreting legal rules and in the filling of gaps found in less developed legal systems with principles taken from a more developed legal system. Roman law was not felt as something alien but as a higher form of the living law, laid down in books almost as sacred as the Bible and taught by men enjoying the highest respect as scholars. In some parts, as in southern France or in regions of Italy, where a good deal of the old Roman law had actually survived, this feeling was not even very remote from reality.

Generally, Roman law followed the line of least resistance, without, however, anywhere completely crowding out local institutions or conceptions. Everywhere the reception was a selective process. Roman institutions and Romanist doctrines helped, in varying degrees, to develop and interpret local laws where these were sufficiently fixed to supply a foundation for the administration of justice. Such was the case, for instance, in Spain (where the *Siete Partidas* served as a semiofficial basis for the application of Roman law), in the lands of the *Sachsenspiegel,* or in France after the codification of the *coutumes.* Roman law also influenced local legislation, as in Italian or German cities; the extent of this influence depended largely on the degree of scholarly training possessed by the men charged with drafting the laws in each given case. Even where Roman law really became the law of the land, as was the case, in the centuries after 1500, in wide areas of the Holy Roman Empire, it was mixed with elements which owed their existence to local traditions; and frequently it had to give way to local statutes or customs deemed to override the common law.

As regards the effect of the reception on the various parts of the legal system, the law of judicial procedure was the branch to feel the impact of Romanization most deeply. What was adopted was not, of course, the classical mode of litigation (which was unknown and would, anyway, have been unfit for reception), but the postclassical forms of procedure, which had survived in canon law. With their emphasis on rational arguments based on fixed principles of law, on the direction of the trial by the presiding judge, and on a free valuation of the evidence, they suited litigation conducted by legally trained advocates before learned official judges. As for substantive law, the reception affected private law more than criminal law, primarily on account of the preponderance of private law in the sources of Roman law. Within the orbit of private law, the Roman law of contracts had the greatest influence, because the simple principles provided by local laws were, as a rule, insufficient for the needs of the growing business of the later Middle Ages and of early modern times.

Other aspects of private law also felt the Roman impact.

The Roman law of property, which in its form as represented in the Digest emphasized the power of the owner more strongly than did either Germanic traditions or feudal law, proved useful to feudal tenants who sought to transform their fiefs into private estates. Likewise was the trend toward more individualistic forms of economic life supported by certain principles governing the Roman law of domestic relations, successions, and wills.

The reception has often been deplored. It has been charged with facilitating unhealthy political and social developments; with substituting a highly technical legal system, intelligible only to specialists, for the living legal conscience of the people;[9] and, especially in Germany, with cutting short the organic development of ancestral institutions. This is not the place to discuss these and other criticisms. Many of the objections are founded on sheer ignorance, although others are worth serious consideration. Whatever one may think about the merits or demerits of the reception, its historical importance and lasting effect on the evolution of the law in all countries of continental Europe are undeniable.

IV. ROMAN LAW IN THE MODERN AGE

1. THE ROLE OF ROMAN LAW

The long process of reception was in the main completed by 1600. For centuries Roman law dominated the legal scene in Europe. The idea of a universal Christian-Roman Empire was dead, but its place was taken by the new humanistic reverence for classical antiquity. This was a purely intellectual attitude and certainly a less durable ideological basis for the continued pre-eminence of Roman law. But it was strong enough to cause the legal scholars of the early Modern Age to

[9] This, in fact, did arouse much bitterness against Roman law and its representatives. (It would seem that here is the origin of the slang expression "baloney": it means *bolonais*, i.e., originating in Bologna—in other words, legal nonsense.)

believe, like their medieval predecessors, that the legal wisdom assembled in the Pandects was timeless *ratio scripta*. Continental lawyers continued to be trained mainly along Romanist lines. Even in England the Romanist tradition not only remained alive but received strong new impulses in Oxford and Cambridge, where the teaching of the "civil"—i.e., Roman—law was never interrupted.

Nor was there any country that did not feel the Romanist impact in its legislation and judicial practice. The extent of Romanism varied in proportion to the strength of the local laws. England, France, and Germany may serve as typical examples. The "common lawyers" of England succeeded in keeping their system pure; and the penetration of "civil" law concepts was confined to matters developed outside the Common law courts, such as probate jurisdiction, administered by ecclesiastical courts, or admiralty law. In northern France the codification of the *coutumes* had given that country a foundation on which a well-organized and excellently qualified judiciary and legal profession were able to build up a French common law, based widely, though not exclusively, on national traditions (see above, page 203). But the scientific spirit in which French jurists interpreted and supplemented their law was determined by their Romanist training. The French law of the seventeenth and eighteenth centuries thus became a blend of Romanist doctrine and traditional institutions, enriched by judiciously selected Roman institutions. The extreme of Romanism was reached in Germany, where *Gemeines Recht* (common law), based immediately on the *Corpus Iuris* as interpreted by contemporary jurisprudence, remained the law of the land in many areas throughout the seventeenth, eighteenth, and nineteenth centuries.

However, these were also the centuries during which Europe, so to speak, outgrew Roman law. The emergence of the modern state, founded on the idea of dynastic, and later, popular, sovereignty and functioning through strong bureau-

cratic governments, changed the conception of law in general
and with it the attitude toward Roman law. A positivist idea
of law was growing, which conceived law as a function of the
state and the creation of legal rules as a prerogative of the
sovereign. Legislation might confirm, modify, or replace Roman law, as it saw fit. Thus new intellectual forces were able
to influence the development of law. The seventeenth and
eighteenth centuries were those of a "Natural law" which was
no longer Roman law, no matter how heavily it drew on Roman sources (see below, page 215). Nationalism was emerging
and brought opposition to Roman law on the grounds of its
foreign origin.

None the less, the time had not yet come for Roman law
to leave the European scene. As a matter of fact, in the nineteenth century, Savigny's Historical School elevated it once
more to a peak of importance. The influence of that school is
not the least among the reasons why Roman law has left indelible marks on the legal systems of many countries. Still, the
days of immediate validity of Roman law drew to a close. The
Corpus Iuris lost its last large area of direct application when
on January 1, 1900, the German Civil Code went into force.

2. SCIENTIFIC APPROACHES

Roman law was necessarily a law of learned men. Thus,
in the centuries after 1500, as in the Middle Ages, the history
of Roman law has been primarily the history of its science.
Not only did doctrines formulated by theorists with respect to
specific legal problems direct the application of the law in
daily practice, but the general attitude of the scholars toward
Roman law both reflected and determined the degree to which
this law was a working force in the intellectual life and in the
positive legal orders of the various states and periods. It was
in the universities that the authority of Roman law as a system embodying final truth for all times was first shaken, when
the theory of Natural law was developed and when the merely

relative character of Roman law as a historical law was discovered.

An outline of the role of Roman law in legal science from the Renaissance to 1900 will show how this transformation came about and how Roman law became one of the foundations of modern jurisprudence.

A. THE HUMANISTS. Lack of historical sense was a characteristic of the Middle Ages. Just as medieval theologians saw in the Bible only the eternal word of God, so the jurists accorded equal authority to every statement in the *Corpus Iuris*. They ignored the fact that the emperors and jurists whose constitutions and decisions are assembled in the Digest lived at different times and long before the compilation was made. They also ignored the circumstance that, according to Justinian's own testimony, the compilers had altered classical utterances by inserting interpolations. Nor was the existence of contradictory statements in the sources admitted. Passages which did not seem to fit together were harmonized by subtle —and sometimes hairsplitting—distinctions. It is undeniable that the approach of the Glossators and Commentators was in perfect agreement with Justinian's express command. Nor is there any doubt that the method of the medieval scholars enabled them—even to Justinian's own age—to discover hidden doctrinal contents of the codification. But the historical evolution of Roman law and the character of that law in periods prior to Justinian lay outside of what those scholars were anxious or able to discover.

The historical and aesthetic interest in classical antiquity as such, which came with the Renaissance, brought a different attitude toward Roman law. A group of scholars appeared whose aim was not the interpretation of the *Corpus Iuris* as it stands, but the reconstruction of that legal system which had governed the life of ancient Rome. This new interest, stressing the legal order that had existed in republican and classical times, required a change of approach to problems and sources. The purely rational analysis of the sources as carried out by the Glossators and Commentators was replaced by a combination of philological methods with juridical analysis. In accordance with the new scientific aims, sources not heeded before came into the sphere of interest: namely, legal texts written prior to the time of Justinian, some Greek passages in the *Corpus Iuris* (the medieval scholars, who knew no Greek, had passed over them), and Byzantine sources. The problem of interpolations was attacked for the first time.

The first to turn to this line of interest were a few Italian humanists in the fifteenth century. But the center of the new historical studies lay in the University of Bourges in France, where in the sixteenth century a group of scholars developed the new method. The school of Roman law in Bourges was, in the thirties of the sixteenth century, founded by an Italian, Alciatus of Milan, and a Dutchman, Viglius ab Aytta. But its two greatest names were those of two Frenchmen of the following generation, Jacques Cujas (Cuiacius, 1522–90) and Hugo Doneau (Donellus, 1527–91). Cuiacius excelled by his profound analysis, passage by passage, of individual titles of Code and Digest and of other sources. Donellus's merits lay in his efforts to present a system of Roman law on foundations laid by philological-juristic research into the sources. A second school with similar tendencies was inaugurated in Louvain by van der Muyden (Mudaeus), a pupil of Alciatus and Viglius.

From these places, their particular type of interest and methods spread into other parts of Europe. Its most important representatives, next to the French, were Dutch scholars of the seventeenth century; it found its way also into Spain, Germany, and England. The humanist type of research lasted into the eighteenth century. But it lost its significance and original freshness of approach when purely doctrinal interests, never completely wiped out by the humanist approach, again came to the fore.

The judgment on humanist jurisprudence has varied in the course of four centuries. Sharply attacked in its own time by the defenders of the older approach or *mos Italicus* (Italian method), the *mos Gallicus* (French method) was highly praised by the historically-minded nineteenth and twentieth centuries. In most recent years some scholars have again become inclined to stress its limitations, without, however, belittling the progress it brought to the science of Roman law.[10]

This progress consisted in the fact that the humanists laid the ground for the historical treatment of Roman law. They were the first to endeavor to separate the old *ius civile* and classical law from later admixtures and to point out that Roman law went through successive phases of evolution—a truism now but a great discovery at their time. They were the first to work out methods for the discovery of interpolations in the Digest and to realize that much juridico-historical information is found in sources outside of Justinian's *Corpus Iuris*. Their humanist interest in bringing back to life the treasures of ancient literature led them to search among the countless manuscripts hidden in monastery libraries; and we owe to them the discovery and first editions in print of much of the postclassical legal literature. Jacques Godefroy's (Gothofredus, 1582–1652) historico-legal commentary on the *Codex Theodosianus* is recognized as a book of high scholarly value, even from the standpoint of present-day Romanistics.

The humanists erred in that they put an exaggerated value on the *ius civile* and classical law and considered only such institutions as existed in these systems as real Roman law and worthy of being taught and held in practical use in their own time. They merely replaced the *ratio scripta* of the *Corpus Iuris,* as accepted by the medieval scholars, by a likewise absolute *ratio scripta* which became apparent after all that

10 See S. Riccobono, "*Mos Italicus* e *mos gallicus* nella interpretazione del Corpus Iuris Civilis," in *Acta Congressus Internationalis Romae, 12–17 Novembris 1934,* II, 377–98.

was condemned as "Tribonianism" was purged from the sources. This dogmatic attitude revealed a lack of genuine historical sense similar to that of the Italian predecessors of the humanists.

At the same time, the rejection by the humanists of much that had found its way into the practice of their own time deprived their teaching of any lasting influence on contemporary legal developments. Many of them, such as Antoine Favre (Faber, 1557–1624), a radical "hunter" of interpolations, or the Dutch Romanists of the seventeenth century, held high positions in the judiciary or wrote practical treatises. But they drew a sharp line between their historical and practical interests; regarding the latter, they followed the *mos Italicus* or, later, the doctrines of Natural law. The "Elegant Jurisprudence," as the humanist science of Roman law was called (the expression indicates its lack of practical importance), remained a purely scholarly phenomenon confined to a comparatively small group of specialists.

B. THE PRACTICAL APPROACH. Italian humanists were the forerunners of the French Elegant Jurisprudence. An Italian, Alciatus, founded the school of Bourges. A German humanist, Ulrich Zasius, also had followed the same line of interest in the early years of the sixteenth century. But neither in Italy nor in Germany was the humanist approach to Roman law a success. As a matter of fact, it was the lack of response in his homeland which caused Alciatus to go to France. Zasius remained without followers in his country; it was much later that historical interests gained a foothold there. An Italian, Alberico Gentili, then professor in Oxford, published in 1582 his book *De Iuris Interpretibus Dialogi Sex (Six Dialogues on the Expounders of the Law)*, a most forceful attack on the methods of the French humanists.

The reasons for the failure of the humanist type of jurisprudence in Italy and Germany must be sought in the position

Roman law had attained in the two countries. Italy was the country of the *mos Italicus*, and the authority of the Commentators there was so great that it could not easily be shaken. Even more important was the dominant position which Roman law held in the actual legal life of both countries. In Italy, Romanist conceptions had exerted a deep influence on the statutory law of the cities, and the works of Bartolus and Baldus were the foremost guides, not only of legal studies in the universities, but also of the activities of the judges. Germany was in the midst of the reception movement. What was needed under such circumstances was books showing the lawyer how to handle the practical problems which confronted him in his daily work, but not the scholarly historicism of the humanists or their philological interest in interpolations.

Thus a jurisprudence akin to that of the Commentators—and strongly influenced by them—remained prevalent in those two countries, just as even in France itself and elsewhere the historical approach to Roman law never became so dominant as to drive the representatives of a more practical approach from the universities. In France, Germany, Italy, and elsewhere, Roman law continued to be taught, and books continued to be written on it from the standpoint of the actual and present needs of the respective countries. Due account was also taken of decisions rendered by high courts, such as the Imperial Chamber Court or the *Parlement* of Paris. In Germany, where the Roman component in this blend of several elements was particularly strong, this type of jurisprudence became known under the name of *Usus Modernus Pandectarum* (the modern use of the Pandects). The systematic work of the theorists of the *Usus Modernus* not only gave direction to the progress of the reception but was largely responsible for its extraordinary depth in Germany.

C. NATURAL LAW. The great time of the *Usus Modernus* was the seventeenth and eighteenth centuries. During these same centuries, however, a new jurisprudence came into being which assumed a critical attitude toward the legal system of the *Corpus Iuris*. Its objections sprang from considerations different from those that had inspired humanist criticism of Justinian's codification. The men who followed the new line of thought did not resort to philological arguments, devised to show that what the Code and Digest presented as Roman law was not really the law of old Rome but a later version of it, distorted and corrupted by interpolations. Their criticism stood on philosophical grounds and was aimed at the law of the classical jurists and of Justinian alike. They undertook to prove that the law of the Romans, like that of any other people, was no more than the positive legal order of one nation. Only such institutions and concepts of Roman law as were held to be compatible with principles believed to be eternally true and therefore fit to govern human relations in any type of civilization were accorded authority.

The new school of thought was that of "Natural law." This name expressed the belief of its followers in the existence of legal principles inherent in the nature of man, so that they might be considered absolutely valid. This theory emanated from the rationalistic philosophy of the seventeenth and eighteenth centuries, although the conception of a "natural" law, common to all men of all times and of higher moral authority than what seemed to be arbitrary rules of individual legal systems, was not new. It had been formulated by Greek philosophy. It had exerted a superficial influence on Rome's classical jurists and on postclassical jurisprudence. It had been given a religious tone by Augustine and had in this form been taken up by medieval Scholasticism, in which it was fully developed by Aquinas. The Protestant rationalists, in their quest for the true natural foundations of human life, as conforming to and perceivable by reason, again raised the postulate of an absolute law, and thus found themselves in line with a long tradition. Refusing to accept theological explanations, however, they sought their backing in ancient statements rather than in those of medieval philosophers.

This made it possible for them to find the roots of their own thinking in Roman law, in spite of their critical attitude toward the *Corpus Iuris*. References in the sources to *ius naturale* and *ius gentium* seemed to connect their own theory with that of Roman jurists. Moreover, many of the legal principles found in the Roman sources appeared to be suitable materials with which to build their own system. To them, it is true, the *Corpus Iuris* was no longer, as it had been to the medieval scholars, the very embodiment of divine reason in legal matters. Actually, German rationalists were by no means reluctant to draw on Germanic laws, which began to arouse the interest of legal historians in the seventeenth century; and, at any rate, Natural law was a system primarily following the lines of an abstract logic.

But many of the solutions proposed by Roman jurists—as well as many of the theories derived from those solutions by expounders from the Glossators to the *Usus Modernus*—were in actual agreement with what seemed "natural" and therefore rational. This is certainly not surprising. The classical Roman jurists had rendered their decisions to meet the needs of an individualistic middle-class society, that is to say, a type of society similar to that envisaged by the scholars of the era of Rationalism, coming, as they did, from the upper strata of an urban middle class. The rationalists did reject such remnants of old Roman formalism as were still apparent in the *Corpus Iuris*—those elements which were indeed overemphasized by the Elegant Jurisprudence. Yet they were able to derive support for their own doctrines from general theories resulting from the interaction of *ius civile* and *ius honorarium*.

The foundations of Natural law were laid by the great Dutch scholar, Hugo Grotius (1583–1645). His work *De Iure Belli ac Pacis* (*Concerning the Law of War and Peace,* 1625) —the book which has ever since remained fundamental for the theory of international law—was the principal statement of his theory. It is not accidental that the legal problems involved in international relations should have provided the occasion for the formulation of a new theory of law. For it was the time when the modern sovereign state was taking definite shape. The principles of feudal law, which in the Middle Ages had governed the relations between rulers, had become obsolete. A new situation called for a new set of principles. This, Grotius supplied, drawing freely on the sources of Roman law whenever general doctrines laid down in them offered solutions, but without accepting these sources—which did not deal directly with the kind of problems he was confronted with—as absolute authority. Succeeding generations, building on foundations laid by Grotius, developed a system of legal principles supposed to cover every branch of the law, especially private law. Among the later scholars of Natural law, Samuel Pufendorf (1632–94), the holder of the first chair of Natural law in Heidelberg, Christian Thomasius (1655–1728), and Christian Wolf (1679–1754) are noteworthy.

In spite of the fact that Natural law was created and built up exclusively by scholars, it proved able to react strongly on the actual law of many countries. International law, in particular, is its product. In many countries, it influenced also judicial decisions concerning cases of private law. Its most important effect, however, lay in the fact that it provoked and deeply influenced the movement toward codification which began in the absolute monarchies of the eighteenth century. The very idea of stating—in theory without gaps—a whole legal system in statutory form is typical of Natural law thinking. Thus the Prussian code of 1794, the Austrian code of 1811, and, most important of all, the French code of 1804, owe their existence and contents in part to the influence of Natural law.

Natural law was doubtless one of the principal factors enabling European jurisprudence to overcome its dependence on Roman law. Yet the Romanist element contained in it made Natural law one of the media through which principles of Roman law survived in the modern world. Even in North America, this influence was considerable from the early Colonial period to the middle of the nineteenth century, and its effect is still apparent in a number of American legal institutions and doctrines. Natural law was not, nor was it supposed to be, Roman law. But it has its place in the history of Roman law and of its science.

D. THE HISTORICAL SCHOOL. Opposition to Natural law arose when the historico-philosophical writings of such men as Montesquieu, Rousseau, and Herder brought a deeper understanding of the interrelations between human activities and institutions and the general conditions of life and culture in each historical period. The belief in the possibility of discovering an absolute system of law, based on pure reason, was destroyed. Moreover, research into the sources of Germanic law had revealed the existence of forms of legal thinking and of institutions which were not found in Roman law. These had proven their practical value and were capable of being assembled in a logically coherent and scientifically satisfactory system. On these grounds a new theory of the origin and ultimate justification of legal institutions was conceived; to wit, that there is no such thing as an eternal and universal law based on any abstract nature of man, but that law, like language and other elements of culture, is one of the characteristic expressions of the individuality of the people which lives by it. Law, therefore, should be understood out of the "spirit of the people" (*Volksgeist*) which varies from people to people.[11]

[11] These ideas were programmatically outlined in Savigny's famous essay of 1814: *Vom Beruf unserer Zeit für Gesetzgebung und Rechtswissenschaft (On the Calling of Our Time for Legislation and Legal Science)*. See H. U. Kantorowicz, "Savigny and the Historical School of Law," in *Law Quarterly Review*, Vol. LIII (1937), 326–43.

The application of this methodological principle introduced a new approach into the study of Roman law. The new school of thought, which had its inception in Germany about 1800, is known as the "Historical School." Returning partly to the methods and aims of Elegant Jurisprudence, it lifted the study of law from unthinking traditionalism, from the somewhat shallow utilitarianism of the *Usus Modernus,* and from the often lifeless abstractions of Natural law. Its goal was the rediscovery of the real character of the historical Roman law without the falsification it had suffered in theory and practice since the days of the Commentators.

The first to postulate a new and more historical approach was a professor at the University of Göttingen, Gustav Hugo (1764–1844). But the real founder of the "Historical School" was Friedrich Carl von Savigny (1779–1861), a professor in Berlin from 1810. In 1803, at the age of twenty-four, he published his book *Das Recht des Besitzes* (*The Law of Possession*), in which he undertook to present the institution of possession as it emerged from the original Roman sources. He attempted to free the concept of possession from the considerable alterations it had undergone at the hands of jurists of Canon law and *Usus Modernus.* The work had a revolutionary effect and brought about a complete reconsideration, by Savigny and his pupils and followers, of all aspects of Roman law. Their objective—greatly aided by the discovery in 1816 of Gaius's *Institutes*—was the reconstruction, directly from the sources, of classical law, purged of the superstructures and admixtures by which medieval and modern jurisprudence had obscured its picture.

However, the efforts of Savigny and his school were not, nor could they be, all directed at the historical exploration of Roman law. Roman law in its form of *Gemeines Recht* (see above, page 207) was still in immediate force in wide areas of Germany. Therefore the historical aim of the school was necessarily coupled with that of a doctrinal interpretation of the system as contemporary law. It was this need which brought forth from 1840 to 1849 Savigny's principal work, *System des heutigen römischen Rechts* (*System of Present-day Roman Law*), in eight volumes.

Unfortunately, the double purpose of the school confronted it with an insoluble dilemma and prevented it from following up to its full consequences the theory of the "spirit of the people," for it was forced to treat Roman law as a law governing the life of German people. The scholars of the Historical School did try to explain the living law in the light of what they believed was classical Roman law, but, for all their opposition to *Usus Modernus* and Natural law on grounds of principle, a total break with the attitudes, methods, and achievements of those theories was not feasible. In consequence of all this, Savigny and his adherents were led—almost against their own wish—to adopt an almost medieval view of the superiority of Roman law, in spite of the fact that, as a matter of principle, they were far remote from the medieval belief in the *ratio scripta*. This attitude, incidentally, earned for the Historical or Pandectistic School, as it is also called, the bitter enmity of the scholars of Germanic law.

The combination of the two aims—with the balance more and more tipping in favor of a primarily doctrinal approach —explains both the shortcomings and the success of the German Pandectistic science of the nineteenth century.

Its principal weakness lay in a trend toward a theoretical doctrinairism, an inclination which increased rather than decreased among the less historically-minded scholars of the generation following Savigny and his immediate disciples. These men were, of course, fully aware of the character of the Digest as a collection of excerpts from legal writings hundreds of years old at the time of the compilation. But the circumstance that these excerpts had to be taken for authoritative statements of valid law compelled the Pandectists to assume too

conservative an attitude regarding the sources. They refused
to pay much attention to the question of interpolations. In
fact, they believed the number and importance of interpolations to be too small to warrant spending time and effort on
searching for them. In part, this was still a belated reaction
against the radicalism of Antonius Faber (see above, page 212),
which had discredited the critical methods of the humanists.

The conservative approach of the Pandectists, it is true,
did not prevent them from crowning their research into the
nature of classical Roman law with lasting results, since most
of the alterations undergone by classical texts do not actually
involve deep changes of the substance of classical law. They
were confronted, however, with the necessity of harmonizing,
in the manner of the Glossators, passages which on the sur-
face seem contradictory and should, as we know now, be
brought into their correct relationship by eliminating the effects of postclassical tampering. This approach brought into
Pandectistic science an increasing tendency of indulging in
ever more subtle and hairsplitting theoretical distinctions and,
thus, of again succumbing to an abstract and unrealistic con-
ceptualism, not dissimilar to that of the school of Natural law
in its later stages. This "jurisprudence of concepts"—as contrasted with a "jurisprudence of interests," i.e., one which takes
into account the actual interests involved in a case and the
desirability or undesirability of the results of purely logical
operations—was criticized by Rudolf von Jhering (1818–92),
the most eminent Romanist of the latter part of the nineteenth
century.

Nevertheless, it is a mistake to underrate the merits and
importance of Pandectistic science, as has been done, on account of this and other criticisms of a more local significance,
particularly in Germany itself. From the standpoint of legal
history, the Historical School must be credited with many
lasting contributions to the historical interpretation of the
Corpus Iuris. It opened the way toward a real understanding

of Roman law as a historical phenomenon. It produced such
lasting results as Bluhme's discovery of the method followed
by Justinian's compilers in assembling the materials used for
the Digest. It inspired research outside private and procedural
law, its principal field. Theodor Mommsen (1817–1903), the
great historian of Rome and of its constitutional and criminal
law, started out from it. The present-day science of Roman
law is its continuation, in spite of its partly oppositional attitude. And it inaugurated, through Savigny's own *Geschichte
des römischen Rechts im Mittelalter* (*History of Roman Law
in the Middle Ages*, 1850–51), the exploration of medieval
Romanistics.

Equally important—and perhaps even more far-reaching
in its consequences—was the impact of the Historical School
on the law and legal science of its time and our own. This effect is due to the doctrinal rather than to the historical element in its make-up. Following in the footsteps of the Glossators, Savigny and his successors brought into the open the
theoretical implications of the classical decisions assembled in
the Digest. It is true that they imputed to the classical authorities ways of thinking that were not really theirs, for the
great lawyers of Rome proceeded from the practical necessities
of the individual cases they were dealing with rather than from
preconceived theories, and the doctrinal logic of their system was felt by them rather than analyzed.

Nevertheless, it was precisely this theoretical approach
which enabled the Pandectists to lay down the results of their
studies in a system of clearly-formulated juridical categories
and to point out the effects of these categories on given situations. These categories were no longer, as in Natural law,
founded on abstract reasoning, but on the actual experience
and practical wisdom recorded in the Pandects. But many of
them were general enough in character to be valid from the
standpoint of any legal system. They proved to be ready tools
for the scientific penetration of other legal systems and for the

analysis, with a view to legal reform, of contemporary social and economic conditions.

These characteristics of Pandectistic science account for its widespread success both beyond the borders of its own field and beyond the borders of its country of origin. It stands to reason that its influence extended chiefly to the scientific treatment of law and to that part of practical application of legal principles which is most immediately exposed and susceptible to guidance by theorists—that is to say, to legislation. The German Civil Code of 1896 (in force since 1900) was the most conspicuous legislative result of Pandectistic science. Prominent representatives of this science participated in the drafting of the Code; and the conceptual framework and technical terminology of the Code (frequently German versions of Latin terms)—as well as a number of its actual provisions and underlying doctrines—show the Romanist impact. The introduction of the Code brought to a close the long rule of Roman law in Germany, but many Romanist theories of the Pandectists have played an important role in the interpretation and further development of the new law.

And not only in Germany was the intellectual force of Pandectistic science felt. Legal scholars in every country of Civil law received from it ideas which they could utilize in the interpretation and development of their own national laws. Even the countries of Common law did not remain untouched by this influence, at least as far as legal theory is concerned. The Englishman John Austin (1790–1859), the founder of the science of jurisprudence as it is taught in the countries of the English tongue, received part of his training in Germany from Pandectistic scholars and reflected in his own work the impression their approach had made on him.

Today Roman law has lost virtually all of its former direct validity. Even in the few countries where it still possesses a degree of authority, as in Scotland, Ceylon, and South Africa, it is giving ground to Common law. In Germany, the Pandectists themselves, by helping to prepare the German Code, dealt the death blow to Roman law as an actually valid law. Moreover, Pandectistic science itself, with its particular approach and methods, has been superseded by modern Romanistics. Yet it is in no small degree due to that science that elements of Roman thinking, in the form the Pandectists have given them, have remained a living force in present-day legal culture in almost every country of Western civilization.

V. ROMAN LAW TODAY

Nineteen hundred may thus be marked as the year in which the long history of Roman law finally reached its terminal point. The history of the science of Roman law, however, has continued to flourish. Furthermore, interest in it has sprung up in countries where formerly it did not exist. Scholars in almost every European country, in the United States, South America, South Africa, Turkey, and even in Japan are actively engaged in Romanist research.

The science, it is true, has changed its character and with it its methods. No longer concerned with the interpretation of a valid law, it has taken a more purely historical slant. Freed from the compulsion to accept the *Corpus Iuris* as an authoritative and therefore inviolable statement of contemporary law and dealing with it as a merely historical source, scholars are able to approach its text in greater freedom and with a more critical attitude. Accordingly, interest in interpolations has been revived; the search for them, greatly refined in its techniques, has in fact become the principal method for the reconstruction of the classical law. More than before, research has turned to problems of the earliest stages of Roman law, on the one hand, and of postclassical law, on the other. The goal of modern Romanistics is to obtain as complete a picture as possible of the evolution of Roman legal institutions and of the forms of juristic thinking revealed by them from the earliest stages discernible down to Justinian and beyond, into the Middle Ages and modern times.

Moreover, this science has burst its old limits and has become a science of ancient law in general. It has embraced the laws of the Greeks, of the peoples of the ancient Near East, and of the Egyptians. We have learned to look upon Roman law in its historical setting as only one legal system among the many that governed the life of the peoples which built the civilizations of the ancient Mediterranean. It has been possible—although the hypothesis appears doubtful—to postulate an ancient legal history in the sense of a history of all the laws of antiquity conceived as one great evolutionary process of convergent lines of legal development, beginning in the individual nations and finally merging in the legal system of the late Roman Empire.[12] Comparative methods have been worked out which make possible the explanation of the phenomena of one legal system in the light of better-known parallel phenomena in others.

One question, however, may be raised: can all this command more than a merely antiquarian interest? The answer is an emphatic yes. As a historical science, the history of the ancient laws—among which Roman law still plays and will always play the central part—traces and explains the origin and background of institutions and concepts. It shows their growth and changes, their spread into other surroundings and systems, and the transformations they underwent on account

[12] This theory was first proposed by L. Wenger, in his inaugural lecture, *Römische und antike Rechtsgeschichte*, delivered at the University of Graz (Austria) in 1905. Wenger has restated his theory several times; for a restatement in English, see his brief essay on "Ancient Legal History," in *Independence, Convergence, and Borrowing in Institutions, Thought and Art*. Wenger's theory was rejected by L. Mitteis, "Antike Rechtsgeschichte und romanistisches Rechtsstudium," in *Mitteilungen des Wiener Vereins der Freunde des Humanistischen Gymnasiums* (1917) and has been much discussed ever since. A detailed discussion of the whole problem is found in J. G. Lautner, "Die Methoden einer antik-rechtsgeschichtlichen Forschung," in *Zeitschrift für Vergleichende Rechtswissenschaft*, Vol. XLVII (1927), 27–76; see also F. de Zulueta, "L'histoire du droit de l'antiquité," in *Mélanges Paul Fournier* (Paris, 1929), 787–805.

of such transplanting. It reveals their function in bringing forth, through the development of their hidden implications, new institutions. It demonstrates the role in the development of legal systems of their intrinsic logic and the dependence of such development on given conditions and on the type and approach of the men charged with the interpretation, preservation, and further elaboration of the laws.

Immediate research into these problems should be conducted from a strictly historical approach—i.e., with the sole aim of illuminating the particular phenomenon under investigation. But its results, through the comparative method, connect the history of ancient law with its sister-sciences: the histories of other legal systems, ethnological jurisprudence, and the exploration of the driving forces of legal development in our own and neighboring civilizations. As has been pointed out, the history of ancient law may, in co-operation with these sciences, contribute to the uncovering of typical reactions of the legal order to certain psychological and social factors which—though outwardly appearing in infinite variety—recur over and over again in the life of human society. In other words, it may lead to a new "natural law"—a natural law, however, not derived from abstract reasoning but from the observation of actual processes at various stages of social development. Thus legal history becomes part and parcel of jurisprudence, especially when this science is considered under the sociological aspect which Roscoe Pound introduced into it. Pound himself has often stressed the necessity and value of historical research into the law.

Ancient legal history—particularly that of Roman law— is one of the most important and most indispensable links in this chain of sciences which, through their combined achievement, will bring us nearer the ultimate goal.

BIBLIOGRAPHICAL NOTE

A NY ATTEMPT to give an even approximately adequate report on Romanist literature would far exceed the limits of the present book. It is therefore fortunate that in the last few decades several comprehensive works have been published in English-speaking countries, which, dealing in detail with the institutions of Roman law as well as with some special aspects of Roman legal and constitutional history, give full information on views held and on controversies debated in Romanist literature.

H. F. Jolowicz, *Historical Introduction to the Study of Roman Law* (2nd ed., Cambridge, 1939) describes the history of Roman political and legal institutions from the earliest times down to Justinian, while Max Radin, *Handbook of Roman Law* (St. Paul, Minn., 1927) and W. W. Buckland, *A Textbook of Roman Law from Augustus to Justinian* (2nd ed., Cambridge, 1932) and the shorter *A Manual of Roman Private Law* (2nd ed., Cambridge, 1939), give systematic presentations of the institutions of Roman private law. Both the history and the system are found in W. L. Burdick, *The Principles of Roman Law and Their Relation to Modern Law* (Rochester, N. Y., 1938), but the value of the book is limited on account of the author's uncritical attitude.

The history and forms of judicial litigation are the subject of L. Wenger's *Institutes of the Roman Law of Civil Procedure* (New York, 1940). F. Schulz, *History of Roman Legal Science* (Oxford, 1946) sets forth the various fields of activity, the social position, and the intellectual attitudes of Roman legal experts in the various periods of Roman legal history from the XII Tables to Justinian; this work also contains detailed surveys of classical and postclassical legal literature. Ethical, political, and intellectual concepts and tendencies underlying the Roman approach to law are also discussed by Schulz, *Principles of Roman Law* (Oxford, 1936).

The constitutional and administrative institutions of Rome and its Empire are described by F. F. Abbott, *Roman Political Institutions* (3rd ed., New York, 1911), L. Homo, *Roman Political Institutions. From City to State* (Chicago, 1929), R. W. Moore, *The Roman Commonwealth* (London, 1942), G. H. Stevenson, *Roman Provincial Administration to the Age of Antonines* (New York, 1939), and J. Kerr Wylie, *Roman Constitutional History to the Death of Justinian* (Capetown, 1948). Reference may finally be made to several brief but highly informative articles in the Cambridge *Histories;* especially, to H. Last's Chapters X and XI in *Cambridge Ancient History,* Vol. XI (1936), and to J. S. Reid's Chapter II in *Cambridge Medieval History,* Vol. I (1924).

Since the reader will find references to general works in foreign languages and to special literature in these books, it will be sufficient here to present a selection of a few works of particular importance, or representative of modern views, which treat topics dealt with in the text; some slight preference will be given to publications written in English. These will be followed by a list of selected source editions and several study and research aids.

The foundations of our knowledge of Roman constitutional law were laid by Theodor Mommsen in his monumental *Römisches Staatsrecht* (3 vols., 3rd ed., Leipzig, 1887–88). Mommsen has remained the leading authority on the Roman constitution, although more recent research has modified some of his views, especially with respect to the archaic period and to the Principate. As regards the latter, Mommsen's characterization of the Principate as a "dyarchy"—i.e., as a form of state in which governmental power was shared by the Senate and the emperor—is generally considered too legalistic and inconsistent with political reality. But no agreement has yet been reached concerning the exact definition of the Augustean political order from the standpoint of constitutional theory. For modern views the following titles may be consulted: V. Arangio-Ruiz, *Storia del diritto romano* (5th ed., Naples, 1947) and P. de Francisci, *Storia del diritto romano* (3 vols., 2nd ed., Milan, 1943); specifically on Augustus: M. Hammond, *The Augustian Principate in Theory and Practice during the Julio-Claudian Period* (Cambridge, Mass., 1933) and H. Siber, *Zur Entwickelung der römischen Prinzipatsverfassung*, in *Abhandlungen der Sächsischen Akademie der Wissenschaften, Philologisch-Historische Klasse*, Vol. XLII, No. 3 (Leipzig, 1933).

Interest in primitive Roman law has greatly increased in recent years. Refined methods have produced valuable results, although lack of direct sources makes every statement inevitably tentative, and scholars have not always escaped the temptation to draw fantastic conclusions. It was, particularly, a group of French and Belgian Romanists who have done much to elucidate the early law; suffice it to give the names of the best-known among them: G. Cornil, F. De Visscher, P. Huvelin, H. Lévy-Bruhl, P. Noailles, and J. G. A. Wilms. But other nations are also represented; R. Düll, V.-A. Georgesco, A. Guarino, A. Hägerström, M. Kaser, F. Leifer, F. De Martino, F. Wieacker, and C. W. Westrup may be mentioned as the most active among them. Kaser's *Das altrömische Ius. Studien zur Rechtsvorstellung und Rechtsgeschichte der Römer* (Göttingen, 1949), the most recent and one of the most thorough of the treatises on the subject, informs fully and critically on current opinions.

Roman criminal law has received comparatively scanty attention from legal historians. Only in recent years has interest been increasing. The most important treatment is still Mommsen's *Römisches Strafrecht* (Leipzig, 1899). An English work is J. L. Strachan-Davidson's *Problems of the Roman Criminal Law* (Oxford, 1912). Of recent works may be mentioned U. Brasiello, *La repressione penale in diritto romano* (Naples, 1937); F. M. de Robertis, "La funzione della pena in diritto romano," in *Studi in onore di Siro Solazzi* (Naples, 1948), 169–96; and G. G. Archi "Gli studi di diritto penale romano da Ferrini a noi. Considerazioni e punti di vista critici," in *Revue Internationale des Droits de l'Antiquité*, Vol. IV (1950), 21–60.

All data concerning Roman legislation were collected and critically discussed by G. Rotondi in *Leges publicae populi Ro-*

mani. Elenco cronologico con una introduzione sull'attività legislativa dei comizi romani (Milan, 1911). More recent are articles on various *leges* and on *Lex Duodecim Tabularum* by A. Berger in *RE*. A highly suggestive discussion of the subject of Roman legislation is F. Wieacker, "Lex publica und politische Grundordnung im römischen Freistaat," in *Vom römischen Recht* (Leipzig, 1944), 38–85. The reconstruction of the Praetorian Edict was undertaken by O. Lenel, *Das Edictum Perpetuum. Ein Versuch zu seiner Wiederherstellung* (3rd ed., Leipzig, 1927). The foundations of present views of Roman civil procedure were laid by the Austrian Romanist Moriz Wlassak: for a list of his principal writings, see Wenger, *Institutes of the Roman Law of Civil Procedure*, 5. Some of Wlassak's conclusions, however, have been modified by more recent research.

For a comparison of Roman and English law, see W. W. Buckland, "Praetor and Chancellor," in *Tulane Law Review*, Vol. XIII (1934), 163–77, and Buckland and A. D. McNair, *Roman Law and Common Law: A Comparison in Outline* (Cambridge, 1936); and generally on the activities of the praetor, see F. Wieacker, "Der Praetor," in *Vom Römischen Recht*, 86–145. The constitutional importance of the imperial administration of justice and its impact on the progress of substantive law have been much discussed in recent years by Italian writers—most recently by F. M. de Robertis, *Sulla efficacia normativa delle costituzioni imperiali*, in *Annali della Facoltà di Giurisprudenza della R. Università di Bari*, Vol. IV (Bari, 1942).

Schulz, *History of Roman Legal Science* is now the most representative authority on Roman lawyers and legal science and literature, although some of his views have been attacked and others can be expected to meet with opposition. F. Wieacker's essay, "Vom römischen Juristen," in *Vom römischen Recht*, 7–37, and *Ueber das Klassische in der römischen Jurisprudenz* (Tübingen, 1950), provide stimulating reading; see also F. Pringsheim, "The Unique Character of Roman Classical Law," in *Journal of Roman Studies*, Vol. XXXIV (1944), 60 ff.

With reference to the questions of the social background of the Roman legal profession and of the foundations of its authority, two articles by W. Kunkel should be mentioned: "Ueber Herkunft und soziale Stellung der römischen Juristen in republikanischer Zeit," in *Festschrift für Adolf Zycha* (Weimar, 1941), 1–52, and "Das Wesen des ius respondendi," in *Z. Sav. St.*, Vol. LXVI (1948), 423–57. All extant fragments of classical Roman jurisprudence have been collected and, as far as possible, rearranged in their original order in O. Lenel's invaluable *Palingenesia Iuris Civilis* (2 vols., Leipzig, 1889); see also Lenel, "Afrikans Quaestionen. Versuch einer kritischen Palingenesie," in *Z. Sav. St.*, Vol. LI (1931), 1–53. An important discussion of early postclassical interference with classical texts is F. Wieacker, "Lebensläufe klassischer Schriften in nachklassischer Zeit," in *Z. Sav. St.*, Vol. LXVII (1950), 360–402.

Concerning postclassical legal science, F. Pringsheim, "Beryt und Bologna," in *Festschrift für Otto Lenel zum fünfzigjährigen Doktorjubiläum am 16. Dezember 1921* (Leipzig, 1922), and P. Collinet, *Études historiques sur le droit de Justinien*, Vol. II: *Histoire de l'école de Beyrouth* (Paris, 1925) are important contributions, although not in every detail borne out by subsequent research. A good survey of postclassical legal literature is found in A. d'Ors Pérez-Peix, *Presupuestos criticos para el estudio del derecho romano*, in *Theses et Studia Philologica Salmanticensia*, Vol. I (Salamanca, 1943), 99–126.

 The basic work on all questions concerning the relationship between Roman and provincial law is L. Mitteis's famous *Reichsrecht und Volksrecht in den östlichen Provinzen des römischen Kaiserreichs. Mit Beiträgen zur Kenntnis des griechischen Rechts und der spätrömischen Rechtsentwicklung* (Leipzig, 1891). Mitteis discovered the survival, even after the *constitutio Antoniniana*, of conceptions and institutions of provincial law in the eastern provinces and proved their influence on imperial legislation. The amount of this influence is in dispute. A recent discussion of the whole problem of foreign and Christian influences on archaic, classical, and late Roman law is E. Volterra's *Diritto romano e diritti orientali* (Bologna, 1937). Volterra stresses the autochthonous character of Roman law at all stages of its development.

There is a considerable amount of literature on the impact

of Christianity on Roman law; included here are E. J. Jonkers, *Invloed van het Christendom op de Romeinsche wetgeving betreffende het concubinaat en de echtscheiding* (Amsterdam, 1938); and U. Brasiello, "Premesse relative allo studio dell'influenza del Cristianesimo sul diritto romano," in volume II of *Scritti in Onore di Contardo Ferrini pubblicati in occasione della sua beatificazione* (Milan, 1947), 1–29. Concerning the western provinces, see E. Levy, "Westen und Osten in der nachklassischen Entwicklung des römischen Rechts," in *Z. Sav. St.,* Vol. XLIX (1929), 230–59. In a number of books and articles, published in Germany, Italy, and the United States, Levy has since been carrying out the program of research laid down in this article; see, in particular, his recent work, *West Roman Vulgar Law: The Law of Property* (Philadelphia, 1951).

Literature concerning Justinian's codification includes G. Rotondi, "Studi sulle fonti del Codice Giustinianeo," in *BIDR,* Vol. XXVI (1913), 175–246, and Vol. XXIX (1916), 104–80; P. Jörs, "Digesta," in *RE* Vol. V, 484–543; H. Krüger, *Die Herstellung der Digesten Justinians und der Gang der Exzerption* (Münster, 1922); C. Ferrini, "Sulle fonti delle Instituzioni di Giustiniano," in *BIDR,* Vol. XIII (1900), 101–207; F. Wieacker, "Corpus Iuris," in *Vom römischen Recht,* 146–94; V. Arangio-Ruiz, "La compilazione giustinianea e i suoi commentatori bizantini (da Ferrini a noi)," in *Scritti di diritto romano in onore di C. Ferrini pubblicati dalla Regia Università di Pavia* (Milan, 1942), 83–117; and F. Pringsheim, "The Character of Justinian's Legislation," in *Law Quarterly Review,* Vol. LVI (1940), 229–46.

Useful introductions into the interpolationist method are F. Schulz, *Einführung in das Studium der Digesten* (Tübingen, 1916) and E. Albertario, *Introduzione storica allo studio del diritto romano giustinianeo. Parte prima* (Milan, 1935). Indispensable aids in interpolationist research are: *Index interpolationum quae in Iustiniani Digestis inesse dicuntur,* edited by E. Levy and E. Rabel (Weimar, 1929–35); E. Volterra, *Indice delle glosse, delle interpolazioni e delle principali ricostruzioni segnalate dalla critica nelle fonti pregiustinianee occidentali,* in three parts in *Rivista di Storia del Diritto Italiano,* Vols. VIII (1935) and IX (1936); and

A. Guarneri Citati, *Indice delle parole, frasi e costrutti ritenute indizio di interpolazione nei testi giuridici romani*, volume IV of *Fondazione Guglielmo Castelli* (Milan, 1927), with supplements in volume I of *Studi in Onore di Salvatore Riccobono* (Palermo, 1936), 701-43, and volume I of *Festschrift Paul Koschaker* (Weimar, 1939), 117 ff.

Byzantine law has been a sort of stepchild of legal historians. C. E. Zachariae von Lingenthal, *Geschichte des griechisch-römischen Rechts* (3rd ed., Berlin, 1892) is still authoritative. More recent works are: G. Maridakes, Τὸ ἀστικὸν δίκαιον ἐν ταῖς Νεαραῖς τῶν βυζαντινῶν αὐτοκρατόρων (Athens, 1922); A. Albertoni, *Per una esposizione del diritto bizantino con riguardo all'Italia* (Imola, 1927); and E. H. Freshfield, *Roman Law in the Later Roman Empire. The Isaurian Period. Eighth Century. The Ecloga* (Cambridge, 1932). A famous treatise concerning the jurists of the period of Justinian, represented in the scholia attached to the *Basilica*, is H. Peters, *Die oströmischen Digestenkommentare und die Entstehung der Digesten*, in *Verhandlungen der Kgl. Sächsischen Gesellschaft der Wissenschaften zu Leipzig, Philologisch-Historische Klasse*, Vol. LXV, No. 1 (Leipzig, 1913); more recently on the same subject is H. J. Scheltema, *Opmerkingen over Grieksche bewerkingen van Latijnsche juridische bronnen* (Zwolle, 1940). A brief survey of later Byzantine and modern Greek legal history is found in G. Petropoulos, Ἱστορία καὶ εἰσηγήσεις τοῦ ῥωμαικοῦ δικαίου (Athens, 1944), 219-83, 362-78. See also N. J. Pantazopoulos, "Aspect général de l'évolution historique du droit grec," in *Revue Internationale des Droits de l'Antiquité*, Vol. V (1950), 245-79.

The reception of Roman legal principles into Visigothic law was discussed in two recent articles of E. Levy's: "Reflections on the first 'Reception' of Roman Law in Germanic States," in *American Historical Review*, Vol. XLVIII (1942), 20-29, and "The Reception of Highly Developed Legal Systems by Peoples of Different Cultures," in *Washington Law Review and State Bar Journal*, Vol. XXV (1950), 233-45. A recent and authoritative treatise on the whole problem of survival and importance of Roman law in Western Europe is P. Koschaker, *Europa und das römische Recht*

(Munich, 1947). P. Vinogradoff, *Roman Law in the Middle Ages* (2nd ed., Oxford, 1929) is a brief but very useful introduction; short bibliographies attached to each chapter inform about important literature. Though antiquated in many respects, Savigny's *Geschichte des römischen Rechts im Mittelalter* (translated by E. Cathcart, Edinburgh, 1829) is still the basis of research into the subject. H. Fitting, M. Conrat, S. Pescatore, E. Seckel, E. Besta, H. U. Kantorowicz, and E. Genzmer are other outstanding authorities on medieval Romanistics; references to their works may be found in Vinogradoff.

A more recent work on the method of the Glossators is E. Genzmer, "Die iustinianische Kodifikation und die Glossatoren," in volume I of *Atti del Congresso Internazionale di Diritto Romano—Bologna—17–20 aprile 1933* (Pavia, 1934), 347–430. Works on the Commentators include W. Engelmann, *Die Wiedergeburt der Rechtskultur in Italien durch die wissenschaftliche Lehre* (Leipzig, 1938) (see, however, exceptions taken to some of Engelmann's conclusions by E. Genzmer, "Kritische Studien zur Mediaevistik I," in *Z. Sav. St.*, Vol. LXI [1941], 276–354; J. L. J. Van de Kamp, *Bartolus de Saxoferrato 1313–1357, leven, werken, invloed, beteekenis* (Amsterdam, 1936); and E. Bussi, *Intorno al concetto di diritto comune*, volume XLVII of the *Pubblicazioni dell'Università Cattolica del S. Cuore, Scienze Giuridiche* (Milan, 1995). R. W. Lee, *A Historical Conspectus of Roman Law* (London, 1948) has briefly treated the role of Roman law in the Middle Ages from the British standpoint. For a brief survey in English, see Q. Breen, "The Twelfth-Century Revival of the Roman Law," in *Oregon Law Review*, Vol. XXIV (1944–45), 244–87.

Information on the reception of Roman law in the various countries is found in the historical literature on national laws. The problem in its totality is considered by Koschaker, *Europa und das römische Recht*, where references to special literature may be found. See also F. Wieacker, "Ratio scripta. Das römische Recht und die abendländische Rechtswissenschaft," in *Vom römischen Recht*, 195–284. With particular regard to England, see T. F. T. Plucknet's important article, "The Relations between Roman Law and English Common Law down to the Sixteenth Century," in *University of Toronto Law Journal,* Vol. III (1939–40), 24–50.

Concerning eastern and northern Europe, see S. Estreicher, *Ueber die Rechtskultur Polens im XVI. Jahrhundert* (Cracow, 1931); V. Gsovski, "Roman Law and the Polish Jurists from the Later Middle Ages to the Partition of Poland," in *Seminar,* Vol. 1 (1943), 74–98; and N. B. Skavang, "Some Salient Traits of the History and Development of Skandinavian Law," in *Seminar,* Vol. VI (1948), 60–71. J. P. Dawson's paper, "The Codification of the French Coutumes," in *Michigan Law Review,* Vol. XXXVIII (1940), 765–800, is interesting for the light it sheds on the limits of Romanization in sixteenth-century France. For an appraisal of certain causes and effects of the reception, see H. F. Jolowicz, "Political Implications of Roman Law," in *Tulane Law Review,* Vol. XXII (1947), 62–81.

For the history of Roman law in modern Europe, the reader may likewise be referred to Koschaker and literature cited by him. See also F. W. Maitland's famous lecture on *English Law and the Renaissance* (Cambridge, 1901); H. D. Hazeltine, "The Renaissance and the Laws of Europe," in *Cambridge Legal Essays* (Cambridge, 1926), 139–71; E. Sachers, "Die historische Schule Savignys und das römische Recht," in volume II of *Atti del Congresso Internazionale di Diritto Romano—Bologna* (Pavia, 1934), 215–50; and H. F. Jolowicz, "Some English Civilians," in *Current Legal Problems 1949* (London, 1949), 139–54. For Roman and Natural law influences on American law, see M. Radin, "Roman Law in the United States," in volume II of *Atti del Congresso Internazionale di Diritto Romano—Bologna* (Pavia, 1934), 343–60; see also H. E. Yntema, "Roman Law and its Influence on Western Civilization," in *Cornell Law Quarterly,* Vol. XXXV (1949), 87f. The importance of Roman law for the modern world, especially the United States, has been discussed also by E. Rabel, "Private Laws of Western Civilization. Part I: Significance of Roman Law," in *Louisiana Law Review,* Vol. X (1949), 1–14.

SOURCE EDITIONS:

There are many editions of Gaius, made in various countries. Most convenient for American readers is F. de Zulueta, *The Insti-*

tutes of Gaius, Part I: Text with Critical Notes and Translation (Oxford, 1946). The *Codex Theodosianus* is available in the edition by T. Mommsen and P. M. Meyer, *Theodosiani libri XVI cum constitutionibus Sirmondianis et Leges Novellae ad Theodosianum pertinentes* (Berlin, 1905). The standard edition of the *Corpus Iuris* is that of P. Krueger, R. Schoell, and G. Kroll: *Corpus Iuris Civilis, editio stereotypica* (Berlin, 1900–1905). The first volume contains the Institutes and the Digest, the second volume contains the Code, and the third volume (by Schoell and Kroll) contains the *Novellae*. Krueger's edition of the Digest is based on Mommsen's critical edition, *Digesta Iustiniani Augusti* (2 vols., Berlin, 1870). Another convenient edition of the Digest, likewise based mainly on Mommsen's authoritative text, is the *Digesta Iustiniani Augusti,* by P. Bonfante, C. Fadda, C. Ferrini, S. Riccobono, and V. Scialoja (2 vols., Milan, 1908).

Other pieces of legal literature, as well as laws and documents, compiled from literary sources or preserved in inscriptions or on papyrus, can best be found in the following collections: C. G. Bruns, *Fontes Iuris Romani Antiqui* (2 vols., 7th ed., Tübingen, 1909); P. F. Girard, *Textes de droit romain* (5th ed., Paris, 1923); S. Riccobono, G. Baviera, G. Furlani, and V. Arangio-Ruiz, *Fontes Iuris Romani Anteiustiniani* (3 vols., 2nd ed., Florence, 1940–43); P. Krueger, T. Mommsen, and G. Studemund, *Collectio Librorum Iuris Anteiustiniani in usum scholarum* (3 vols., Berlin, 1878–1923); and P. E. Huschke, E. Seckel, and B. Kübler, *Iurisprudentiae Anteiustinianae Reliquiae* (3 vols., Leipzig, 1908–27).

The *Basilica* and their scholia are available only in an antiquated edition by C. G. E. Heimbach, *Basilicorum libri LX* (6 vols., Leipzig, 1833–97), with supplements by C. Ferrini and G. Mercati. For Theophilus, see C. Ferrini, *Institutionum Graeca paraphrasis Theophilo antecessori vulgo tributa* (2 vols., Berlin, 1887–89). Many other Byzantine sources are easily accessible in J. Zepos and P. Zepos, *Ius Graecoromanum* (8 vols., Athens, 1931).

The only edition made in modern times of the *Breviarium Alarici* is still G. Haenel's *Lex Romana Visigothorum* (Leipzig, 1849). But its component parts and *Interpretationes,* with the exception of the *Interpretatio* of the *Sentences* of Paulus, can be found, partly in the edition of the *Cod. Theod.* and partly in Riccobono and others, *Fontes Iuris Romani Anteiustiniani.*

STUDY AND RESEARCH AIDS:

To the knowledge of the author, there is no English translation of the Corpus Iuris as a whole. But British and American scholars have edited individual titles of the Digest, with translation and commentary. The translation of Gaius's *Institutes* has already been mentioned. For Justinian's Institutes, see T. C. Sanders, *The Institutes of Justinian with English Introduction, Translation, and Notes* (London and New York, 1922). A huge work, containing translations of many sources but not entirely reliable, is S. P. Scott, *The Civil Law, including the XII Tables, the Institutes of Gaius, the Rules of Ulpian, the Opinions of Paulus, the Enactments of Justinian, and the Constitutions of Leo, Translated from the Original Latin and Compared with All Accessible Systems of Jurisprudence Ancient and Modern* (17 vols., Cincinnati, 1932); the work includes Justinian's Code and *Novellae* but not the Digest or Institutes, nor does it give translations of imperial constitutions issued and transmitted in the Code in Greek. A translation of the *Codex Theodosianus* is in preparation at Vanderbilt University, under the direction of Clyde Pharr.

There is no English dictionary for the sources of Roman law. A German dictionary is E. Seckel, *Heumanns Handlexikon zu den Quellen des römischen Rechts* (9th ed., Jena, 1907). A French dictionary is R. Monier, *Vocabulaire de droit romain* (4th ed., Paris, 1949).

A valuable aid to research are word lists, which have been compiled for most of the legal sources. The *Vocabularium Iurisprudentiae Romanae* (Berlin, 1903– ?), although incomplete, covers the Digest, Gaius, *Fragmenta Vaticana, Pauli Sententiae,* and *Ulpiani Epitome;* for Gaius there is also P. P. Zanzucchi, *Vocabulario delle Istituzioni di Gaio* (Milan, n.d.), and for the other sources just named, except for the Digest, E. Levy, *Ergänzungsindex zu Ius und Leges* (Weimar, 1930), which covers also a considerable number of other postclassical sources. For the *Codex Iustinianus,* see R. von Mayr and M. San Nicoló, *Vocabularium*

Codicis Iustiniani (Prague and Leipzig, 1923–25). For the *Codex Theodosianus* and the post-Theodosian *Novellae,* see O. Gradenwitz, *Heidelberger Index zum Theodosianus* (Berlin, 1925) and *Ergänzungsband* (1929), covering chiefly the *Novellae.* A word list for the *Novellae* of Justinian is in preparation under the direction of L. Wenger.

A complete bibliography of Romanistic literature since 1800 is being prepared by L. Caes and R. Henrion under the title of *Collectio bibliographica operum ad ius Romanum pertinentium* (Brussels, 1949 ff.).

INDEX